ACTION RESEARCH
ESSENTIALS

ACTION RESEARCH ESSENTIALS

DOROTHY VALCARCEL CRAIG

JOSSEY-BASS
A Wiley Imprint
www.josseybass.com

Published by Jossey-Bass
A Wiley Imprint
989 Market Street, San Francisco, CA 94103-1741—www.josseybass.com

Jossey-Bass books and products are available through most bookstores. To contact Jossey-Bass directly call our Customer Care Department within the U.S. at 800-956-7739, outside the U.S. at 317-572-3986, or fax 317-572-4002.

Jossey-Bass also publishes its books in a variety of electronic formats. Some content that appears in print may not be available in electronic books.

Library of Congress Cataloging-in-Publication Data

Craig, Dorothy Valcarcel (date)
  Action research essentials / Dorothy Valcarcel Craig.
    p. cm.
  Includes bibliographical references and index.
  ISBN 978-0-470-18929-0 (pbk.)
1. Action research. I. Title.
 LB1028.24.C73 2009
370.7'2—dc22

                              2008041911

Printed in the United States of America
FIRST EDITION
PB Printing   10 9 8 7 6 5 4 3

CONTENTS

FIGURES, TABLES, & EXHIBITS

FIGURES

TABLES

EXHIBITS

To PAC, the two runaways, and the two rescues. The five of you were always in my thoughts, especially while writing this book.

PREFACE

Action Research Essentials is designed primarily for use by graduate students in education and other fields, professors, and professional development trainers who work with practitioners in settings where action research is applicable. As a university professor, I am constantly searching for new materials to integrate into my research courses. As a course developer, I am required to peruse and examine texts on a weekly basis with the sole purpose of identifying a text that complements course requirements, content, and student needs. The philosophy that guided the design and development of this text was the framework that action research may be an integral part of different courses as well as a component of a course devoted entirely to research methods that could be used by graduate students, practitioners enrolled in graduate coursework, and professional development leaders. My vision was to create a text that encouraged students to become familiar with the action research process while engaging in inquiry in order to improve practice. To accomplish this, the book's content encompasses the rationale for action research, steps in the process, information regarding the institutional review board, components of a research report, conducting and writing a literature review, and relevant examples that could be used by professors, graduate students, teachers, administrators, and others interested in conducting action research. An underlying theme in the text is that action research plays an important role in the practicing environment in that the process prompts an examination of practice, reflection, and action.

INSPIRATION OF THIS TEXT

My initial impetus for writing *Action Research Essentials* was driven by three key factors. These factors emerged as I examined my own practice and the practice of colleagues, graduate students, and practitioners. First, graduate-level programs in the field of education typically attract practicing teachers, administrators, and individuals who are seeking both the degree and professional licensure. In working with students enrolled in a variety of courses, I found that many were being encouraged to engage in action research as a means of examining and improving practice within their own classrooms and schools. The required coursework—unless it was a research class—did not integrate action research into the existing content. As universities revise programs and coursework, however, action research began appearing in graduate coursework across disciplines. Although there are several texts devoted to the cyclical process of action research, most take a theoretical stance. The theoretical text is not appropriate for a non-research-based course; the information is better suited to situations that require attention to research practices only. In addition, teacher preparation programs that offer alternative routes to teaching require field experience as part of the program. The field experience integrates inquiry and action research, as students enrolled in such programs are in the classroom while simultaneously completing licensure coursework. My vision for *Action Research Essentials* was to create a text that would be ideal for use in different courses, including leadership courses, curriculum courses, methods courses, and licensure-based courses. My intent was also to design a tool that could easily be integrated into a research course as one component of the research process.

Second, a big part of my own research involves collaborative efforts with practicing teachers and administrators—most of whom are not enrolled in graduate programs. As part of a federal grant that I implemented, school administrators revealed their goals of addressing problems and improving practice through action research. However, they made it clear that most of their teachers—although very aware of their own practice—did not consider themselves researchers. These conversations led me to the idea that a text that was reader-friendly for graduate students who were also practitioners would also be ideal for professional development conducted by teachers and administrators. Effective professional development is designed in a longitudinal manner that provides relevant information and opportunities for application and reflection. *Action Research Essentials* may easily be used in professional development workshops, as the information is integrated with examples, applications, and organizers to assist the practitioner.

The third factor involved my observations and conversations with full-time graduate students across a number of disciplines. I found that full-time graduate students enrolled in education programs as well as those enrolled in other programs such as nursing, social work, aerospace, and marketing were being encouraged to engage in research prior to enrolling in their research block courses. The students were confused about the process and did not see relevancy in the practice of conducting research. In addition, the full-time graduate students—prior to enrolling in a course devoted entirely to research—did not regard themselves as researchers, nor did they possess the confidence to conduct research. Most didn't know where to begin. Without knowledge of the institutional review board, ethical research guidelines, or the differences among research methods, the students were in need of a process that would help them see the relevancy in conducting research. I have therefore intentionally written *Action Research Essentials* in a general manner that is applicable across disciplines. The text incorporates a variety of examples and may be used with graduate students enrolled in education programs as well as in programs that require student research.

ORGANIZATION OF THE TEXT

The book may be read from beginning to end in a sequential manner, or the reader may select particular chapters out of sequence as needed. Instructors may rearrange the chapters to reflect assignments, tasks, and course requirements. Students may revisit chapters as they design proposals, conduct individual studies, complete literature reviews, and write the action research plan and report. Each chapter begins with learning objectives and includes key terms highlighted in the text and listed at the end of the chapter; all key terms are defined in the Glossary at the back of the book. Examples and organizers are integrated throughout each chapter. Suggested application activities are blended with discussion topics and questions. Discussion questions are intended to encourage reflection and dialogue. In addition, a special section devoted to online learning activities and discussions is included. Each chapter includes a summary of key points and topics.

Chapter One begins with an introduction to the action research process. The chapter lays the groundwork and provides background for readers who are new to the process as well as relevant information for those intending to use the text for professional development workshops. Key information presented in this chapter includes a discussion of definitions of action research, data, code of research ethics, introduction to the institutional review board (IRB), and the rationale behind using action research.

Chapter Two covers the steps involved in action research and offers several tools—such as the Planning Log—to get started. The reader is encouraged to begin identifying research ideas and possible topics. Strategies for identifying research topics are discussed. The role of reflection is presented as part of the process. The IRB is revisited with an in-depth discussion of the review process. Examples illustrating an exempt study, an expedited study, and a full review are presented. Sample IRB forms are included with the online resources.

Chapter Three is devoted entirely to the literature review. The chapter carries the reader through the literature review process and offers suggestions for locating, evaluating, and identifying appropriate electronic sources. Suggestions for organizing the review are included as well as a discussion of the summative style versus the expert style of writing an effective literature review.

Chapter Four focuses on developing and writing appropriate research questions. Readers are encouraged to reflect on research topics and to develop sound research statements that convey the focus of the inquiry. The research umbrella is introduced, and the literature review is revisited.

Chapter Five addresses the differences between quantitative methods and qualitative methods. A discussion of quantitative data and qualitative data follow. Introduced in an earlier chapter, the triangulation matrix is revisited. The data collection schedule is discussed, as well as methods for collecting and organizing data.

Chapter Six is devoted to the action researcher's tools. These include the field journal, the participant journal, and elements of recording. Reflection as a tool for research is discussed. Artifacts—as a data form—are addressed, as well as types of electronic tools such as the online journal, blogs, and online forums.

Chapter Seven returns to data. Collecting, organizing, and means for analysis are discussed. The coding of qualitative data is addressed, with a good amount of attention given to the coding process, types of codes, categorizing, and assigning attributes.

Chapter Eight examines the action research report and provides a rationale and tips for writing the report and presenting and sharing findings. A sample action research assignment complements this chapter and is included with the online resources.

Chapter Nine covers the action plan and how it relates to the action research process. Components of the plan and implementation are discussed. Instructors may combine Chapters Eight and Nine as needed to meet course and student needs.

FEATURES

Action Research Essentials includes several features to assist instructors, students, and practitioners. Each chapter includes examples that complement the information presented. Examples are grounded in real-world experiences and reflect actual research. Key terms introduced in each chapter are highlighted and defined in context. These terms are listed at the end of each chapter and also included in the Glossary at the back of the book. Tables embedded in the chapters illustrate important information to assist and aid understanding. As noted earlier, the chapters may be read in any sequence.

The text is accompanied by a variety of online resources. Instructors will find the graphic organizers helpful when engaging students in application tasks. Related materials such as rubrics and checklists are provided to assist students in designing questions, evaluating online sources, writing the literature review, and writing the action research report. Please visit josseybass.com to access these online materials.

NOTE TO STUDENTS

You will find the learning objectives helpful, as they provide an introduction to the text and help focus the chapter material. The key terms may be reviewed prior to reading each chapter, as the definitions will promote understanding. Students are encouraged to use the rubrics and checklists to assist with their research or as self-evaluation tools. Last, the chapter examples illustrate the material and are provided to enhance the information.

NOTE TO PROFESSIONAL DEVELOPMENT TRAINERS

The online resources contain organizers to promote application of content, strategies, and processes. Organizers may be used as part of a training session or workshop or as part of follow-up assignments. Rubrics and checklists may also be used as part of professional development sessions or as self-evaluation tools for participants.

NOTE TO ONLINE INSTRUCTORS

Online discussion forum questions are provided. Forums may be structured for small group or team discussion. Questions may also be used for class forums as well. A rubric for evaluating online discussion is included with the online resources.

ACKNOWLEDGMENTS

I would like to acknowledge Dr. Bennie and Dr. Dillon. Thank you for providing peace, solace, and a place to write. Thanks to K.S., who provided motivation, color, and style. Special thanks to Paul, my best friend and gazebo partner—I couldn't have completed this book without your encouragement and support.

Thank you to the graduate students and teachers that collaborate with me every day. I continue to observe in wonder as you travel on your research journeys.

I sincerely thank Andy Pasternack and Seth Schwartz at Jossey-Bass for their guidance and assistance with this project. It's been a pleasure working with you.

THE AUTHOR

Dorothy Valcarcel Craig holds a bachelor of science degree in elementary education and a master of arts in education with an emphasis in diagnostic and prescriptive reading from East Carolina University; a specialist in education degree in curriculum and instruction from Middle Tennessee State University, and a doctorate in education with specialization in instructional technology from Tennessee State University. She completed postdoctoral studies in English as a second language at the University of Memphis. A former classroom teacher and curriculum writer, Dr. Craig joined the faculty at Middle Tennessee State University in 1996. She holds the rank of professor and teaches undergraduate and graduate courses online. She directs the university's specialist in education program in curriculum and instruction, with a specialization in technology and curriculum design, and serves as a faculty mentor for online instructors and course developers. From 2002 to 2007, Dr. Craig was the principal investigator for the ESL Enterprise Project, a U.S. Department of Education professional development grant. Her research endeavors include technology integration in K–12 and higher education, use of iPods in second-language instruction, second-language acquisition, early literacy, and online learning. Dr. Craig's publications have appeared in the *International Journal of the Book*, the *Journal of the Arts in Society*, the *Journal of Educational Technology Systems*, the *International Journal of Learning, Higher Learning*, the *Journal of Elementary Science Education*, and *Work-Based Learning in Primary Care*. She is an editorial reviewer for *Current Issues in Education*, the *Journal of Ethnographic and Qualitative Research*, the *Tennessee Association of Middle Schools Journal*, and the *TNTESOL Journal*.

ACTION RESEARCH
ESSENTIALS

CHAPTER

1

INTRODUCTION TO ACTION RESEARCH

LEARNING OBJECTIVES

After reading Chapter One, you should be able to:

- Discuss several definitions applied to action research
- Identify the steps involved in the action research process
- Examine the rationale for selecting action research as an appropriate method
- Discuss the role and responsibilities of the ethical researcher

INTRODUCTION

We live in an information age driven by accountability issues that influence practice across many disciplines. The classroom teacher faced with designing effective instruction that meets the needs of a diverse population of students must also address the demand to prepare students for end-of-year standardized tests. Social workers—in order to give attention to multiple cases—must examine procedures and practices to develop effective strategies that reflect sound performance. Professionals in the field of nursing—faced with budget cuts and shortages—examine current practices as they address accountability concerns in order to support needs and improve conditions. Graduate students are encouraged to examine a variety of issues in their field of study—many of which involve some type of accountability related to practice—as they build skills needed to be effective researchers. These are just a few examples of practitioner-based environments where professionals—whether it be teachers, nurses, social workers, graduate students, or human resource coordinators—face the need to examine a variety of issues and concerns in order to gather information systematically and formulate a plan to improve practice. This chapter presents information that is covered in depth in later chapters. Examine the information presented here, and seek additional explanations in other chapters.

Although conditions for inquiry are present in a variety of practitioner-based settings, this text will specifically focus on teaching and learning environments such as classrooms and will present information to help graduate students build skills needed to identify problems, carry out research, and develop action plans to improve practice. Therefore, the expressions "work-based environment" and "practitioner-based environment," although they may be applied to a variety of settings, should be understood as specifically referring to the classroom setting in the P–16 environment.

WHAT IS ACTION RESEARCH?

Within the realm of teaching and learning comes the blended challenge of addressing accountability issues while at the same time using available information and experience to improve practice. Once immersed in the classroom, teachers often find the role of teacher expanding to that of teacher-as-researcher. This is in part based on their experience as professionals as well as their knowledge base as experts in the field. Elliot Eisner (1998), in *The Enlightened Eye*, suggests that experience has its genesis in the transactions one has with the environment. There is no better catalyst to inform practice than the teacher who interacts in the classroom on a daily basis. Drawing on professional experience, classroom teachers often find themselves engaged in inquiry regarding the intricacies of teaching and learning. This is possible due to the expertise of the practicing teacher and the *data* available in the environment. Data are sets of information collected during inquiry. They may consist of sets of numerical information. Data may also take the form of interview responses, observations, or survey responses. When considering the type of data typically available in the classroom environment, one might think of classroom test scores, recorded observations of interactions, inventories, journal entries, interview responses, standardized test scores, projects, and writing samples, to name a few. The inquiry process involves identifying problems, gathering data, analyzing data, and designing a plan of action. The plan is implemented—based on the inquiry—in the practicing environment. Additional data are collected and analyzed, which leads to conclusions—all for the sake of improving practice. This type of research is known as *action research*.

Action research is a common methodology employed for improving conditions and practice in classrooms and in other practitioner-based environments such as administrative, leadership, social, and community settings. Kurt Lewin, who was instrumental in establishing a research center at the Massachusetts Institute of Technology, was perhaps one of the first researchers to use the term *action research*. Lewin (1951) suggested that in an effective community of practice, comparative research takes place. This comparative research consists of an examination of conditions and effects of different forms of social action. Unlike research that produces findings without action, the spiral and cyclical research process leads to action and improvement.

Through action research, teachers and others working in a practitioner-based environment use their expertise and knowledge to conduct systematic inquiry that helps improve conditions and solve problems. As practitioners interact in the environment, they gain experience. They use this experience to inform practice. However, experience must be matched with evaluative skills to improve the practicing environment. Effective evaluation of a program, situation, or condition—which is in essence based in systematic analysis—can be facilitated through action research. Action research encourages the researcher to consider the interconnectedness of the environment and everyone in it, the conditions present in the environment, and the interactions among the individuals in the environment. Action research is typically community-based. *Community-based research* is usually conducted in the practicing environment, individually or in teams. It involves the parties who naturally interact in that environment and is ordinarily conducted to improve the community as a whole. The community may be the individual classroom, a grade level of classrooms, the school, or the entire school system. Lewin (1951) uses the term *community of practice* to describe the community-based quality of action research.

In addition, action research is considered a *field-intensive process*. A *field-intensive process* is one that requires the researcher to take an active part in the environment being studied. The researcher is expected to be a *participant observer* as well as a *researcher-as-instrument* involved in the research process. A *participant observer* is a researcher who takes part in all activities in the environment being studied and interacts naturally with subjects in the environment. A *researcher-as-instrument* is able to rely on expertise, draw on experience, and use research skills in an unbiased manner in tasks such as conducting interviews and recording notes during observations. The field-intensive process also requires the researcher to collect multiple forms of data, organize the data effectively, analyze the data, and use the findings to design an *action plan*. The researcher uses the findings—matched with knowledge of the environment, expertise, and experience—to develop a plan for improvement. The *action plan* is a framework or blueprint that is implemented to improve practice, conditions, or the environment in general. The design of the action plan is based on the inquiry and findings. All of these things make action research an ideal methodology for practitioners.

For example, one classroom teacher may observe certain interactions among students in the classroom environment, which leads the teacher to believe that the reading material currently being used is not challenging enough. The teacher over-hears students admitting that they had read the book and done the same activities the year before. The teacher also notices that most of the students breeze through the comprehension tasks and related writing activities with ease. Consulting with grade-level teams, the teacher discovers that other teachers are seeing the same things in their classrooms. This prompts a grade-level survey of all students, observations over a period of time, and group interviews with students in order to gather information regarding previous reading experiences, interests, and preferences. Each teacher compares results with colleagues. The grade-level team decides to gather additional data consisting of student classroom reading scores, writing samples, standardized test scores, inventories of reading materials, compiled lists of library resources, and parent or guardian input based on a short survey. The data are organized and analyzed. This leads to a redesign of the reading program and a plan of action for implementation. The teachers involved in this action research example relied on their experience as experts in the field. They were participant observers in the environment as they interacted with students, observed, and collected data. They organized the classroom data and used them to design an action plan to improve their own practice and the community of practice as a whole.

ACTION RESEARCH: SOME DEFINITIONS

Although there are many definitions of action research, most have common threads that illustrate the key theoretical points of the method. Several of these points have already been mentioned. First, action research is typically conducted by teachers for teachers. It may also be conducted by practitioners for practitioners. The process focuses on practice in order to improve practice. Action research may result in positive change in the form of action. It is participatory in nature and involves the community of learners, the community of the environment, and the community of practice. The focus of action research inquiry is related to all of these. It is systematic and structured. Last, action research focuses on problems, issues, or concerns present in the practicing environment.

Many definitions imply that action research consists of research for the sake of taking action. The process requires the researcher to become actively involved in the study of the environment and the parties who interact naturally with each other and with the environment. The process is practical in that data and the analysis of data lead to improvement and change. The process is also participative because it encourages collaboration among colleagues. The collaborative quality of action research is empowering due to the fact that participant researchers are able to effect change and make improvements. The collaboration is imperative because social reality is determined and improved as part of the overall common goals and visions of an entire school. The process is also tentative in that the inquiries may result in change in particular situations and may then be reexamined as needed. Finally, the process is critical for practitioners because they are able to search together for practical solutions and improvements.

Action research is both proactive and reactive. A *proactive research process* is prompted when a practitioner researcher—operating naturally in the environment—uses expertise to identify potential problems and then conducts systematic inquiry in order to improve conditions. A *reactive research process* is prompted when a practitioner researcher—interacting naturally in the environment—identifies an existing problem and then conducts systematic inquiry to correct the problem and improve conditions.

For example, a proactive study may require the teacher researcher to try a new practice, collect data, and reflect on alternative behaviors and results, which may lead to yet another new practice—all for the sake of positive change. A reactive study may involve collecting data to diagnose a problem, using results to implement a plan, and then distributing data and findings to others in order to effect change and improve practice. Whether proactive or reactive, the characteristics and components of action research and the process itself are continuous inquiry, reflection, and continuous improvement.

According to Sohng (1995), action research is premised on the principle that the parties in an environment carry out the investigation themselves; it therefore excludes techniques that require a separation of the researcher from the people being researched—as when experimental subjects are kept ignorant of the purpose of the study. The participatory nature of action research enables the researcher to study the natural practicing environment, engage in a methodical examination from inside a particular environment, examine the environment and all it entails, collect data, analyze the data, design an action plan for positive change, and draw conclusions and present findings to inform practice. It should be noted that the results of action research may not always require a formal presentation of findings. In many cases, action research conducted by individual teachers is not shared formally. The results may, however, be shared in an informal manner with colleagues and administrators. Although the action research process is aimed at improving practice and effecting change, the process is also a journey that tells a story. The journey of action research conducted by individuals tells a story of thought processes, solutions, and strategies. The story may be personal in a specific classroom and environment or public across several grades or even the entire school or institution.

Various researchers examine the definitions of action research further and suggest that multiple definitions are necessitated by the nature and uniqueness of the process (Noffke & Stevenson, 1995). Perhaps the most distinctive aspect of action research is that researchers can evaluate the situation and conditions from inside the environment, thereby obtaining authentic data and firsthand information. For example, practicing teachers who engage in action research as a means for bringing about the essential aspects of a more genuine profession are true researchers in that they are able to share a base of knowledge and expertise common to their profession. As practitioners, they are able to use their knowledge to drive systematic inquiry because they are aware of the standards of their practice. Practicing teachers—and practitioners in general—understand the differentiated roles in the profession and are fully competent to make professional decisions with regard to improving a specific situation. And they are able to engage in continuous reflection in order to improve the working environment (Meyers & Rust, 2003).

Action research has also been defined as the process of studying a "real" environment to understand and improve the quality of actions or instruction (Henson, 1996). It is a systematic and orderly way for classroom teachers to observe their practice or to explore a problem and a possible course of action. It is preplanned inquiry that is systematic and organized and can be shared with others in order to improve practice (Johnson, 2002). Sagor (2000) sums up action research as a disciplined process of inquiry conducted by practitioners who want to improve their own situation. The primary reason for engaging in action research is to assist the "researcher" in improving or refining situations, environments, and practice.

WHY ENGAGE IN ACTION RESEARCH?

Action research enables the researcher to study a particular situation and then to design and implement a plan to improve practices, conditions, and environments. Although there are numerous reasons to employ action research as a method for conducting research, there are basically three main purposes for selecting the approach.

1. Action research is selected as a method for conducting research by those who want to solve problems, address issues, and improve situations and conditions because the process promotes professional growth, improvement, and change. The process enables teachers and practitioners to become "experts in the field" because findings are based on true inquiry and therefore inform practice.

2. The method is ideal for addressing specific targeted goals and objectives that are within the realm of possibility for the practitioner to achieve. By actually

conducting an action research study, teachers are able to experience success firsthand.

3. Action research promotes collaboration and encourages "community" among all parties involved in a specific learning situation, leading to results that have the potential to improve conditions and situations for all members of the learning community.

These three basic reasons for selecting the method are also the reasons that make the process effective.

In its truest form, action research enables the researcher to provide valuable information—supported by facts and data—to individuals in decision-making positions. The process provides information that may assist in providing measures of accountability and support for specific practices. The information resulting from an action research study is used to inform practice and assist decision making. Action research is selected as a method because it provides a means for collaborative reflection, which encourages researchers to examine practice in order to make positive changes.

Osterman and Kottkamp (1993) provide a rationale for action research as a professional growth process in their "credo for reflective practice," which holds that everyone needs professional growth opportunities, all professionals want to improve, all professionals are capable of assuming responsibility for improving practice, and the process enriches the professional environment. Action research is characterized by the following components:

1. The study takes place in the "natural setting."

2. Before the study begins, the researcher examines his or her own biases in order to remove them and to use professional judgment and background in developing into a researcher-as-instrument.

3. Throughout the study, multiple forms of quantitative or qualitative data (or both) are collected—including primary data, secondary data, cued data, and artifacts.

4. Findings are typically rich in description.

5. Process, not product, is stressed.

6. Inductive analysis is ongoing.

7. Meaning is derived from data analysis, findings, and conclusions.

8. Findings inform practice.

It should also be noted that as a study progresses, the role of the researcher changes as the study evolves and the situation becomes clearer. Researchers must trust their instincts and rely on themselves as instruments in carrying out the study, collecting the data, analyzing and coding the data set, and reporting findings. Data consist of information collected as a result of any particular study. Data are used to inform the study. In qualitative studies, data may be grouped into sets; therefore, qualitative studies may use the term *data sets.*

Baskerville (1999) suggests that action researchers are among those who assume that complex social systems cannot be reduced for meaningful study. They believe that human organizations—as an interactive context—can only be understood as whole entities. The key assumptions of the action researcher are that social settings cannot be reduced for study by outside investigators and that action brings understanding leading to insight. One must keep in mind that it is these key assumptions that make action research uniquely different in form and structure from lengthy, more traditional research conducted for the sake of research alone, which in many instances is not possible within the confines and time limits of teaching and learning environments.

For further clarification, a comparison between the action process and the more traditional approach must be explored. To begin this exploration, the term *research* is defined as an organized and systematic means of finding answers to questions. *Theoretical* or *traditional research* is concerned with knowledge for the sake of theory as well as adding to the existing body of knowledge. Its design may be quantitative or qualitative. *Quantitative research* typically consists of a systematic examination of specific factors and includes numerical information as data. Quantitative studies usually involve a large number of subjects as the researcher attempts to quantify attitudes or behaviors in order to correlate or compare. Large quantitative research studies are not controlled by the practical usefulness of the findings. Other designs may take a qualitative approach. *Qualitative research* studies are broad and extensive, and typically require a much longer timeline. A qualitative study involves small groups of subjects and may even consist of an examination of one person operating and interacting in a particular environment. Qualitative studies attempt to provide insight into behaviors that occur among a specific number of subjects, at one given time, in one very specific setting.

Some theoretical research may be further divided into two broad categories of quantitative research—experimental research and descriptive research. Although action research may be based on theory derived from a previously done theoretical study, it may adopt a *qualitative research approach,* a *quantitative research approach,* or a mix of the two, depending on the nature of the inquiry (Henrichsen, Smith, & Baker, 1997). Table 1.1 provides a brief exploration of studies that follow a quantitative or qualitative approach and compares these approaches to the characteristics of action research.

A lengthy research study that takes a quantitative approach requires the researcher to identify a problem, collect data, and run a statistical test in order to draw conclusions. In many cases, the researcher is not present at the actual research site. Longitudinal qualitative studies do enable the researcher to interact regularly with participants; however, studies of this nature take place over a period of months or even years. Action research requires that practitioner researchers look at what they

TABLE 1.1. **Quantitative Approach, Qualitative Approach, and Action Research Characteristics**

Quantitative Approach	Qualitative Approach	Action Research
Specific focus or variable	Focus on broader problems	Focus on the "big picture" in examining a multitude of variables at work in a real-world environment
Operates on the basis of hypotheses	Uses overarching questions and themes	May operate on the basis of overarching questions that serve as a framework for examining themes or may require a hypothesis
May reveal degree of causality	May provide insight in the form of themes and patterns	May reveal degree of causality or may provide insight with the purpose of improving practice
May involve large groups of subjects Subjects may be divided into groups (control group and experimental group) May involve multiple research sites	May involve a very small group of participants or a limited number of subjects Subjects may be divided into smaller groups and may even consist of one subject as a case study Focus of inquiry typically involves one particular situation	Involves a limited number of subjects of one particular group within one specific environment May involve a larger number of subjects if the goal is systemic improvement May involve multiple research sites (classrooms)
May involve multiple instruments and analysis procedures Research may be removed from the actual research setting (Example: Phone or e-mail surveys)	Multiple forms of data are necessary in order to ensure triangulation Triangulation occurs when multiple forms of data yield similar results Involves fieldwork (researcher on research site)	Multiple forms of data selected to specifically inform practice Requires fieldwork (researcher on research site)

Continued

(Table 1.1 continued)

Quantitative Approach	Qualitative Approach	Action Research
Analysis uses statistical tests	Analysis involves coding, categorizing, and examining emerging patterns	Analysis may involve statistical tests or may involve coding, categorizing, and examining patterns
Findings may be applied to many different situations	Findings are rich in description and usually cannot be applied to different situations	Findings are used to design a plan of action Conclusions help inform and improve practice

themselves are doing, reflect on what they are thinking, and seek creative ways to improve their situation. Drawing on both quantitative and qualitative methods, action research reflects a practical blend of traditional (theoretical) research and integrates qualities and characteristics of both into a research process.

STEPS IN THE PROCESS

In essence, action research mirrors the teaching and learning process in that both are recursive. For example, it is sound educational practice to identify goals and objectives prior to presenting a lesson. The goals and objectives are aligned with content, skills, standards, student learning tasks, assessment tools or methods, and materials. The lesson is presented, and learning is analyzed. Assessment is both formative and summative, which helps inform subsequent lessons. Reflection takes place, and results are analyzed in order to make adjustments and revisions. The recursive process then begins again. Key factors and components of the process are thus an organized plan, onsite data collection, analysis, reflection, and use of findings to improve practice.

The process of teaching and learning and the action research process follow somewhat similar steps. First, both begin with identification of information. Next, both processes move to determining what is needed for success. In the case of teaching and learning, this step includes determining skills, content, and prior knowledge. In action research, the step involves designing the overarching questions based on the problem, issue, or concern. The processes move smoothly to an alignment step. Content, skills, tasks, assessment, and resources are aligned in the teaching and learning process. Overarching questions are matched with data sets—*all the collected data*—in action research. Next, implementation takes place. During this step, both processes involve collecting information, analysis, and reflection. Then adjustments are made—in teaching and learning and in action research—based on findings. Finally, the process begins again. The combined steps may be viewed in Table 1.2.

Action research is a *recursive* or *cyclical method*. A research method is recursive or cyclical when it moves through a series of steps over and over again. It does not end when findings are determined and conclusions are arrived at; instead, the process begins anew. Action research does not start from an initial question to the formulation of data collection, analysis, and conclusions. Rather the process begins with problem identification, which leads to research questions. The process progresses in

TABLE 1.2. **Similarities Between the Teaching and Learning Process and Action Research**

Overview of the Combined Process	Teaching and Learning Process	Action Research
Information identification	Identify targeted goals and objectives.	Identify problem, issue, or concern related to the work-based environment.
Determine what's needed	Determine content, skills, and prior knowledge.	Design questions based on problem, issue, or concern.
Alignment	Align content, skills, tasks, assessment tools, techniques, and resources.	Align questions with data sets.
Implementation	Implement lesson, conduct ongoing assessment, and engage in reflection.	Implement study, collect data, conduct ongoing analysis, and engage in reflection.
Adjustments	Make adjustments in teaching based on information from prior lesson.	Design action plan based on findings.
Success and change	Make informed decisions based on the previous steps. Begin process again.	Make informed decisions based on previous findings. Begin process again.

a manner that recognizes the need for ongoing, continuous inquiry. Regardless of the structure of the study, the researcher identifies types of data collected. These sets of data may be quantitative (numerical), qualitative (descriptive), or both. *Quantitative data* consist of numerical information. *Qualitative data* consist of writing, diagrams, pictures, and other products. Then the researcher engages in analysis leading toward an informed plan for improving practice. The plan of action and implementation of the plan assist the researcher in drawing conclusions, offering suggestions, and making changes to improve practice.

Steps in the action research process are similar to those typically followed with any type of research. The exception is the addition of an action plan integrated into the study. In the recursive or cyclical process of action research, also described as spiral or dynamic, the researcher begins by identifying a problem; develops a research statement, questions, and sometimes a hypothesis; collects data; analyzes the data; interprets the data; takes action; engages in reflection; and uses the findings to effect change (Creswell, 2002). Being part of the teaching and learning environment helps teacher researchers identify problems, issues, or concerns. After identifying a problem, the design of any action research study demands that the researcher develop research questions. Depending on the focus of the inquiry, the questions may be specific or broad and overarching. The questions become the blueprint or framework for the inquiry. The research questions of any action research study determine if the study will take a qualitative or a quantitative research approach because the questions guide the data identification. A qualitative research approach would require a set of broad research questions that are matched with multiple data sets consisting of a variety of information such as recorded notes, journals, and student writing samples. A quantitative research approach would require a hypothesis and numerical data. For example, depending on the type of questions and the focus of the inquiry, the study may require a *hypothesis statement*—typically part of a quantitative study. A *hypothesis statement* enables the researcher to make a prediction regarding the outcomes of the inquiry. Studies that take a quantitative approach include a hypothesis statement. The questions may require the researcher to use a qualitative approach and to collect data sets that match each overarching research question. This information is covered in depth in a later chapter.

In summary, action research typically includes research questions that provide a focus as to what will be examined and who will be involved. The questions encourage the researcher to focus on problems specific to a particular environment and to examine what takes place, how subjects interact and behave, and what is needed to improve conditions. The questions focus the study and lead the researcher in selecting the approach needed—either quantitative or qualitative—to best inform the inquiry. These steps are summarized in Figure 1.1.

In many cases, practitioner action research is conducted by individuals; however, it may be conducted by teams of teachers or collaborative groups including parents, teachers, students, and administrators. It may also be conducted by graduate

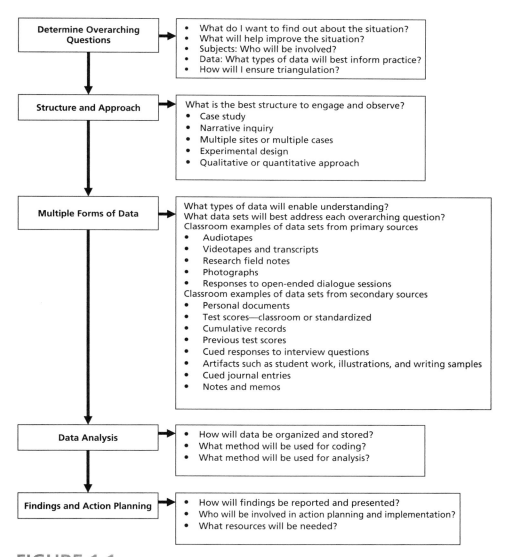

FIGURE 1.1. *The Action Research Process*

students working together or individually. Depending on the group, action researchers typically follow these steps in conducting a study:

- Selecting a focus
- Reviewing helpful theories that apply to the problem, issue, concern, or situation
- Identifying research questions

■ Narrowing the questions

■ Identifying subjects and participants such as colleagues, graduate students, administrators, parents, or community members

■ Selecting the method to best inform the inquiry

■ Identifying data sets

■ Collecting relevant data

■ Analyzing the data

■ Designing the action plan and taking informed action

■ Reporting results to all parties involved in order to improve conditions and situations related to teaching and learning

This multistep process may seem daunting to the beginning researcher. However, by working in the teaching and learning environment on a daily basis, the process becomes a natural part of the classroom. Beginning researchers may find the accompanying examples helpful as they embark on the action research journey. Exhibit 1.1 illustrates a teacher's planning log. Exhibit 1.2 illustrates the process from a graduate student's perspective.

PHASES OF AN ACTION RESEARCH STUDY

It is always a good idea for anyone who is new to the action research process to think in terms of three phases in completing an action research study: prestudy planning, implementation and analysis, and poststudy action planning. Several research-based tasks take place during each phase. By systematically moving through the phases, the process becomes easier and more fluid. Although the components and steps in the action research process are fully covered in subsequent chapters, the following are several suggestions illustrating activities that might take place during each phase in the process.

Prestudy Phase: Observations

Occasionally, when working in the classroom environment, observations of the subjects reveal problems, issues, and concerns. Before selecting a focus, it is sometimes beneficial to identify the subjects. This works well when a suspected problem involves several students or a particular group of students. Since action research revolves around practice, it is typical to select students that interact with the researcher in a routine fashion. The subjects may be part of the teacher researcher's own classroom or may be enrolled in another teacher's class. Researchers may begin by conducting at least three very focused participant observations of the subjects for approximately forty-five minutes to one hour. In participant observation, the researcher interacts with the subjects while observing. The interaction may be combine observation, interacting, and conversing. In many instances, the teacher researcher will be

EXHIBIT 1.1. Getting Started with Action Research: A Teacher Researcher's Planning Log

Problems, Concerns, and Questions	Subjects Involved	Possible Data Sources	Collection Timeline	Reflections, Ideas, and Emerging Patterns
Problems and Concerns Students are breezing through reading. Comprehension tasks seem relatively easy. Overheard conversation that students read this particular book last year. Activities they spoke about are very similar. Spoke with grade-level team to see if others are observing a similar situation. All expressed the same concern. Consulted with the principal regarding a possible study to determine what we can do as a team to challenge students. *Questions* What interests do students have that may assist teachers in identifying appropriate reading materials? What types of reading materials will appropriately challenge our students and help encourage students to read for a variety of purposes? What materials are readily available and which of these may be integrated effectively into the sixth-grade curriculum? *Needs* Interview instrument Parent survey Student survey Library inventory	HMS sixth-grade students HMS sixth-grade teachers	Reading comprehension tests (classroom) Standardized test scores (reading subtests) Small group interviews with students Parent/guardian survey (home reading habits and interests) Student surveys Classroom inventory Library inventory	Design timeline at next grade-level meeting. *Bring* Reading comprehension test scores (September and October) State assessment scores for reading subtests Classroom inventory of books	

EXHIBIT 1.2. Getting Started with Action Research: A Graduate Researcher's Planning Log

Problems, Concerns, and Questions	Subjects Involved	Possible Data Sources	Collection Timeline	Reflections, Ideas, and Emerging Patterns
Problems and Concerns As a graduate teaching assistant in the Foreign Language Department, I noticed that many undergraduate students majoring in Spanish do not fluently engage in conversations. Typically, they can be overheard integrating a few words in Spanish into primarily English conversations. In an informal conversation with other GTAs, they noticed the same thing. Out of curiosity, I examined student fluency test results. The test—taken after the students complete 12 credit hours of Spanish—indicate that almost half of the undergraduate students fail the fluency test on the first attempt. *Questions* What existing factors are preventing students from moving to a conversational level of fluency? What strategies may be integrated into Spanish coursework that will promote and encourage fluency? What information from this study may help improve practice? *Needs* Undergraduate student survey Student fluency exam results Interview department chair	Undergraduate students enrolled in SPAN 1101, SPAN 1102, SPAN 1103, and SPAN 1104 Instructors and graduate teaching assistants	Fluency tests In-class assignments Class participation grades Observations of class sessions Interviews with undergraduate students Interviews with instructors Examination of current textbooks and syllabi	Design timeline at next faculty meeting. Meet in library in order to examine current textbooks. Bring syllabi and other related materials such as assignments.	

able to identify emerging problems that surface during the interactive observations. In addition, the focused observations usually reveal problems in the environment that point to concerns that may develop into the focus of the study. Graduate students also benefit from this preplanning process.

Prestudy Phase: Finding a Focus

Whether working alone or collaboratively, teachers as well as graduate students may reflect on certain key questions:

1. What do I want to find out about these specific students or situation?
2. What is important, and what do I want to improve in terms of meeting the needs of this special group of students?
3. What are the problems, issues, and concerns in this specific environment?
4. What issues and concerns emerge that need to be addressed in order to improve the situation?

Two simple strategies that usually help beginning researchers are keeping a reflective journal and conducting informal reflective interviews.

Reflective Journal   Practitioner action researchers commonly keep reflective journals documenting their ongoing research. These may be in the form of spiral note-books, three-ring binders, decorative journals, or electronic files. Begin by recording thoughts in a reflective journal. Jot down initial responses to the questions. After a day or two, return to the responses to record any additional thoughts or reflections that come to mind.

Informal Reflective Interview and Analytical Dialogue   It is always a good idea to talk to colleagues, administrators, parents, and community members when appropriate. Engage in informal dialogue. Discuss the problems surrounding teaching and learning that have been identified. Ask questions regarding the problems, and record the informal responses for later reflection. In many cases, the informal dialogue helps focus the study more tightly and provide additional insight.

Prestudy Phase: Reviewing Helpful Theories

Considering the nature of action research, the teacher researcher must be able to explore existing theories in order to gather information to make informed decisions and to design the action plan. Calling on personal expertise and experience as a practicing professional, explore underlying feelings, beliefs, and insights regarding teaching and learning. Revisit entries recorded in the reflective journal. Conduct a personal brainstorming session to further explore the problems, issues, and concerns. Record the responses. Conduct an intuitive assessment by prioritizing the responses. Next, organize the responses in a list, chart, or some other graphic form. Some researchers find it helpful to reorganize responses and ideas into a concept map, as the process helps in expanding ideas and revealing additional details regarding the issue, concern, or problem.

Prestudy Phase: Brief Review of Literature

With the focus of the study now well defined, a brief, preliminary literature review can help support the rationale for research. The *literature review* is a process that enables the researcher to identify and evaluate studies conducted by other scholars and practitioners. The review is a systematic examination of existing research related to the focus of the study. The literature review may also serve as a fact-finding process to help the researcher narrow the research focus.

Prestudy Phase: Designing Research Questions

The refined and narrowed focus calls for a strong set of overarching questions. Three or four well-written questions will get the study moving.

Prestudy Phase: Identifying Data Sets

Reexamine the overarching questions. Ask yourself, what type of data will best inform? Carefully select data that will provide insight. Remember that as the study progresses, additional data sets may be added.

Implementation and Analysis Phase

It is strongly suggested that a data collection schedule be prepared. The collection schedule should be followed throughout the study. Ongoing analysis is conducted as the study progresses. A timeline illustrating activities from beginning to end will keep the study on track.

Poststudy Phase: The Action Plan and Reporting Findings

The ongoing analysis aids the recursive process and helps the researcher draw conclusions. The findings are used to design the action plan, which is implemented in a timely manner. The findings should be formally reported to all parties involved. The dissemination of information based on research is the key to improving practice because positive change is the basis of systematic inquiry. To succeed in the role of researcher, one must be able to substantiate the process. Action research is the perfect tool to answer the question "So what?" In other words, if a study is conducted and the findings yield little relevant information to effect change and to improve practice, people may ask, "So what?" The action researcher is in a professional position to provide the answer to this basic question because the results from the action plan can be directly linked to improving practice.

WHAT ARE DATA?

To offer further clarification regarding the data, teacher researchers need to revisit the need for multiple data sets. The classroom and work-based environments are rich with naturally occurring data. For example, teachers come in contact with multiple data sets on a daily basis. Data in the form of observations, classroom test scores, student artifacts, standardized test scores, discussion responses, and informal conversations are abundant, and all may inform practice. It is the systematic matching of overarching questions with data sets that is the key to a successful study. No amount of data will inform practice if it is not considered or used. Therefore, it is critical for the teacher researcher to be able to match data carefully with inquiry, know which data will best inform, identify effective analysis methods, and consider all data as sources of information.

For example, a study that focuses on a new math program that is being implemented to improve test scores would require the action researcher to collect information—possibly pre- and poststudy implementation—regarding student progress. The data may consist of test scores before and after program implementation. In addition, the action researcher may want to find out how the students liked working with the math manipulatives that are part of the program; in that case, a student survey may be administered. The data collected would then be statistically analyzed using a test. Even though several forms of data were collected, the methodological approach of the study would be considered quantitative. However, if the researcher just wanted to find out how the students liked the manipulatives that were part of the math program, the research design would require different types of data. For example, the researcher might collect test scores, interview students, conduct open-ended discussions, and videotape classroom sessions. This study would be taking a qualitative approach. Both studies described have similar research goals, which require a certain type of data. In addition, both studies require the researcher to collect several types of data. This is often the case. This is due in part to the research environment, which is also the practicing environment, where multiple forms of data are readily available.

One reason for collecting multiple data sets when the action research takes a qualitative approach is to ensure triangulation. *Triangulation* occurs when multiple forms of data, when analyzed, show similar results, thus confirming the researcher's findings. Typically, a qualitative action research study includes two or three overarching questions. Data sets are identified based on their ability to assist the researcher in answering each question. It is recommended that at least three data sets be identified and collected for each question in order to establish triangulation.

Triangulation of the data provides validity to what was studied. Sagor (2000) suggests that action researchers use a graphic organizer or triangulation matrix to show the various data sets that will be used to answer each overarching question. The triangulation matrix helps the researcher formulate thoughts and visualize the process. The matrix is also helpful in determining what data sets will best address the overarching questions as the study progresses. Exhibit 1.3 illustrates a simple triangulation matrix. (For further discussion regarding developing questions, identifying data sets, and matching data for triangulation purposes, see Chapter Five.)

Although not always required, a triangulation matrix is also beneficial when the action research takes a quantitative approach. The matrix helps the researcher think systematically about what types of data will best inform the study, even if the data are quantitative.

EXHIBIT 1.3. A Completed Triangulation Matrix

Focus of the Study

Preservice teachers' perceptions and views of diversity as related to today's classrooms and what is needed to prepare for ever-changing populations in public schools

Overarching Questions	Data Set 1	Data Set 2	Data Set 3
Question 1 What views and perceptions regarding diversity are held by predominantly white preservice students?	Student responses to a diversity survey	Discussion responses to a Socratic seminar based on *Educating Esme*	Response papers based on diversity issues presented in *Educating Esme*
Question 2 Would an examination of historical issues and current issues within the context of a beginning education course alter these views and perceptions?	Student-created concept maps focusing on concerns about the first year of teaching	Student responses to open-ended questions	Instructor field notes
Question 3 How do students of the "digital generation" view the role of the teacher in meeting the needs of diverse populations?	Revised concept maps (after viewing two popular movies depicting teachers)	Online discussion forum response to *Freedom Writer's Diary*	Student-designed "plan for a successful first year"

Considering the fact that data are the heart of any action research project, the researcher must select data sets that assist in making decisions, narrow the study, and determine the path that must be taken with regard to the methodological approach. In addition, the action research process calls for both ongoing data analysis and summative data analysis. *Ongoing data analysis* helps the researcher formulate hypotheses. The continuous analysis of data also helps the researcher develop and revise analytical questions, if needed. Ongoing analysis also helps identify any additional data that may be needed. When planning the research timeline, ongoing analysis should be integrated into the schedule in all phases of the study. Ongoing analysis promotes continuous data collection based on the data previously collected. It encourages the researcher to record observer notes, which help direct the study. For qualitative action research, ongoing analysis prompts the researcher to explore metaphors, analogies, and concepts in order to identify any patterns that emerge in the environment. In quantitative action research, ongoing analysis carries the study forward and provides a continuum on which to plot the research. And in all action research, regardless of whether a qualitative or a quantitative approach is used, ongoing analysis helps the researcher design the action plan based on the inquiry because the history of the analysis provides a clear picture of what took place and what is needed to improve practice.

WHEN IS ACTION RESEARCH THE APPROPRIATE CHOICE?

To say that the action research process is appropriate in every research situation would be untrue. However, there are factors present in specific situations that demand an action research approach. In addition, perhaps the critical factor in selecting action research is that the researcher is also the practitioner operating in the work-based environment in which the study will take place; a specific problem, issue, or concern has been identified; and the results from the study will improve the environment, situation, or conditions. Keep in mind that action research is an approach as well as a process method. A researcher in any given situation must identify a focus, determine subjects and participants, identify data sets to inform, and select a methodology. Sound research is driven by the problem at hand. Researchers may review a number of methods before selecting the one that is well matched to the problem or focus of the study, will best inform the situation, and will enable the inquiry to yield the results in order to make valid contributions to the related field.

Two Scenarios

Consider the following two scenarios. Which of the two is the better match for an action research approach?

Scenario 1 An eighth-grade English teacher notices that several female students are arriving at school three days each week dressed in scrubs, which are normally worn by people in the medical profession. He begins to take note that on the two remaining days, the same female students wear outfits that are typically worn by any other middle school female student. Upon further examination, he notices that on days when scrubs are worn, the female students take part in discussion at a higher rate, offer to assist others with writing tasks, and are generally more involved in classroom tasks.

Focus

Clothing choice and interactions among eighth-grade female students enrolled in an English/Language Arts class

Overarching Research Questions

1. Does choice of clothing have an effect on the rate of interactions among female students, and if so, what is the connection?

    Data set 1: Recordings (on calendar) of daily outfits

    Data set 2: Audiotaped recordings of interactions among students during focused discussion

    Data set 3: Teacher observations of voluntary help sessions

2. Would the absence of choice in this particular situation hinder the high rate of interactions?

    Data set 1: Field notes recording interactions on days when scrubs are not worn

    Data set 2: Informal interviews with students regarding "free choice" of clothing

    Data set 3: Survey administered to students regarding choice of clothing

3. Do the interactions carry over to other subject areas and does this behavior affect academic success, and if so, what suggestions can be made to help content area teachers be more tolerant of student choice of attire?

    Data set 1: Interview responses from non–English/Language Arts content area teachers

    Data set 2: Classroom grades for one marking period (gathered from all content area teachers)

    Data set 3: Observations of interactions in non–English/Language Arts content area classes

The nature of the inquiry in this scenario demands a qualitative approach. There are a small number of subjects involved. The researcher must collect multiple forms of qualitative data. The data must be coded and compared in order to make meaning of the situation. The researcher looks for emerging patterns and gleans key points from the patterns. Findings are shared with non–English/Language Arts teachers in order to provide insight and make changes in classroom instruction.

Scenario 2   As part of her responsibilities, a graduate teaching assistant (GTA) is assigned to teach a freshman-level Introduction to Biology class. Her office happens to be located next to that of an adjunct professor in the same department. In conversation, the GTA learns that the adjunct is teaching another section of the same Intro to Bio class. As the semester progresses, the GTA notices that students are disrespectful and condescending to her. She discusses this with the adjunct, and he expresses a similar concern regarding his own class.

Focus

Views of graduate teaching assistants and adjunct professors held among freshmen at a large state university in the northeastern United States

Overarching Research Questions

1. What views regarding the expertise of GTAs and adjunct professors are held among freshmen at a state university, and do these views differ with regard to tenure-track faculty?

    Data set 1: Online survey administered to freshmen enrolled in the Intro to Bio classes that focuses on perceived levels of expertise among instructors

    Data set 2: Student enrollment numbers at the start, midpoint, and end of the semester

    Data set 3: Drop and add records across all sections

2. Do these views—whether positive or negative—hinder or enhance success at the university level?

    Data set 1: Student test scores

    Data set 2: Student lab scores

    Data set 3: Final grades

3. What can be gleaned from this study that would assist future GTAs and adjuncts in preparing for the teaching and learning experience at the university level?

    Data set 1: Satisfaction surveys administered at the end of the semester (classes taught by GTAs, adjuncts, and tenure-track professors)

    Data set 2: Faculty evaluation data

    Data set 3: Surveys administered to GTAs, adjuncts, and tenure-track professors

The nature of the inquiry in the second scenario demands a quantitative approach. The number of participants is large. Data consist of multiple survey results, test scores, grades, evaluation results, and related numerical information. A statistical analysis is required in order to make sense of the information. Findings are shared with department chairs, GTAs, adjuncts, and tenure-track professors in order to provide insight and improve practice.

Analysis

Every study is unique. Methodological approaches—qualitative and quantitative—differ. Scenario 1 focuses on a small, specific population, while scenario 2 targets a large population. The similarities, however, are what make action research appropriate in both situations. First, both scenarios describe situations where the researcher is also the practitioner. Second, the practitioners—one a teacher and the other a GTA—are immersed in the environment. Third, change and improvement are within the realm of possibility for both the practitioner researchers described. Finally, each study has the potential to yield information that may be used to improve practice. It is these factors, present in both situations, that lead the researchers to action research.

HOW CAN THE PROCESS EFFECT CHANGE?

The essence of all inquiry is to gain knowledge or to inform in some way. The inquiry is driven by a set of questions, which guide the researcher. Typically, the research concludes with information gleaned from data, thus leading to new knowledge. The application of such knowledge beyond the study is one reason action research is effective in promoting change. Consider the amount of research that is conducted in all walks of life on a daily basis. Think about the potential findings of medical research and market research. In the medical field, research conducted usually leads to new procedures, techniques, and medicines. Market research results in new products. Even though the researchers may not be involved in the actual "practitioner-based" environments that the findings relate to, the results are beneficial and serve as a catalyst for change and improvement. Classroom research—conducted using the action research approach—has the same potential to improve teaching techniques, classroom environments, and student learning. However, action research—conducted by researchers who are also operating in the practicing environment on a daily basis—has even greater potential because practitioners are able to use their own experience and expertise. The process prompts overt ownership because the researchers are also the practitioners and teachers. The degree of relevancy is highest when the researcher is also the practitioner who is able to make sense of the findings and use the results to take action for improvement and change.

Consider a common occurrence that takes place in most public schools across the United States every year: the process of administering standardized tests. The students are prepared, tests are given, and compiled results are sent to the schools. Teachers review the scores and share the results with parents. Copies of the score reports are filed in student cumulative folders and kept in a designated place. Are the results of the tests useful? If the reports are never used as diagnostic tools to improve instruction, the answer is no. However, if teachers and administrators review the score reports and use the findings to inform instruction, the tests have value in improving practice.

The same is true for research. Action research encourages the systematic study of a particular problem but carries the research to the point of using findings for the specific purpose of taking action and improving practice. The action plan is informed by research results, thereby assisting in effecting change through the experience and expertise of the teacher or practitioner researchers, new knowledge, "inside information" gleaned from the researchers, and the researchers' ability to connect the research process with the actual practice of the field.

THE ETHICAL RESEARCHER

Important to the ethics of research is the *institutional review board (IRB),* a team of peers that works as part of a university or school with the goal of protecting the rights and welfare of human research subjects. Many school systems, even those without IRBs, have guidelines for conducting research. Most universities that require students to conduct research do have an IRB, which issues guidelines for conducting research that involves human subjects. Whenever research involves human subjects—which action research almost always does—the researcher must consider the ethics involved in maintaining the confidentiality of participants in the study. For example, an action research study may involve photos of students as one form of data in order to explore group dynamics. At the least, the researcher must obtain parent or guardian consent to use the photos if the findings are to be shared outside the research site. Despite good intentions, a well-meaning teacher researcher may design an action research study that violates ethical rules. When in doubt, there are many online resources that may be consulted.

The *Code of Ethics for Institutional Research* published by the Association for Institutional Research (2001) is available on the organization's Web site (http://airweb.org). The code outlines critical items that must be considered when conducting research that involves human subjects. It covers the following topics:

1. *Competence.* The code discusses the auspices under which a researcher accepts an assignment for conducting research and states that the researcher must not—under any circumstances—assume a role for which he or she cannot claim a specific degree of competence. This discussion also addresses the assumption of duties that would require a researcher to train subordinates or educate subordinates regarding research practices and procedures.

2. *Practice.* Objectivity, use of accepted technical standards, initial discussions regarding special techniques and procedures, responsibilities, data collection and storage, reporting, and documentation are addressed. The ethical researcher must follow guidelines for data storage as well as accurately reporting what took place.

3. *Confidentiality.* One critical factor in conducting research with human subjects is to make sure that their anonymity is protected. Other guidelines govern treatment, exclusion, and inclusion based on specific criteria that must be considered.

4. *Relationship to the community.* Equal treatment, local codes, archiving and custody of information, assessment, integrity and accuracy of reports, and external reporting are discussed. Although action research is conducted for improving practice, the relationship to the community at large is important in that findings may be used by others in a school or school system.

5. *Relationship to the craft.* The ethical researcher must address research responsibilities such as acknowledging co-researchers and maintaining integrity throughout the study. In addition, the research must report any unethical conduct of colleagues even if it means that an uncomfortable situation may develop.

SUMMARY

The action research process encourages participatory change. The process promotes using teacher or practitioner expertise in identifying a problem, designing inquiry-based questions, designing a study, implementing the study, and using findings to design an action plan for the sake of improving practice. The process employs elements of traditional research approaches but is unique in that the study restarts itself after information gleaned from the initial inquiry is used to design the action plan. Steps in the process include selecting a focus, identifying research questions, selecting data and analysis procedures, drawing conclusions, and designing and implementing the action plan. In addition, there are specific research-oriented tasks that teacher researchers may engage in at the prestudy phase that help refine a study and focus the inquiry more tightly. Multiple forms of data—carefully matched with the overarching research questions—ensure triangulation, thereby providing additional reliability. The method is ideal for addressing specific problems, goals, and objectives that are within the realm of possibility for the practitioner to solve and achieve. The field-intensive process of action research is practical, empowering, and critical in searching for solutions and ways to improve conditions and practice.

The action research process is an appropriate method for those who operate in the practicing environment on a daily basis. It is an effective process that promotes improvement and change because it enables practitioners to use their experience and expertise while taking ownership of the research process. Last, all researchers must follow guidelines provided by individual institutional review boards at their particular institutions or research sites or else other authoritative professional research ethics and codes of conduct. The following chapters provide in-depth discussion of all these steps, along with strategies for conducting action research studies.

KEY TERMS

Action plan
Action research
Community-based research
Cyclical method
Data
Data set
Field-intensive process
Hypothesis statement
Institutional review board (IRB)
Literature review
Participant observer
Proactive research process
Qualitative data

Qualitative research
Qualitative research approach
Quantitative data
Quantitative research
Quantitative research approach
Reactive research process
Recursive method
Research
Researcher-as-instrument
Theoretical research
Traditional research
Triangulation

DISCUSSION QUESTIONS

1. Compare the teaching and learning process with the action research process. How are the two related, and why is the relationship important?

2. Compare the characteristics of action research and qualities and elements of quantitative and qualitative research approaches. How does the action research process use key elements of both quantitative and qualitative methods and in doing so make the process a sound educational choice?

3. What is the value in completing the prestudy research tasks? How do the tasks assist the researcher in refining and focusing the study?

4. Discuss the conditions under which action research is appropriate. How does the action research process help the practitioner?

SUGGESTED TOPICS

1. Compare action research as a method and an approach to the quantitative and qualitative approaches. Identify key elements drawn from quantitative and qualitative research. Provide an explanation as to why the elements make action research a sound educational choice for research.

2. Brainstorm possible problems, issues, and concerns that may become the focus for an action research study. Use a planning log like the ones in Exhibit 1.1 and Exhibit 1.2 to record thoughts and ideas.

3. Study the following scenarios to determine which would work best with action research.

a. A university department is planning to add a diversity strand to all under-graduate courses. However, after several preliminary discussions, the faculty members are not sure if integrating a diversity strand would be as effective as developing a new course devoted entirely to diversity and cultural issues.

b. A team of first-grade teachers would like to implement a new vocabulary strategy but are concerned that it might not work. Their school administrator agrees to purchase the necessary materials if the teachers would study the effect of the new strategy and report findings to the PTA.

c. High school dance team leaders decide to implement a peer-coaching system to help team members learn dance routines. Team members respond well after just two sessions. The team leaders decide to continue the peer-coaching system, study progress, and report findings to other athletic teams.

d. A middle school English as a Second Language teacher would like to examine the progress of non-English-speaking students as he implements a multisensory approach to teaching.

ONLINE ACTIVITIES

1. Select one or two of the discussion questions provided to set up an online forum. Have students support their ideas with outside sources. Use a rubric for evaluating the postings. (Note: This may be completed in small groups or with the entire class.)

2. Brainstorm and complete the pre-planning log. Exchange the completed log with group members. Pose at least two questions to assist the researcher who completed the log in refining and focusing the study.

3. Using the scenarios provided, set up a dedicated discussion forum for each. In small groups, have students discuss the possibilities of action research. Would it work? Is action research best suited for the inquiry? What methodological approach would be required for the inquiry? Why?

4. Set up an open discussion forum. Encourage students to post questions regarding action research along with ideas they have for action research projects.

CHAPTER

THE PROCESS BEGINS

LEARNING OBJECTIVES

After reading Chapter Two, you should be able to:

- Explore, consider, and evaluate possible topics for action research through brainstorming, concept mapping, and use of a simple rubric
- Engage in evaluative reflection regarding action research topics and problems
- Examine the differences between exempt, expedited, and full proposal reviews
- Identify commonly used forms and procedures in order to submit a proposed study to an Institutional Review Board (IRB)

THE ACTION RESEARCH ENVIRONMENT

Beginning the research process may seem overwhelming for readers new to action research or any other type of research, for that matter. Whatever the reason for conducting research, the process may be daunting at first. If you were to ask ten researchers how to begin, each would offer unique techniques and strategies for identifying problems and narrowing the research focus. In some cases, the process begins with ideas. The ideas branch out to a focused problem. The focused problem is then refined until the researcher arrives at the actual questions that frame the study. In other instances, the research is prompted by a previous study that is repeated. In the case of action research, however, research is prompted by a problem that is present in the practitioner's own environment. The need for change, matched with a desire to improve, is often the catalyst for ideas that lead to problem identification for possible inquiry.

As a method for school and work environment improvement, action research is not only for people already working in the field. It is becoming increasingly popular for graduate programs to integrate action research into coursework in order to prepare teachers pursuing graduate degrees to face the challenges of research in the classroom. It also provides opportunities for full-time graduate students to gain skills needed to conduct research in the work environment. Typically found in master's-level coursework, action research is making its way into doctoral programs and is becoming an approved method for dissertation research in many universities. Burnaford, Fischer, and Hobson (1996) suggest that traditionally, researchers would distance themselves from the research in an attempt to make their work more credible. Teachers—who are immersed in the classroom—have a research-rich environment at their fingertips. Consider the classroom environment for a moment. Teaching and learning flow each day. As a teacher presents new information, students connect new to old learning and construct meaning. The new information helps the students move forward and make adjustments in schemas that enable them to gain skills needed to advance. This is also true for action research in the classroom or practitioner environment.

The work of many of the same theorists who have influenced classroom instruction can also be applied to the action research process. From John Dewey (1929) and his work with laboratory schools, where discovery learning and "learn by doing" were established as sound educational approaches, to Piaget, Vygotsky, and more recently, Gardner, the same principles of learning theory are revealed when conducting action research in classrooms. They promote self-discovery, learning by doing, learner construction of meaning, collaboration and learning together, and developing multiple intelligences and a strong sense of self. It is the process of self-discovery learning that influences behavior, along with the capacity to know and truly understand oneself, others, and the environment (Gardner, 1983; Rogers, 1961).

Action research is the natural outcome of combining this sense of self with the expertise of the practitioner and the research-rich environment of the classroom. The classroom becomes the laboratory for promoting learning by doing, self-discovery learning, and construction of knowledge and meaning, thus leading to continuous improvement. Needless to say, problem identification is natural for the action researcher because it is part of self-discovery in the learning environment.

IDENTIFYING PROBLEMS SUITABLE FOR ACTION RESEARCH

People who are already working in the classroom or other environment are aware of abundant problems and critical issues that might be considered as a focus for action research. Graduate students—who are not already in the classroom—find it a bit more difficult to determine which problem or critical issue is worth pursuing. In both cases, the interests of the research typically drive problem selection. Because the classroom is also an environment where naturally occurring events take place, numerous problems arise that might be suitable for action research. Also present in the classroom environment are outside influences—such as school improvement goals, the need to improve test scores, new program implementation, and system-wide goals—that may require research. Researchers must remember, however, that not all problems will demand that an action plan be put in place to achieve improved conditions.

When deliberating on problems for research, be sure to consider the following points.

■ Is the topic of interest to the researcher, and if so, will pursuing the problem via action research enhance knowledge, build research skills, and contribute to improvement? It is very important that graduate students consider this question first and foremost. The degree of interest must be considered first. If the problem exists but is of little or no interest to the researcher, it should not be pursued. Lack of interest will have a negative impact on critically evaluating the data, keeping the research on track, and completing the study. The same holds true to some degree for teachers and practitioners. However, the nature of teaching and the structure of schooling may in some cases demand that a teacher or practitioner pursue a study that is not of great interest but is critical to improving practice and effecting change.

■ Can the researcher provide a convincing explanation for the choice of problem? If not, a different problem should be selected.

■ What impact will the findings have on the teaching and learning process, and will the findings lead to change and improvement? There is no point in pursuing action research if the findings will have little effect on improving the environment.

■ Are there adequate resources in place to support the action research, and are there others who deem the problem important enough to pursue? For example, if the research requires resources that are beyond the scope of the researcher, it will become burdensome and may not be effective. The action research process promotes collaboration, so if resources are scarce, consider teaming up with another researcher, administrator, or colleague.

TABLE 2.1. Problem Identification Rubric

Criterion	Take Immediate Action	Place on Hold	Discard
Interest	High degree of interest Excellent potential to enhance knowledge Interest sparks the development of skills Inquiry will contribute to improvement	Some interest Good potential to enhance knowledge May help with developing research skills May assist in promoting improvement	Little interest
Explanation	Problem choice can be easily explained and supported Researcher feels comfortable explaining problem selection to colleagues and administrators Researcher is passionate about the problem	Problem choice can be explained Researcher is somewhat comfortable providing an explanation	Researcher has trouble explaining why this problem should be selected
Impact	Findings have great potential for contributing to the existing body of knowledge Findings have potential to effect change and improve practice Findings have potential to inform those in decision-making positions	Findings have some potential for adding to the existing body of knowledge and effecting change	Finding may have some potential for adding to the existing body of knowledge
Resources	The research does not require resources that are beyond the researcher's environment	The research may require resources outside the researcher's environment	Pursing this problem will require more resources than are available
Existing goals	The problem is related to existing goals and objectives Findings may be beneficial to specific environments and may be applied to other situations to improve practice	The problem is somewhat related to existing goals and objectives Findings may be beneficial to others in the same environment	The problem has little relationship to specific classroom goals or schoolwide or systemic goals

■ Is the problem integrated and related to existing goals or objectives? Although pursuing a problem related to schoolwide or departmental goals is always a good idea, there may be times when a problem specific to one particular learning environment is so consistent that it demands a solution. In cases such as this, action research is a natural process, as a solution is within the realm of possibility for the practitioner.

For teachers, more often than not, it is difficult to determine which of many problems is worth pursuing through the research process. Full-time graduate students have an equally difficult quandary because they may not be operating in the practicing environment on a regular basis. Table 2.1 provides a simple rubric that may help with problem identification and determining if the problem should be pursued immediately, be placed on hold for the time being, or discarded as a potential action research project.

SOURCES FOR PROBLEMS OR RESEARCH TOPICS

Reason and Marshall (2001) suggest that research may sometimes arise from commitments to students, work, collaboration, or something close to the heart of the practitioner. In many cases, the potential research problem or topic is in plain sight, but the teacher or practitioner may not be able to determine what is important because he or she is totally immersed in the situation. Herr and Anderson (2005) add that often the research is a puzzle that teachers or practitioners have been mulling over for some time. The formal identification of the problem or topic solidifies the need to pursue the action research and thereby helps support the inquiry. Although the classroom and practitioner environment presents research-rich opportunities for action research, there may be times when other sources need to be considered due to the numerous problems typically present. Graduate students in particular may find it helpful to examine several other options for possible action research.

Even if the problem is easily identifiable, there are several excellent sources of help in refining research topics. Consider the teacher or practitioner who is in the process of identifying a problem. Several problems have the potential to develop into an action research project. To help narrow the problem, consider a brief literature review. Conducting a preliminary review of literature via an Internet search can help by prioritizing a list of topics. New ideas may be gathered in addition to a variety of sources that may be consulted later when developing the action research plan. Discussions with colleagues—and in the case of graduate students, with peers, professors, and administrators—may reveal information and opinions that aid problem identification and determining the potential for the research to improve practice. Observations in the classroom or work environment lead to additional insights and may prompt pursuing a specific problem whose findings may effect universal change among similar environments. Considering other researcher projects is also a way to view a problem from multiple perspectives. The process

TABLE 2.2. Sources for Selecting Problems and Research Topics

In the Classroom or Work Environment	Outside the Classroom or Work Environment
School or system goals	Brief review of literature
School improvement plans	Professional literature
Specific problems related to teaching and learning	Conference presentations
Curriculum development or content	Professor or peer research
Professional development initiatives	Professional organizations
Specific methods or materials	Web sites and blogs related to practice
Programs implementation	Professional workshops
Testing and student achievement	National trends and critical issues
Student products and artifacts	National initiatives
Observations	National data related to practice
Discussions and dialogue with colleagues	Discussions with professors and peers
Existing or revisited problems	Informal interviews with colleagues
Researcher interests	Researcher interests
Team or school interests	Previous studies completed that relate to a specific problem or issue
	Observations

in itself provides the researcher with another practitioner's viewpoint on a similar problem or situation.

One of the greatest resources for help with problem identification and selection is professional conference sessions that focus on practitioner research. Formal research presentations conducted by other researchers may spark interest in a particular problem or topic. For graduate students, professional conference sessions provide a wealth of ideas and research possibilities that may be adapted to a more specific situation. National trends and critical issues noted by professional organizations may also be present in local classrooms. The need to address the trends and issues at the individual or systemic level may prompt the need for an action research study in order to improve the situation at hand. Examining existing problems or revisiting old problems is always worthwhile, for a more specific focus for action research may emerge. Finally, examining test scores, classroom grades, student products, writing samples, and other classroom artifacts may help in prioritizing and determining which problem or issue to pursue for action research.

Whether you are just beginning the research process or a seasoned researcher, look to the environment first; however, keep in mind that there are other sources to assist with problem identification, topic selection, and refining focus. Table 2.2 provides an overview of the sources discussed.

CONSIDERING THE VALUE OF A PROBLEM OR TOPIC

The collaborative nature of the action research process allows for ongoing discourse and discussion regarding relevant issues, concerns, and problems related to the practitioner environment. The collaboration also enables *evaluative reflection.* Evaluative reflection involves examining problems, issues, and concerns in order to determine relevance, prioritize, and pursue inquiry that will lead to change and improvements. Evaluative reflection also helps when implementing the action plan because it encourages ongoing revisions, interventions, and adjustments—all part of the recursive process of action research. Reflection is a vital component of practice and has been proved to be an effective tool in many walks of life. When conducting individual or collaborative action research, the process is repeated continuously. During problem identification, evaluative reflection comes in handy in determining if the problem has value in terms of immediacy, urgency, and relevancy. The value criteria work rubric (see Table 2.3) provides a tool for individual researchers or collaborative teams.

In addition to the rubric, researchers working individually or in teams may also use the following questions for evaluative reflection:

- Is the identified problem widespread and present in several learning environments, or is this an isolated problem?
- If isolated, what conditions, issues, or factors may have contributed to it?

TABLE 2.3. **Value Criteria Work Rubric**

Determining the Value of a Problem, Concern, or Issue

Criterion	High Value	Some Value	Little Value at This Time
Immediacy	Need to solve problem or improve situation is high. Problem demands immediate attention, as results have great impact on the environment.	Problem is important; however, there are at least two other problems that demand attention. *Identify them here:*	More than five other problems are present that demand immediate attention. *Identify them here:*
Urgency	Urgency is high, as findings from research surrounding the problem, concern, or issue will greatly improve the situation.	There is some urgency. Findings would improve the situation to some degree.	Although urgent, there are other concerns or problems that must be addressed first. *Identify them here:*
Relevancy	The problem will have a significant impact on related instruction, teaching, and learning environments.	The problem may have an impact on instruction, teaching, and learning environments.	Although relevant, the problem may be isolated due to certain conditions. *Identify these here:*

- What populations are affected by the problem, issue, or concern, and will the inquiry benefit these populations?
- Are there other problems that are more urgent? If so, what are they?
- Is the degree of urgency so high that deterioration will take place if the inquiry is not pursued?

NARROWING THE FOCUS

In typical research studies, once a problem, issue, or concern has been identified, the researcher faces the task of narrowing the focus of the inquiry. The process of refining a broad problem into a specific focus flows naturally in action research because the researcher draws on expertise and observations while working in the classroom environment. The events of the classroom occur on a continuum such that the practitioner researcher is generally aware of the events that led to the current situation, the events or activities that contributed to the problem, and behaviors that preceded the problem. Even if the problem or concern is identified at the beginning of the school year, the researcher has resources in the form of conversations with colleagues, cumulative records, previous school improvement plans, and results from standardized tests that may be reviewed and examined. The data-rich environment provides the means to construct a timeline or continuum of events that led to or contributed to the identified problem, which in turn guides the researcher in refining and narrowing the focus of any action research study. The example in Exhibit 2.1 illustrates an identified problem and available data sources that may help in narrowing the focus.

The disconnection between home and school and lack of parental communication is too broad a topic in that it does not lead the researcher to a specific research question. However, after examining the available sources of data, the researcher may see a pattern emerge that will help narrow the focus. For example, the student contact

EXHIBIT 2.1. **Narrowing the Research Focus: Classroom Example**

Identified Problem

Disconnection between home and school (fifth-grade teachers and parents)

Available Sources of Data to Assist in Narrowing the Identified Problem

- ▦ Informal conversations with fourth-grade teachers: What previously worked, and what did not?

- ▦ Examination of school improvement goals and suggested strategies regarding increasing parental involvement and communication

- ▦ Electronic (e-mail) discussions with sixth-grade teachers at the middle school the fifth graders will attend

- ▦ Student contact records, including phone numbers and possible e-mail addresses

- ▦ PTA attendance records and observations of meetings

- ▦ Copies of parent newsletters sent in previous years by fourth- and sixth-grade teachers information may reveal that every parent or guardian who has a student enrolled in the fifth grade also has e-mail either at home or at work. In addition, discussions and informal conversations with fourth- and sixth-grade teachers may reveal that parents respond a little better to e-mail than to other contacts. Finally, the researcher may discover, after attending one or two PTA meetings, that attendance records indicate that most parents provide an e-mail address instead of a phone number. Based on available data sources, the researcher may draw the conclusion that communicating with parents electronically, via e-mail and an electronic newsletter, may help build a stronger connection between home and school. The problem now has a good, strong focus from which specific research questions could be designed.

Consider the following example, which illustrates a similar process that might be following by a graduate student. Exhibit 2.2 outlines a broad problem identified by the graduate student. A student working on an action research project at the master's, specialist, or doctoral level is not yet considered a practitioner. However, since the university is also a practitioner-based environment, graduate students have resources available due to the nature and structure of the environment. Consequently, graduate students, following the same process as practicing teachers, can explore prestudy data and resources that are readily available on campus. Observations, records, informal discussions with peers, informal interviews with professors, and other related library resources typically found on university campuses lead the researcher to the narrow focus needed.

The identified topic is too broad and does not provide a good, solid framework for building research questions. The graduate student may begin by conducting

EXHIBIT 2.2. Narrowing the Research Focus: Graduate Student Example

Identified Problem

Using technology at the university level

Available Sources of Data to Assist in Narrowing the Identified Problem

- Informal conversations and observations with graduate professors
- Examination of workshops and technology training sessions available to professors, making note of how many are offered onsite and online
- Informal inventory of equipment available in a variety of classrooms where class sessions typically take place
- Attendance records gleaned from workshop attendance or training
- Informal discussions with peers
- Observations recorded after sitting in a few different classes taught by graduate faculty

several observations of graduate faculty teaching in classrooms that seem to be well equipped with technology. However, after several informal conversations and discussions with professors and peers, the action researcher may decide to examine what type of technology workshops and training sessions are offered for faculty. This examination may lead to an analysis of attendance records taken after workshops and training sessions have occurred. The combination of workshop content with attendance records may lead the graduate researcher to the conclusion that although workshops are offered, the content presented is more directive ("how to") and does not include actual pedagogy. Based on available resources, the graduate researcher may conclude that if workshop content focused more on pedagogical skills, technology, and curriculum development, more professors would integrate technology into class sessions. The problem now has a strong focus that may provide a solid framework for designing specific research questions. Thus the action research process encourages the use of available resources in the practicing environment that can provide additional knowledge to help focus the inquiry, inform the process, and provide the framework for the study.

THE REFLECTIVE JOURNAL REVISITED

The *reflective journal* was discussed in Chapter One. The journal is one of the greatest tools that any researcher may possess. Think for a moment about the process of narrowing the focus I have just described. The thoughts and reflections of the researcher when examining all of the available resources should be recorded. Notes from informal conversations, discussions, and observations all help the researcher reflect and further narrow the focus. Once recorded, the researcher's journal entries—whether on paper or electronic—become yet another rich source of data. The notes recorded when examining resources prior to the study help the researcher do all of the following tasks:

- Explore all available resources before the study begins

- Record important information that leads to a strong, narrow focus for the inquiry

- Identify valuable data sources that may be revisited later in the study

- Uncover information that may assist in narrowing the focus

- Develop a strong research framework from which specific research questions can be designed

For many people, the use of paper and pencil has become obsolete. Electronic journals kept on a laptop, Blackberry, or the Notes option on an iPhone now serve the purpose. It is the act of recording that makes the journal a valuable tool for research because it provides a record of the process from which the researcher may draw from beginning to end. The research continuum begins with the initial thoughts and ideas identified by the researcher. It moves to the exploration of available resources in the practitioner environment. Conclusions are drawn as patterns are revealed and information is examined. Finally, the topic is refined and narrowed to the point where actual research questions can be designed.

CONCEPT MAPPING AND FOCUS

Related to the reflective journal, *concept mapping* is another useful tool in refining and narrowing focus for an action research study. Concept mapping may be used by individual researchers as well as collaborative teams and provides an excellent illustration and visual. According to Maykut and Morehouse (1994), concept mapping involves generating ideas through brainstorming and then creating a physical "map" of relationships among ideas that helps focus and narrow the inquiry. Novack (1998) suggests that concept mapping—typically used in education settings—involves drawing a graphic representation of ideas and how each idea is related to a general theme or question. The actual mapping may be completed in free form or in fixed form. *Free-form mapping* involves a type of brainstorming in which the researcher records whatever information comes to mind. *Fixed-form mapping* has the researcher record ideas and then connect each idea to the general theme in some manner. The resulting maps, of either form, illustrate a general theme, concept, or question; related subthemes; sets of ideas related to the subthemes; and connections between subthemes and the general theme, concept, or question.

Concept maps are especially helpful in designing action research projects because they allow the researcher to examine the overall focus of the research as well as a variety of related and connected information. By examining the related information, the researcher is able to do the following:

- Explore related ideas, concepts, and issues surrounding the general research focus in greater detail
- Refine the focus and explore options, avenues, and themes
- Use the information as a basis for a literature review
- Develop and refine specific research questions
- Narrow the focus by determining which information is essential to the action research
- Identify relevant data sets that will inform the inquiry

Much like action research itself, concept mapping is recursive in that once completed, the map can be revisited at any time throughout the action research study.

Four steps are involved in concept mapping: recording the general concept, question, or issue for research; engaging in either free-form or fixed-form mapping; connecting the ideas; and revisiting the completed map (see Exhibit 2.3).

As the researcher moves through the steps, information is usually recorded in the reflective journal. Once again, the journal serves as a vital purpose in the research

EXHIBIT 2.3. **Steps in Concept Mapping**

1. *Recording the general concept, question, issue, or problem.* The process begins with a statement of the general concept, question, issue, or problem. Initial ideas and thoughts may also be recorded.

2. *Free-form or fixed-form mapping.* The researcher reflects on the general concept or problem, recording any additional thoughts related to the why, where, when, and how of the research as well as other information that might show cause, effect, or connection. Typically, beginning with free-form mapping works best. After the ideas and thoughts are recorded, the researcher may reexamine the map and engage in fixed-form mapping to rearrange ideas, make connections, and prioritize.

3. *Connecting ideas.* Reflecting on the concept map, the researcher connects ideas and then reexamines the map, looking for themes that may have emerged. Next, the researcher analyzes the map to refine the focus further. The themes are examined, and specific research questions are designed. Finally, the researcher reflects on the questions and themes and identifies data sets that will inform the inquiry.

4. *Revisiting the map.* Once the study begins, the researcher revisits the map on a continual basis in order to keep the study on track, collect all necessary data sets, refer to the specific research questions when designing the action plan, and write the final research report when presenting findings.

process because once the map is completed, the researcher may review it at any time by returning to the journal to add more information, record notes, and make adjustments. Figures 2.1 and 2.2 provide examples of concept maps.

As you can see from Figure 2.2, information is organized around central themes, and specific research questions are already forming naturally. In addition, there are several categorical themes that lead the researcher to identify the types of data that may inform the study.

REFLECTING ON RELEVANCY

Since the driving force behind action research is to improve practice, the actual act of concept mapping helps the researcher uncover the relevancy of a given potential study. For example, after recording the main issues and related ideas (Figure 2.1), the researcher may determine that although funding and support are both vital to the success of an after-school program, these factors may be beyond the researcher's ability to change. However, the relevancy of student success—within the realm of possibility to effect change and improvement—may have a direct link to funding priorities and ultimately influence the level of support and funding for after-school

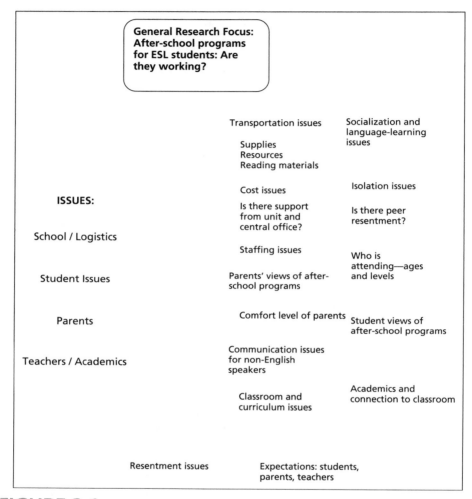

**General Research Focus:
After-school programs
for ESL students: Are
they working?**

Transportation issues

Socialization and
language-learning
issues

Supplies
Resources
Reading materials

Cost issues

Isolation issues

ISSUES:

Is there support
from unit and
central office?

Is there peer
resentment?

School / Logistics

Staffing issues

Who is
attending—ages
and levels

Student Issues

Parents' views of after-
school programs

Parents

Comfort level of parents

Student views of
after-school programs

Teachers / Academics

Communication issues
for non-English
speakers

Classroom and
curriculum issues

Academics and
connection to classroom

Resentment issues

Expectations: students,
parents, teachers

FIGURE 2.1. *Concept Map: Steps 1 and 2*

programs. Further examination of the completed concept map (Figure 2.2) provides a stronger illustration that there are logical links between teachers and students working or collaborating with after-school services. Therefore, a practicing teacher—who is also a researcher—may decide that there is high degree of relevancy in an action research study that examines issues related to students, teachers, and after-school programs and that such a study would yield findings that will result in an action plan that in turn will assist in improvements and change. The map helps the researcher reflect on the degree of relevancy of an action research study and assists in further narrowing the specific focus of the inquiry.

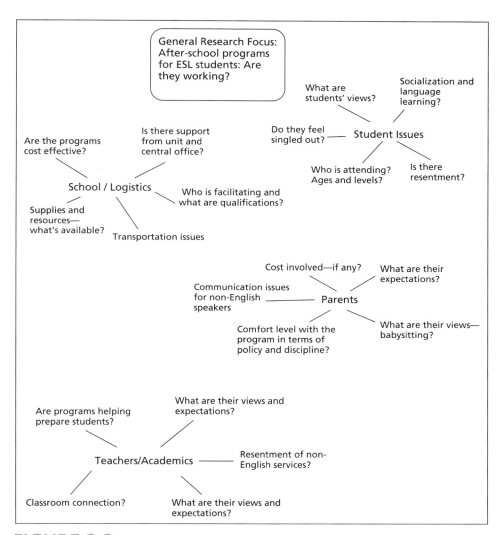

General Research Focus:
After-school programs
for ESL students: Are
they working?

What are
students' views?

Socialization and
language
learning?

Do they feel
singled out?   Student Issues

Are the programs
cost effective?

Is there support
from unit and
central office?

Who is attending?
Ages and levels?

Is there
resentment?

School / Logistics

Who is facilitating and
what are qualifications?

Supplies and
resources—
what's available?

Transportation issues

Cost involved—if any?

What are their
expectations?

Communication issues
for non-English
speakers

Parents

Comfort level with the
program in terms of
policy and discipline?

What are their views—
babysitting?

Are programs helping
prepare students?

What are their views and
expectations?

Teachers/Academics

Resentment of non-
English services?

Classroom connection?

What are their views and
expectations?

FIGURE 2.2. *Concept Map: Steps 3 and 4*

INQUIRING, QUESTIONING, INTERVIEWING, AND GATHERING INFORMATION

There are several other techniques that help researchers narrow and refine the focus of a research study. Particularly helpful to beginning researchers is to engage in questioning, interviewing, and gathering information prior to a study. The act of inquiry involves a continuous stream of questions and "wonderings." The data-rich environment is full of interactions, questions, and though-provoking acts. When a teacher or practitioner begins to observe, note, and reflect on the environment systematically, the transition is made from teacher to researcher. Being aware of the dynamic environment is the first step in making the transition. The next step is to begin seeing oneself as a researcher and to engage in self-inquiry—always keeping in mind that inquiry will lead to change and improvement.

One technique to assist beginning action researchers is to engage in *questioning and discussing with self.* This involves engaging in self-reflection and exploring questions related to practice and related inquiry that may result. Most effective teachers do this automatically. The following illustrate several questions that teachers may think about daily—all imply a desire for change and improvement.

- What can I do to make this lesson better?

- How can I get through to this student?

- What forms of technology will capture the attention of my students?

- What techniques will help me present this information most effectively?

- Where can I find related resources to make this unit more interesting?

- How can I involve parents more in the education of their children?

- What can I do to encourage students to get involved in clubs and after-school activities?

Reflecting on and recording ideas and responses related to questions such as these carries the practitioner farther down the road toward the transition from teacher to researcher. In addition, the act of questioning oneself helps pinpoint specifics within the broad research focus.

Another helpful technique is to engage in *informal interviewing* with colleagues. The process promotes collegiality, builds collaboration, and helps the researcher determine which questions, topics, and issues are critical and vital to improving practice. Informal interviewing may be in the form of conversations about practice. They may also be centered on a specific problem that is common to a number of colleagues. Last, informal interviewing may focus on topics specific to a larger community of practitioners, such as the school as a unit, the system, the local community, state initiatives, or national issues pertaining to the profession. Informal interviewing may consist of discussions, dialogues, e-mail exchanges, and any other type of communication with others in the field that help the researcher obtain information regarding the research topic (see Exhibit 2.4).

Again, the reflective journal comes in handy for recording notes and ideas gleaned from the informal interview sessions.

One final key component in narrowing a research focus is to put all of the information together in an organized manner. Information gathered during topic identification, concept mapping, and informal interviewing adds to the researcher's expertise and provides additional background material to work with. However, if left unorganized, the information is worthless and in many cases bogs down the

EXHIBIT 2.4. **Informal Interviewing**

Interviewees	Sample Questions
Colleagues	What do you think about integrating literature into science instruction?
	Have you every tried using podcasts in teaching social studies?
	What types of things are you doing to promote student research?
Administrators	What resources are in place to assist first-year teachers?
	Do you feel that a mentoring program would help?
	How does this fit in with school improvement plans and goals?
University professors	Do you feel that preservice teachers are prepared to work with diverse learners?
	How is technology being used in your department?
	Is this a campuswide problem?

researcher and prevents the process from moving forward. If the information is organized, the researcher is able to make sense of the information and see relationships, determine which information is most useful in structuring the study, and narrow the topic enough to start designing the actual research questions. One suggestion is to use a graphic organizer like the one in Exhibit 2.5 to record the most relevant information gathered.

As the researcher enters the information, ideas, thoughts, and reflections can be added. First, the researcher revisits the problem identification rubric. A re-examination of the concept map enables the researcher to select important information and categories. A return to the responses that resulted from questioning self may be added to the chart. Notes taken during informal interviewing are selected. Last, the reflective journal is examined and ideas are revisited with key ideas noted. Information selected from each of the processes is recorded on the chart, allowing the researcher to view combined critical information. The researcher now has a visual representation of how the study moved from just an idea or thought to a refined, narrow, research focus (Exhibit 2.5).

THE IRB—FRIEND OR FOE?

Before any research involving human subjects is conducted, the study should be approved by the *institutional review board (IRB)* wherever the researcher intends to conduct the study. As explained in Chapter One, an IRB, working as part of a university or school, protects the rights and welfare of human subjects. If the researcher is associated with a school, the individual unit as well as the school system

EXHIBIT 2.5. Sample Graphic Organizer

Source of Information	Key Points Critical to the Study	Ideas and Reflections
Problem identification chart	Use of student-designed rubrics in English II as a means of improving writing High priority due to past scores and upcoming state writing test	School improvement goal Team goal Check other high schools to see if others are working on this
Concept map	Improving writing Student preferences to work in groups Teacher expectations Student perceptions as authors Rubric design—may help students as well as teachers across subjects Student views of writing—high priority	Way to engage students in groups May encourage discussing writing Give students opportunities to self-assess and peer-assess
Questioning and discussing with self	Is this a viable technique for English II? Can high school students handle this? What do I need to know about rubrics?	See Atwell & Graves See rubrics design book
Informal interviewing notes	Team members are interested and would like to collaborate on this. Cox has several good books on rubrics and will share Wells and Nance (U.S. history) both used rubrics designed by students to assess projects Mr. Rouse is supportive and suggested that the team speak with our feeder schools	Team goal: all on board Checked with feeder schools—would like to observe our process Professional development program will offer a rubrics design workshop. We can get the presenter to hold an after-school session next month.
Reflective journal	Viewed example rubrics on Web E-mailed SHS to see if there are others interested there Observation: Tested the rubric idea by giving the students a rubric that was partially completed; they added the remaining criteria—pretty harsh on themselves!	Possible research question: Will the use of student-designed rubrics promote effective writing?

or district usually has a procedure in place for designing research that protects human subjects. In some cases, the IRB may consist of the superintendent as well as the members of the board of education. In the university setting, the IRB is a committee that reviews and approves research that involves human subjects. Graduate students who conduct research in the university setting typically follow guidelines issued by the university IRB. However, graduate students conducting research in public or private schools must follow not only their university IRB guidelines but also school procedures for conducting research involving minors.

At the university level, professors and advisers guide the graduate researcher through the process of designing a research proposal and submitting the proposal for IRB approval. However, it is ultimately up to the researcher to find out the procedures and policies in effect wherever the research will take place. University Web sites contain comprehensive resources outlining IRB procedures. Most public and private school sites also set out the policies and procedures for conducting research in the classroom setting.

The difficulty of gaining IRB approval depends on several factors. First, if the university is committed to research in general, chances are good that there are resources and procedures in place that advise the researcher on preparing and submitting the proposal and obtaining approval. However, if the university is committed to scientific research—the type that does not typically involve teaching, learning, and classrooms—then it is up to the researcher to help inform the process. Consider the following example,

A graduate student enrolled in a master's-level education research class intends to study online learning in the high school classroom. The proposal is written and submitted to the university IRB. The IRB is made up of faculty members representing biology, chemistry, physics, and psychology. They typically review proposed studies based in the hard sciences or studies that do not involve minors. The board members question the graduate student's proposal regarding the value of such a study because they are unfamiliar with life in a K–12 classroom, are apprehensive about approving a study that involves minors, and do not view educational research as having value because it does not usually involve hard science.

This is a common occurrence that presents a great obstacle to graduate research in education. However, it is the responsibility of the researcher to inform the process and to provide additional information to clarify the study. A well-written proposal will leave no doubt as to the value of the research. The researcher must support the idea behind the inquiry with expertise in the field and make a case for why the inquiry is needed. Using the theory behind the action research process helps in building a strong case for inquiry that results in improved practice and change in the practicing environment. Research that results in a viable plan of action to improve practice makes a strong statement to any institutional review board. The IRB should not be viewed as an obstacle to research. Rather, the IRB and the process involved should be regarded as a resource to facilitate and encourage ethical research.

Generally, an IRB conducts three types of review—exempt, expedited, and full board, depending on the nature of the research, the level of potential risk involved, and the involvement of human subjects. An *exempt review* can be given to a study that involves no more than minimal risk to human subjects. The term *minimal risk* implies that the nature of the study involves no more risk than typically experienced in daily life. An exempt review may also be given to a study that involves the examination of data only. Examples include studies that examine test scores over a period of years or data that are in the public domain.

An *expedited review* is given to a study including minors that involves no more than minimal risk to human subjects. Closer examination is deemed necessary due to the age of the minors involved. Examples of expedited reviews include studies involving routine classroom activities that involve minors.

A *full board review* is required for studies that involve greater risk to the subjects or vulnerable populations—such as the terminally ill, the elderly, or people with special needs—that require special protection. Table 2.4 gives examples of all three IRB review types.

Researchers should consult IRB information provided by their individual schools and universities to determine which of the three types of reviews the proposal falls under. It is always best to request a higher review—such as expedited rather than exempt—and leave it up to the IRB to determine which review category the study falls under.

There are several steps in gaining IRB approval. Although the process may vary depending on the institution where the study will be conducted, most institutions require a researcher to complete a course of training in research with human subjects. Many universities provide training in the form of workshops or online modules. Some have a designated *compliance officer* to provide the training and will test workshop attendees to be sure that they have completed the training. The compliance officer is designated by the institution and is the person who oversees and facilitates research training and approval for research conducted by individuals associated with the institution. There are several excellent sites that researchers may access to complete the training online. These include the University Committee on Human Subjects Training Modules (at Cornell University: http://www.osp.cornell.edu/HSCompliance/index.html) and the Human Participants Protection for Research Teams Training (from the National Cancer Institute: http://cme.cancer.gov/clinicaltrials/learning/humanparticipant-protections.asp). Both programs are available free and online, and the completion certificates are accepted at most universities and school systems as evidence of training in human subjects protection. It is highly recommended that researchers consult with their specific institutions to be sure what type of training is required when working with human subjects.

Most institutions also require that the researcher prepare and submit a research proposal. The proposal consists of researcher contact information; an abstract of the research; a description of the research—where it will be conducted, method, data

TABLE 2.4. **Examples of Studies Subject to Exempt, Expedited, and Full Board Review**

Type of Review	Sample Action Research Study	Evaluation
Exempt review	*Title: An Examination of Music Preferences Among Teens as Displayed on MySpace Sites* *Rationale for the study:* Music teachers at a large, urban high school intend to examine music preferences in order to integrate student interests into instruction in the hope of generating interest in and enthusiasm for music education.	Data for this particular study would be selected from public domain (not private) MySpace sites. Therefore, the study does not directly involve human subjects. However, all information would require *deidentification* so that the individuals who designed the MySpace sites would remain anonymous.
Expedited review	*Title: Use of Electronic Primary-Source Documents and Project-Based Learning in an Advanced Placement History Class* *Rationale for the study:* AP U.S. history teachers in a suburban high school setting intend to use electronic primary-source documents for a six-week period to determine if use of this method and materials improves students' preparation for and performance on the AP exam.	Since the student population consists of minors, an IRB may require an expedited review to ascertain that the study involves minimal risk to the participants and that the activities involved present no greater risk to subjects than typical, daily classroom tasks.
Full board review	*Title: Better Eating for Developmentally Delayed Preschool Children* *Rationale for the study:* Teachers in a public pre-K class for developmentally delayed four-year-olds intend to work with a local hospital and dietitians in providing breakfast and lunch menus that reflect healthy eating (as determined by hospital staff) in order to determine if healthy eating habits promote success in school.	This study may require a full board review because the population consists of minors who also have special needs and because the study involves changes in eating, which may involve greater than normal risk.

that will be collected, and how data will be analyzed; a description of the subjects, how they will be selected, and who will be included and excluded; an explanation regarding how participant confidentiality will be ensured; copies of informed consent forms for adults and assent forms for minors (to be discussed shortly); any instruments that the researcher will use for the study, such as surveys or interview instruments; and letters of approval from school administrators and superintendents, when applicable.

Some universities require that a researcher obtain approval from the school system IRB before the study is approved by the university committee. Some school systems require approval from the university prior to approval at the superintendent level. Again, it is strongly suggested that the researcher review the policies and procedures in place at the individual school, system, or university where the study will be conducted.

INFORMED CONSENT FORMS AND ASSENT FORMS

One component of any IRB proposal is the *informed consent form*. The informed consent form is used to gain consent of any adult participating in a study. Informed consent forms must be signed by all adult participants. The consent form typically contains the following information:

Title of the study

Institution

Compliance officer or IRB contact information

Researcher contact information

Faculty adviser contact information (if researcher is a graduate student)

Description of the study

Duration of the study

Why the participant is being asked to take part in the study

"No harm" statement—detailed assurance that the participant will not experience bodily harm

"Compensation for participation" statement—explanation regarding compensation provided to participants, if any

"Unforeseeable risks" statement—explanation of steps that will be taken if any unforeseeable risks occur and any compensation that will be provided

Benefits of the study

Consequences if a person withdraws from the study

"Confidentiality" statement—explanation of how participant confidentiality will be ensured

Signature and date (applied by the participant)

When conducting research with minors as subjects, a *parental consent form* is required along with an *assent form* for minors. Many beginning researchers become easily confused regarding the forms needed for conducting research with minors. The parental consent form is adapted from the typical informed consent form, worded to address parents of participants rather than the participants themselves. For example, an informed consent form may begin with a statement such as "You are being asked to participate in this study . . ."; on a parental consent form, this would be changed to "You are being asked to allow your child to participate in this study . . ."

All components listed for the informed consent form would appear on the parental consent form. Furthermore, an assent form is typically required when working with minors. The assent form consists of a set of questions that potential participants might ask, with provided answers written in a way that the targeted age group can easily understand. For example, an assent form used for research involving high school students would be written in a manner understandable to that particular age group, whereas an assent form used for research involving kindergarten students would be written much more simply, both because of the participants' age and because it may have to be read aloud to students participating in the study. Typical questions and responses on an assent form for minors might look like this:

Question: Why are you doing this research project?

Response: I am doing this research project to help students learn to read and write.

Question: What will I have to do?

Response: You will be working in literature groups and will be writing stories about what you read.

Question: How long will it take?

Response: You will be reading in groups for the next month.

Question: Could it make me sick?

Response: The project will not make you sick at all.

Question: Will anyone know I am participating in this research project?

Response: No one will know you are in this project. I will make copies of your stories and will put a sticker over your name so that no one else will know which story is yours.

Question: Can I do something different instead of this project?
Response: You can read by yourself in the reading center.

Question: Whom do I talk to if I have any questions?
Response: You can talk with me, your teacher.

A FEW MORE WORDS ON THE IRB

The IRB can be of great assistance to both researchers and participants. The IRB serves as a resource for researchers by providing training and information needed to conduct successful research. The IRB also serves as a protective shield for research that involves human subjects. Researchers should draw on the resources and training provided by the IRB when preparing research proposals, working with human subjects, and implementing a study. All researchers should consult the IRB operating at each specific institution prior to preparing a research proposal, as specific requirements may differ from one institution to another. When working with several institutions and IRBs, the researcher should become familiar with each board and the procedures involved. The training and information help researchers build background and versatility in terms of developing proposals, working within compliance guidelines, and designing informed consent, assent, and parental consent forms.

SUMMARY

The process of considering topics and problems for research as well as analyzing the value of a topic leads to several techniques that help the researcher narrow and refine the research focus. Strategies including concept mapping, reflective journaling, informal interviewing, and a variety of preresearch techniques were discussed.

Researchers should pay careful attention to the guidelines of the institutional review board (IRB) governing research at the specific institution regarding procedures for gaining approval of research involving human subjects. The type of approval review depends on the design of the research and the participants. Various forms are required for adult and minor participants. It is important that anyone who is designing an action research study master all these particulars before preparing a proposal for action research.

KEY TERMS

Assent form
Compliance officer
Concept mapping
Evaluative reflection
Exempt review
Expedited review
Full board review

Informal interviewing
Informed consent form
Institutional review board (IRB)
Parental consent form
Questioning and discussing with self
Reflective journal

DISCUSSION QUESTIONS

1. Discuss the process of selecting a problem or topic for action research. What types of activities may assist the beginning researcher in identifying a focus for action research?

2. Reflect on the process of concept mapping in action research. How is the process helpful?

3. Consider the IRB process. What key components must be addressed when preparing a proposal?

4. Discuss the assent form and the parental consent form. How do they differ?

SUGGESTED TOPICS

1. In collaborative groups, decide on an identified problem. Using the key questions near the beginning of this chapter, critique the identified problem in terms of a possible action research study.

2. Design a simple concept map. In small groups, examine each other's maps and make suggestions. Then refine your map to focus more tightly on the problem or topic for action research.

3. Consider the typical IRB approval process. Develop an informed consent form, an assent form, and a parental consent form.

ONLINE ACTIVITIES

1. After designing a simple concept map, post the map to an online discussion forum. Discuss the maps and offer suggestions in order to assist in refining the maps and further focusing the identified problem or topic.

2. Examine the following examples. Identify which would require exempt, expedited, or full board review. Post and discuss responses to an online forum.

   a. A proposed study that will examine two groups of students and the effect of a high-carbohydrate lunch with regard to performance in math. The first group will eat lunch at the normal, scheduled time of 11:00 A.M. (prior to math instruction) and will be offered a high-carb menu. The second group of students will eat lunch at the normal, scheduled time of 11:00 A.M. (prior to math instruction) and will be offered lunches consisting of a dietitian-designed balanced diet.

   b. A proposed study that will examine standardized reading test scores available on a state department of education Web site in order to determine the effectiveness of a new reading program.

   c. A proposed study that will examine perceptions of teaching held by undergraduate students enrolled in teacher education courses.

3. Consider the typical IRB approval process. Discuss the pros and cons. Be sure to support views with outside sources.

4. Develop an informed consent form, an assent form, and a parental consent form. Post the forms to the online forum. Examine and critique in small groups.

CHAPTER

3

THE LITERATURE REVIEW

LEARNING OBJECTIVES

After reading Chapter Three, you should be able to:

- Locate and identify appropriate sources to be included in a literature review
- Use a rubric to evaluate print and electronic sources
- Conduct a keyword or phrase search using a search engine
- Identify primary, secondary, and tertiary sources
- Write a literature review that accurately reflects the existing body of knowledge regarding the action research focus

THE LITERATURE REVIEW AND ACTION RESEARCH

In a recent discussion, a graduate student stated that the most difficult part of the research process was the literature review. When asked to explain further, she described a grueling process that involved hours spent browsing through online sources and numerous trips to the library—all of which resulted in an enormous number of disconnected sources that had no relation to the topic of her research. All too often, researchers—both experienced and inexperienced—believe that this is an accurate account of the literature review process. Researchers in today's information age have a seemingly limitless number of sources at their fingertips, making it difficult as well as time-consuming to sort through them all and select the appropriate ones. In addition, given the nature of the action research process, many feel that a literature review is not necessary due to the fact that action research is prompted by a practitioner's expertise and experience in a specific environment. What they overlook is that the literature review provides evidence, support, and credibility to each action research study. An effective literature review complements and supports the individuality of the study's focus by offering additional insights. The insights of others in the field add to the researcher's own expertise and help affirm the value of the concern, issue, or problem. The information uncovered in the literature review helps the researcher make a strong case for conducting the study and helps solidify the need for it. In addition, by including a literature review in action research, the researcher is able to provide background information that clearly illustrates the importance of the study.

WHAT IS A LITERATURE REVIEW?

Fink (2005) states that a *literature review* is a systematic process that allows the researcher to identify and evaluate existing studies conducted by scholars and practitioners. The term *literature review* may also be used to describe one component of a research report in which the researcher describes and discusses reviewed articles, books, and other sources related to the study (Gay, Mills, & Airaisian, 2006). Typically, a literature review consists of locating and selecting sources in order to conduct analysis, synthesis, and integration of the work of others as related to the problem or focus of the action research study. Sources included in a literature review may consist of online materials as well as hard copies selected from a library search. Thanks to the plethora of accurate, quality resources available, many researchers conduct the literature review entirely online by accessing notable sites, university libraries, and professional organization Web sites. However, it is ultimately up to the researcher to locate, select, analyze, and synthesize the sources most relevant to the focus of the study.

In lengthy studies such as dissertations, the literature review may consist of a somewhat exhaustive search in order to determine what other studies related to the topic have been conducted. The process of "reviewing related literature" assists the researcher in identifying gaps in the research area and helps focus the study while providing support that the study is of value to the field. A substantive literature review is required as one component of a thesis, dissertation, and—in many cases—a grant proposal. The literature review component presents information that relates the research to previously conducted studies, provides additional background, and substantiates the need for the study. Although an action research literature review is not as exhaustive as a literature review conducted for a dissertation, the review is critical for the following reasons:

- To establish a connection between previously conducted studies and the focus of the action research study
- To connect the expertise of the practitioner to experts in the field
- To make a strong case that the study is needed
- To provide background information for people in decision-making positions

RATIONALE FOR REVIEWING LITERATURE

In the field of action research, there is a current debate whether or not a literature review is appropriate. Some researchers feel that due to the nature of action research, a literature review is not needed. If action researchers are also practicing experts, why consider other expertise in the field? Others feel that by conducting a literature review, action researchers add to their own expertise while connecting the important issues, problems, and concerns in their practicing environment to those of others in the field. Also, as researchers, we must consider that the premise of inquiry—including action research—is to contribute to the field and to offer additional knowledge, insight, and expertise in order to improve practice. Going beyond the debate, one must consider the rationale for conducting a literature review, which in any type of research provides a framework for the researcher and helps identify appropriate methods, data sets, and processes. Table 3.1 gives an overview of the critical factors and rationale for conducting a literature review as part of the action research process.

LITERATURE REVIEW FOR ACTION RESEARCH

The literature review reveals whether similar studies have been conducted. Many beginning researchers are under the assumption that if multiple studies have been conducted on the selected topic, focus, or problem, their own study may not be valid or may even be a waste of time. This is not entirely true when it comes to action research. That a wealth of information regarding the selected topic or focus of an action research study exists does not necessarily mean that further inquiry should be discouraged. On the contrary—action research promotes individualization in inquiry. Although related to a previously conducted study, the action research environment, situation, problems, subjects, and data may be very different; consequently, additional

TABLE 3.1. Rationale for Conducting a Literature Review: Critical Factors

Critical Factor	Explanation
Connections	Reviewing sources promotes an examination of how the focus of the study relates to the work of others. The literature review enables the researcher to connect the work of experts in the field and previously conducted studies to the problem and focus of the action research study.
Themes	Selected sources provide an overview of themes as related to previously conducted studies and how these themes relate to the action research study.
Context	The organized sources assist the researcher in providing background information, which integrates a body of knowledge with the action research study. The integration helps place the focus of the study within the context of research, expertise, and field knowledge.
Gaps	The organized sources help the researcher determine if there are any gaps in previously conducted research. By identifying gaps in the body of knowledge, the researcher may further define the study or extend the original focus of the action research study.
Method and data	The process allows the researcher to explore possible methods and consider possible data sets and analysis procedures. By reviewing the work of other experts, the researcher is able to relate the project to other studies and is therefore more equipped to select a method, generate ideas for data sets, and determine appropriate analysis methods.
Relevancy	A well-written, highly organized literature review provides a clear picture of how the action research study relates to other relevant studies and generates discussion among practicing professionals, which further supports the need for the action research.

inquiry will add to the existing body of knowledge. The literature review helps the researcher determine if additional inquiry is needed.

Although a literature review for an action research study is not as lengthy as that for a dissertation, the review should accomplish all of the following:

- Provide an overview of related, previously conducted research presented in an organized manner

- Help the researcher in *delimiting* the scope of the study by describing the boundaries of the action research as related to the existing body of knowledge

- Explore contradictory findings as reported in previously conducted studies

- Connect the action research to relevant, previously conducted studies

- Identify any gaps in the existing body of knowledge and provide an explanation as to how the action research will attempt to address these gaps

- Provide a basis and rationale for the action research

- Clarify the direction of the study in terms of methods, data sets, and analysis procedures

Some experts feel that there are differences between a literature review conducted for a quantitative study and one conducted for a qualitative study. Since action research may take a quantitative, qualitative, or mixed-method approach, the literature review process is similar in all three approaches. A literature review for an action research study mirrors the action research process in that the review is not linear but cyclical (see Figure 3.1).

An action research literature review may continue throughout the project as the researcher moves through the study. Searches may be conducted multiple times as the study progresses in order to add to the expertise of the action researcher. The literature review may be revisited, extended, and added to as needed. The need to revisit the literature review is determined by the structure of the study as well as what emerges as the study progresses. In most cases, the action researcher naturally revisits the literature review in order to gather additional information regarding events, outcomes, and processes. The natural flow of inquiry blends with the need for additional information, thereby leading the action researcher to revisit the literature review.

CONDUCTING A GENERAL LITERATURE REVIEW: PROCESSES AND STEPS

The initial steps involved in the literature review process are as follows:

1. Based on the research problem, write out the questions you need to ask.

2. Identify types of resources.

3. Identify specific titles of resources.

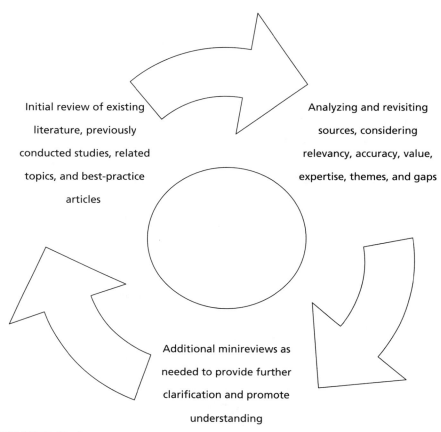

Initial review of existing literature, previously conducted studies, related topics, and best-practice articles

Analyzing and revisiting sources, considering relevancy, accuracy, value, expertise, themes, and gaps

Additional minireviews as needed to provide further clarification and promote understanding

FIGURE 3.1. *Cyclical Nature of the Literature Review*

4. Identify databases.
5. Search appropriate materials (books, articles, dissertations, papers, and so on).
6. Follow the bibliographies for additional sources.
7. Evaluate what you have found.
8. Revise your search or focus.
9. Organize sources.

With action research, the literature review is driven by the focus of the study and the identified problem. The process begins with an initial review of previously conducted studies with a similar focus. Also involved in the beginning stages is a review of sources that relate the project's focus. For example, if the focus of the study is to determine which strategies and methods work best for teaching an advanced placement biology course, the literature review might consist of a review of previously conducted studies with a similar focus, strategies for teaching biology, professional teaching standards in the area of biology and scientific inquiry, and articles written by practicing teachers describing successful techniques. The literature review should be broad in scope, allowing the researcher to uncover themes and related topics that may be helpful in supporting the study.

Once a good amount of sources have been reviewed, the researcher examines each source in order to determine relevancy to the project, value and accuracy, expertise presented, and any themes, gaps, and connections. Additional minireviews are then conducted in order to provide depth, offer expert background information, and support the need for conducting the action research. In addition, the minisearches assist the researcher in clarifying the problem and promoting understanding. The minireviews are driven by the themes uncovered in the initial review and may continue throughout the project if needed. Last, action researchers should consider how the findings and action plan will be shared and the composition of the audience. Additional minireviews may be needed, depending on who will be reading the final report, as the audience may or may not need detailed background in order to understand the findings or the rationale behind the action plan (see Table 3.2). Always remember that the action research literature review is cyclical—never-ending—and depends on a number of factors including the structure of the project, the methodological approach, and the audience for the final report and action plan.

IDENTIFYING AND SELECTING APPROPRIATE SOURCES

With the amount of information that is available online, the literature review may become a daunting task. Graduate students often have a difficult time getting started on the actual review because the gathering process seems to go on forever. Even experienced researchers often wonder when to stop gathering sources and begin reviewing. Keep in mind that an action research literature review does not have to be an exhaustive review—a good rule of thumb is to collect a variety of *primary, secondary*, and *tertiary sources* before delving into the analytical review (see Tables 3.3 and 3.4). A *primary source* reports original, firsthand research. The author of a primary source provides a detailed description of the study in terms of method, participants, data, findings, and conclusions. A *secondary source* typically consists of a summary, report, or review of research. The source may consist of a review of multiple studies or an overview of practice. A *tertiary source* is a collection of primary or secondary sources (or both). Many researchers begin with a review of tertiary sources in order to gain background information and direction before gathering and reviewing primary sources. However, it is entirely up to the researcher to determine which sources are reviewed first. In most cases, researchers naturally gather a variety of primary, secondary, and tertiary sources before analyzing and engaging in the actual review. Selecting a few from each category typically provides a general overview of the existing body of knowledge and a good starting basis for the literature review.

TABLE 3.2. Steps in the Literature Review

Step	Tasks
1. Initial review of related literature	Begin with an initial review of previously conducted studies on similar topics. Look for studies conducted in a variety of settings in order to provide a more global picture of what has already been done. Check professional organizations for articles and reports. Examine government—national and state—reports and related documents. Review sources written by practitioners describing best practices related to the focus of the study. Locate and select a variety of sources that present original research, best practices, and information regarding expertise in the practicing environment.
2. Review sources	Review sources gathered in order to uncover gaps in the research. Examine sources for recurring themes among authors. Consider relevancy to the focus of the action research. Note interesting related topics and ideas. Review each source with regard to the author's expertise in the field or related fields.
3. Minireviews	Conduct minireviews as needed throughout the study. Consider who will read the final report and action plan. Conduct additional minireviews accordingly in order to promote understanding and establish need. Repeat step 2 as minireviews are conducted.

It should be noted that if the researcher determines that minireviews are needed, it is a good idea to return to the secondary sources to generate additional information. Since some secondary sources consist of overviews, reviews, and summaries, they may also provide bibliographies that direct readers to additional materials relevant to the study. Figure 3.2 provides a framework for minireviews.

TABLE 3.3. **Sources for the Literature Review**

Primary Source	Secondary Source	Tertiary Source
Original article written by the researcher who conducted the study Reports firsthand research Provides detailed information regarding methodological approach, nature of the study, subjects, data, analysis, findings, conclusions, and action plan results	Reviews, summarizes, or discusses the research of others Provides overviews	Reproduces a collection of primary or secondary sources (or both) Helps readers understand primary and secondary sources
Examples	**Examples**	**Examples**
Articles appearing in refereed (peer-reviewed) journals Dissertations Theses Technical reports Diaries Transcripts of interviews and field journals Books Newspaper articles reporting firsthand events Conference proceedings Conference presentations Unpublished research papers Some government reports Blogs from notable sites (may also be secondary and tertiary) Original documents (birth certificates, school records, and so on) Podcasts (may also be secondary and tertiary) YouTube videos (may also be secondary and tertiary)	Articles appearing in refereed (peer-reviewed) journals Articles appearing in nonrefereed journals Literature reviews included in dissertations Popular magazines (may also be tertiary) Newspaper articles presenting commentary (may also be tertiary) Books and textbooks Reviews of research Commentaries Related scholarly books Conference proceedings Government reports Handbooks (may also be tertiary) Indexing and abstracting tools (may also be tertiary) Podcasts (may also be primary and tertiary) Blogs from notable sites (may also be primary and tertiary) Wikis (may also be tertiary) YouTube videos (may also be primary and tertiary)	Yearbooks Reference books "Fact-related" books Dictionaries Directories Guidebooks Newspaper articles presenting commentary (may also be secondary) Popular magazines (may also be secondary) Handbooks (may also be secondary) Indexing and abstracting tools Podcasts (may also be primary and secondary) Blogs from notable sites (may also be primary and secondary) Wikis (may also be secondary) YouTube videos (may also be primary and secondary)

TABLE 3.4. **Comparison of Primary, Secondary, and Tertiary Sources**

Topic	Primary Source	Secondary Source	Tertiary Source
Science mentors	Article appearing in a refereed journal that describes original research conducted by university professors and classroom teachers	Textbook lesson used by classroom teachers working as science mentors	Online nonfiction catalogue of books that may be integrated into science lessons for elementary students
Online research	Dissertation describing a study that focused on high school students conducting online research in an advanced placement history class	How-to article appearing in a popular technology magazine that describes the use of popular search engines	*New York Times* article or editorial on Internet use in classrooms
Perceptions of gender and race	Field notes recorded from a qualitative researcher working onsite	Government report discussing several studies previously conducted	Blog entries posted on a popular Web site

RELEVANCY, ACCURACY, AND VALUE OF ONLINE SOURCES

As you can see from Tables 3.3 and 3.4, numerous resources may be gathered by conducting just one Internet search, which makes it all the more difficult for a researcher to determine which sources should be included in the literature review. To assist in the selection process, consider the following questions regarding each source:

- *Expertise:* Is the author well known in the field?
- *Scope:* Has this author completed extensive studies in the field or in a related field?
- *Recency:* What is the date of publication? (A source published within the last five years is typically more timely than one published ten years ago.)
- *Relevancy:* How relevant is the information in the source to the focus of the action research?

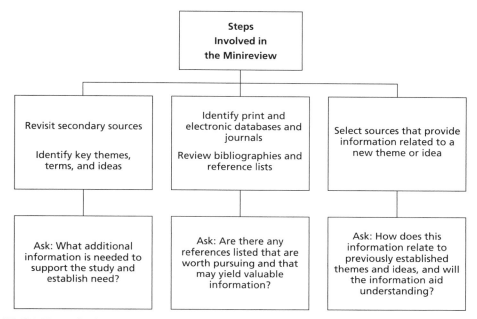

FIGURE 3.2. *Conducting Minireviews*

■ *Accuracy:* Is the information accurate, to the best of your knowledge?

■ *Quality and quantity:* How much relevant information does the source yield, and is the information of sufficient quality that it will support the action research study and provide rich background information?

Even after considering these six key questions, it may still be somewhat difficult to decide which sources should be included in the written literature review. Some researchers find it helpful to use a simple rubric for evaluating sources. The rubric helps them select sources that may best be integrated into a cohesive literature review that supports the action research study. Exhibit 3.1 illustrates a rubric for evaluating sources to be included in a literature review. The criteria are based on the six questions and qualities listed. A comments section allows the researcher to note pages, paragraphs, topics, and other pertinent information that come in handy when writing the literature review. The comments may be revisited to expand themes and conduct additional minisearches as the study progresses.

ONLINE LITERATURE REVIEW

With the seemingly infinite amount of information available online, many researchers elect to conduct literature searches on the Internet. The information contained on Web sites is available at any time. This makes conducting an online literature review

EXHIBIT 3.1. Rubric for Evaluating Sources

Category	Evaluative Criteria	Comments
Expertise	Author is well known in the practicing field. Author's research is recognizable across related fields. Research encompasses multiple projects and reflects a wide breadth of knowledge. Research findings have been applied in multiple settings.	
Scope	The scope of the research is broad and cuts across several related areas. Research projects reflect a variety of subjects and locations. Findings may be applied in many situations.	
Recency	Research was conducted within the last five years. Publications describing findings have been released within the last five years. Findings are timely and reflect related topics.	
Relevancy	Information is directly related to the action research study. Related topics reflect similar situations, problems, or issues. Findings reported are relevant and informative. Information supports the focus of the action research.	
Accuracy	Information is accurate and informative. Participants and locations are portrayed accurately. Background information is accurate and detailed.	
Quality and quantity	Writing is scholarly and descriptive. Material is from a referred journal, professional Web site, conference proceeding, or other reliable source. If a secondary or tertiary source, it is closely related to the focus of the action research.	

ideal for researchers who may have scheduling conflicts, difficult work schedules, or family responsibilities. Accurate, relevant information generated from online literature reviews may be easily gathered from Web sites such as business sites, personal sites, and electronic newspapers and from university or professional Web sites such as those sponsored by professional organizations, online libraries, and other education-related institutions and agencies.

Although university or professional sites yield the best sources for scholarly literature reviews, many other reliable Internet sites may be helpful when gathering sources for literature reviews. As with all sources, the researcher needs to carefully evaluate each source to determine which ones support the action research focus most effectively. Criteria for evaluating sources are presented in Exhibit 3.2; in addition, online sources must be judged on the authenticity of the site as well as the quality of the material provided by contributors.

Online literature reviews are conducted in a similar manner as those completed onsite. The steps—and even some of the tools—are similar. For example, when conducting a literature review at an onsite library, a researcher would use keyword searches, browse online catalogues, and examine databases, directories, and indexes to locate possible sources.

The first decision a researcher must make when conducting an online literature review is to select a *search engine (SE)*. SEs are tools that enable a researcher to search numerous sites for appropriate sources related to any topic or interest. Once the keywords are entered, the SE instantaneously scans sites to produce a list of related links that contain the keywords. Some SEs are more effective than others when it comes to academic and scholarly research. Several of the most popular, in the suggested order of use, are these:

Google Scholar   http://scholar.google.com

AltaVista   http://www.altavista.com

Yahoo   http://www.yahoo.com

Lycos   http://www.lycos.com

Researchers may also use a *metasearch engine (MSE)*. An MSE searches multiple SEs simultaneously to produce a list of possible sources. Some researchers prefer using an MSE for reasons of time efficiency. Again, some are more effective in conducting research in specific fields while others are better for simply surfing the Internet. These are among the most popular MSEs:

Copernic Agent   http://www.copernic.com

Dogpile   http://www.dogpile.com

Metacrawler   http://www.metacrawler.com

iBoogie   http://www.iboogie.com

DMOZ   http://www.dmoz.org

Note that DMOZ is human-edited and maintained entirely by volunteers. Information obtained from DMOZ should be evaluated carefully when considering if a source should be included in a written literature review. Also note that iBoogie is the only MSE listed that will present results in the form of a *concept cluster,* grouping the generated list into categories. The categories help the researcher determine which sources are most relevant to the action research focus, and clustering helps cut down on time spent viewing multiple sites.

Both SEs and MSEs allow the researcher to conduct a keyword search or a phrase search. To conduct a *keyword search,* one or two words very closely related to the topic are entered. It is always best to develop a list of keywords prior to conducting the first search. To conduct a *phrase search,* a simple phrase, enclosed in quotation marks, may be used. This is important because when conducting a literature review, many phrases emerge that later become crucial to the research focus. A phrase also helps refine the search by clarifying the information being sought.

In addition to SEs and MSEs, researchers may make use of subject directories, online databases, research sites, and online document repositories. Most are free of charge and may be accessed without a username or access code. Subject directories are useful for quickly locating relevant sources, as all information contained on the site is already grouped into categories. Online databases such as the National Center for Education Statistics (http://nces.ed.gov) provide valuable information when gathering sources for literature reviews. Document repository sites house copies of scholarly and research papers and abstracts available for public use. The following sites are often especially useful:

Librarian's Internet Index   http://lii.org

LibraryThing   http://www.librarything.com

Infomine   http://infomine.ucr.edu

Yahoo Directory   http://dir.yahoo.com

California Digital Library   http://www.cdlib.org

arXiv at Cornell University Library   http://arxiv.org

Online libraries are also an excellent resource for locating information that is useful in a literature review. Public libraries as well as universities and schools offer resources online. However, most universities and school libraries will require a username and password—which in many cases also requires admission status. Online libraries contain information organized in areas and topics. Most offer e-reference links, online databases, reference books, and e-books. In addition, popular databases may include access to such sites as *Dissertation Abstracts*, ERIC, JSTOR (a scholarly journal archive), MLA Bibliography, Project Must, and Lexis-Nexis. If possible, select documents with full text whenever available. This may be an option offered when searching. Also look for articles and related materials contained in peer-reviewed (refereed) journals as well as those that are included in the library holdings, just in case an onsite visit is necessary. Finally, select the option to view documents with the most recent publication dates, as this will reduce the time spent searching. In most cases, materials and resources obtained from a university library or a public library online will be the most reliable to use in a literature review.

As noted earlier, the literature review process requires the action researcher to evaluate sources based on relevancy, accuracy, and value. Exhibit 3.2 identifies key

EXHIBIT 3.2. **Rubric for Evaluating Online Sources**

Category	Evaluative Criteria	Comments
Site authenticity	Site is a university site, professional organization site, or online library. Site provides a variety of unbiased information on a wide range of topics related to the action research study. Site is highly organized and well known. Content may be verified via other sources. Domain (.edu, .org, .gov) gives confidence in the reliability of the materials stored on the site.	
Expertise	Authors are well known in the practicing field. This research is recognizable across related fields. Some information is a result of federally or privately funded grant projects. Research encompasses multiple projects and reflects a wide breadth of knowledge. Research findings have been applied in multiple settings.	
Scope	The scope of the research is broad and cuts across several related areas. Research projects reflect a variety of subjects and locations. Findings may be applied in many situations. Contributors represent a variety of cultural and educational backgrounds. Level and depth of information meet the needs of the literature search as well as the action research study.	

(Exhibit 3.2 continued)

Recency	Contributor's research was conducted within the last five years.
	Publications describing findings have been released within the last five years.
	Findings are timely and reflect related topics.
	Site is updated regularly, with dates posted.
Relevancy	Information contained on the site is directly related to the action research study.
	Related topics reflect similar situations, problems, or issues.
	Findings reported are relevant and informative.
	Information supports the focus of the action research.
Accuracy	Information is accurate and informative.
Quality and quantity	Contributor's writing is scholarly and descriptive.
	Secondary or tertiary sources are closely related to the focus of the action research.

criteria for evaluating online resources for literature reviews. In addition to the criteria listed in the exhibit, each online source must be carefully examined to determine how well the source relates to the study, the accuracy of the source, and the value in terms of providing support and establishing need for the action research. In addition, the authenticity of the site where the resources was located must also be taken into consideration. Although blogs, podcasts, and videos posted on YouTube may be of value, resources from more notable sites will usually prove to be more reliable.

WHAT EXPERTS HAVE TO SAY

The literature review should be a rich, integrated summary of previously conducted research related to the action research at hand, an organized presentation to support the study, detailed background information that promotes understanding of the focus, and an overview of related themes, ideas, and topics that address similar situations, trends, and problems. Although it is important to include an overview of the work of experts in order to support the research, it is not as important as providing background information and support as to why the study is needed to improve practice.

The review should include information on a sufficient number of previously conducted studies—keeping in mind that if there are no more than one or two, that may actually indicate that there is a great need to address the problem or focus. In general, a search is exhausted when several reliable and accurate primary, secondary, and tertiary sources have been gathered and evaluated. It is not necessary to conduct a dissertation-type literature review for an action research study. Researchers should use their professional judgment when gathering sources. It is more important to have a good variety than an exorbitant number of sources.

If few previously conducted studies related to the focus of the action research study can be found, the researcher should look for related themes and ideas. Once identified, additional minisearches should be completed. Related topics can spark additional thought and inquiry. Also, if the only studies previously completed are on related but not identical topics, the researcher must synthesize the information from those findings and apply them to the action research study. Finally, the related themes and ideas prompt the need for ongoing reviews and minisearches as the study progresses, further adding to the background and expertise of the practicing researcher.

ORGANIZING SOURCES AND THEMES IN THE LITERATURE REVIEW

In a good literature review, the researcher doesn't merely report the related literature but also evaluates, organizes, and synthesizes what others in the field have done. Through careful evaluation, the researcher is able to uncover subproblems and related themes. These later serve as an organization tool for data collection and help inform and guide the research. Although all effective researchers develop their own means of organization, the beginner may find it useful to organize the sources in a chart such as the one shown in Exhibit 3.3. An organizational table or chart can be reviewed and revisited as the study progresses in order to clarify and gain additional knowledge. Another way to organize sources is to use a field journal and record relevant information (author, journal or source, date, overview of the study, and so on). Last—and perhaps most time-consuming—the researcher may elect to gather hard copies of books, articles, Web resources, and other materials for review. After careful examination, the sources are physically organized in folders with additional notes highlighting relevant information along with themes uncovered, commonalities in ideas and among authors, and other observations. With experience, each researcher comes to know which method of organization works best.

As sources are examined, reflecting on the following questions helps identify sources that best matches the action research framework.

Why is this research important to the focus of my study?

Does the described research relate to the action research project?

EXHIBIT 3.3. Organizing Sources: An Example

Type of Source	Title and Author	Page or Chapter	Publication Information and Date	Comments
2	*Introduction to rubrics: An assessment tool to save grading time, convey effective feedback and promote student learning.* Stevens, D. D., & Levi, A. J.	Chapters 1–3	Sterling, VA: Stylus, 2005	Appropriate information for use in the higher education classroom. Authors provide a rationale for using rubrics in performance-based teaching and learning.
2	*From standards to rubrics in steps.* Burke, J.	pp. 23–70	Thousand Oaks, CA: Corwin Press, 2006	Provides information regarding rubric design.
1, 2	*Rubrics in the age of accountability: Transparent assessment in support of learning.* Ronkowitz, K., & Mullinix, B. B.	Web resource: NJEDge.net videoconference	Newark: New Jersey Institute of Technology (organizer), February 16, 2005. Retrieved July 14, 2008, from http://web.njit.edu/~ronkowit/teaching/rubrics/index.htm	Multiple resources—more examination needed. Check conference proceedings and research papers listed.
3	NCSU Libraries, North Carolina State University	Web resource: NCSU library site	Raleigh: North Carolina State University, updated daily. Retrieved July 14, 2008, from http://www.lib.ncsu.edu	Use "Search the Collection" link

*1 = primary, 2 = secondary, 3 = tertiary.

To what degree do the findings contribute to the field?

What was measured?

What information does the author provide regarding the participants?

Do the participants mirror the participants of my action research study in some way?

How were the data collected? Does the article or source include a data collection schedule?

Do data sets relate to the hypothesis or overarching questions described in the article?

What were the results, and how did these results inform practice?

Can this source be effectively integrated into the literature review?

Before making final decisions on sources, the researcher should reexamine each source and regroup the sources according to theme, findings, conclusions, ideas, and relevancy. For example, after reviewing several sources, the researcher may find that three or four sources present information focusing on a similar theme. These sources are then reexamined and regrouped, making sure that the authors of each source are of the same mind or, in the case of a primary source, that the research studies presented have a common thread. One easy means of reorganizing is to use a chart similar to that shown in Exhibit 3.3, adding notations regarding the central theme, ideas, or findings with a brief explanation regarding similarities. Another means of organizing sources by theme is to use a simple flowchart. The flowchart can later be used in writing the literature review.

Of course, there are many researchers who will prefer to use hard copies of all sources and physically organize them using highlighters, sticky notes, and tabs. The tables and charts are just one means to expedite the process and to get sources organized for the actual writing of the literature review. Again, the personal preferences of each researcher will determine how the sources will be organized. The important factor, however, is to group sources by common themes in order to present information in the literature review in a more comprehensive manner.

WRITING THE REVIEW

Once a reasonable number of sources have been identified, examined, and organized, the researcher is ready to begin writing the literature review. However, several common problems may dramatically halt writing, including these:

Trying to exhaust the topic with endless searches over a lengthy period of time

Attempting to read every word in every source on a particular topic

Forgetting to keep detailed bibliographic notes

Gathering sources without taking time to reexamine, weed, and organize

With a good representation of primary, secondary, and tertiary sources, reviewed and organized, the researcher begins the task of writing the literature review. Basically, there are two approaches to writing the review—the summative approach and the expert approach. The *summative approach* is commonly used by beginning researchers on the first attempt to engage in action research. If a summative approach is taken, the researcher falls into a writing tendency that presents information in short, disconnected paragraphs, which make the literature review read like a list of brief accounts. The summative approach does not illustrate a true synthesis of the sources, nor does it help to present the common themes and ideas. In addition, the summative approach makes it difficult to integrate multiple sources while relating any previously conducted studies to the action research itself. Literature reviews that follow this approach are disjointed, disconnected, and choppy. Although many of the studies may be related, each paragraph has little depth. Needless to say, the summative approach to writing the literature review is not recommended.

An *expert approach* to writing a literature review requires in-depth analysis of sources and thematic organization. The result is a detailed presentation from the standpoint of an authority or expert in the field. Literature reviews that are written using the expert approach enable the researcher to address each source in the context of a central theme as related to the action research. The knowledge gleaned from each source is further synthesized and presented in a scholarly manner that supports the research. This approach uses the commonalities of theme, ideas, findings, or even chronology as vehicles for organization and writing (see Figure 3.3).

The example employs the use of a common theme and relationship, thus providing clarity for the reader. In addition, the expert approach allows the researcher to ask questions such as these:

What do I understand about the research of others, and how do the findings relate to the action research?

Which themes and connections will provide the greatest support for the action research?

How can I define the terms and relationships so as to promote understanding?

Which connections and relationships are essential to the action research study?

What related information is required to establish need and further support?

Typically, a literature review is structured with a beginning or introductory paragraph to provide background. The introductory paragraph sets the stage for the research. This is followed by an exploration and discussion of the literature sources written in a logical, coherent manner. The body of the review is the most important

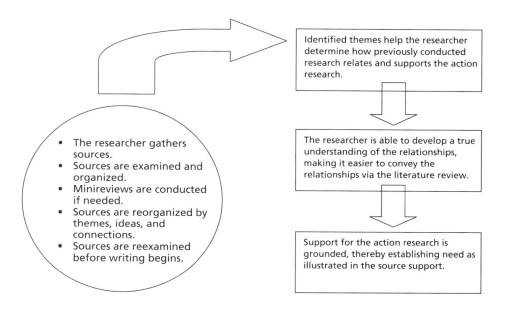

The researcher gathers sources.
- Sources are examined and organized.
- Minireviews are conducted if needed.
- Sources are reorganized by themes, ideas, and connections.
- Sources are reexamined before writing begins.

Identified themes help the researcher determine how previously conducted research relates and supports the action research.

The researcher is able to develop a true understanding of the relationships, making it easier to convey the relationships via the literature review.

Support for the action research is grounded, thereby establishing need as illustrated in the source support.

Example Illustrating the Expert Approach

Findings gleaned from studies conducted by Jones (2001) and Smith (2005) indicate that a strong preference for silent reading was apparent among fifth graders who were involved in the project. In addition, silent reading during "free time" promotes choice among students, which increases vocabulary development, interaction with text, and reading enjoyment (Craig, 2006; Stevens, 2007; Valdez, 2007).

FIGURE 3.3. *Expert Approach: An Example*

component because it includes an in-depth discussion of the action research focus as related to previously conducted research and supporting literature. The conclusion section highlights relevant points and returns to the need for the action research. A concluding paragraph that relates the established research to the action research ends the review (see Table 3.5).

In general, the review should convey an understanding of the action research focus and present information that defines the scope of the study. A well-written literature review sets the stage for the action research and paves the way for

TABLE 3.5. Structure of a Literature Review

Section	Overview	Purpose
1. Introduction	Introductory paragraph followed by a discussion of content in a structured and organized manner	Defines or identifies the general topic Provides a brief background regarding the topic or problem Establishes a rationale for the new research
2. Body	Most important component of the review, containing in-depth discussion of the action research focus as related to previously conducted research and supporting sources	Identifies previous related work Introduces themes, findings, and general information from established research
3. Conclusion	Summary of rationale for the new research	Highlights relevant points and relates key concepts to the need for the action research Briefly discusses and explores the relationship between the established research and the action research

presenting findings later in the study. Here are some general tips for beginners on writing literature reviews:

- Read generally to obtain an overview of the research area and focus.
- Define the limits of the review, setting time aside for conducting searches, ongoing review, and examination.
- Locate a reasonable number of sources.
- Establish criteria (or use a rubric) for selecting and evaluating sources.
- Continue the search until the same sources begin to surface—this is a good indication that enough sources have been gathered.

- Arrange and organize the sources for review and examination.
- Structure the review in three sections: introduction, body, and conclusion.

It may be helpful for beginning researchers to refer to a rubric (see Table 3.6) when writing the literature review. Having detailed guidelines matched with evaluation criteria serves as a blueprint for writing. Many professors teaching graduate

TABLE 3.6. Literature Review Rubric

Component	Excellent	Average	Unacceptable
Introduction	The topic is introduced, and groundwork is laid as to the direction of the research. Background information is offered in a clear, concise manner.	The topic is introduced with some groundwork laid as to the direction of the research. Background information is offered.	Little reference is made to the topic that is to be examined, leaving the reader confused as to the focus of the research.
Body (presentation of themes, concepts, and ideas)	The information is organized in clearly related themes, concepts, or ideas. The writing takes an expert approach by illustrating the relationship between themes, concepts, and ideas reported in the literature and links these to the focus of the action research. A variety of appropriate sources are integrated in a smooth and logical manner.	The information is organized by themes that are roughly related. Ideas are explored as the writing attempts to take an expert approach; however, some themes appear to be disconnected. Sources are integrated in a fairly organized manner.	The review belies a summative approach, with information presented in a disconnected, disjointed manner and not clearly tied to the action research.

(Table 3.6 continued)

Writing style	Writing style is scholarly and flows naturally, presenting information in a clear, concise, and descriptive manner. Voice is active and devoid of bias.	Writing style is academic and flows by presenting information in a concise manner. Voice is active and devoid of bias.	Writing style is somewhat immature, with repeated technical and grammatical errors.
Conclusion	The conclusion makes a convincing link between the existing body of literature and the action research. The conclusion offers support and further establishes a strong need for the study.	The conclusion attempts to make a convincing link between the existing body of literature and the action research.	The conclusion leaves the reader wondering how the existing body of literature relates to the action research.
Citations and references	All sources are cited (in the text) and referenced (at the end of the review) according to American Psychological Association (APA) guidelines with virtually no errors.	Most sources are cited and referenced using APA style, although there are occasional errors in formatting or other details.	APA format was not used in this literature review.

courses that focus on the research process use a rubric as an evaluative tool for the literature review. The criteria listed on the rubric may encompass writing, technical aspects, content, and analysis. In addition, for those who are new to the research process, the rubric helps guide the process, thereby alleviating a certain amount of stress. Just as some researchers prefer a rubric when writing the literature review, others would rather have a checklist to help cover all key points and components during writing (see Exhibit 3.4).

EXHIBIT 3.4. Checklist for Writing the Literature Review

- ❑ Introduction
  - ❑ Strong opening statement
  - ❑ Concise background information provided
  - ❑ Writing takes an expert approach in presenting information
- ❑ Body
  - ❑ Themes presented in an integrated, connected manner
  - ❑ Authors grouped logically
  - ❑ Information presented chronologically (if applicable)
  - ❑ Relationship between themes and action research presented in an organized, logical manner
  - ❑ Connection established between previously conducted research
- ❑ Conclusion
  - ❑ Conclusion offers additional support for the action research
  - ❑ Conclusion provides the final link between previously conducted research and the action research
  - ❑ Conclusion revisits the need for the action research through connections and relationships
- ❑ Overall
  - ❑ APA formatting utilized in the body of the paper
  - ❑ APA formatting utilized in the References
  - ❑ Writing is free of mechanical and technical errors
  - ❑ Careful editing

SUMMARY

The action research literature review provides evidence, support, and further credibility to each action research study. An effective literature review complements and supports the individuality of the study's focus by offering additional insights. The literature review may be completed onsite using university or public libraries. It can also be completed entirely online using electronic libraries, databases, directories, and indexes. Researchers may use online tools, such as search engines and metasearch engines, to assist in conducting literature searches. Keyword searches and phrase searches yield possible resources that are then reviewed, examined, analyzed, and organized into themes.

The literature review may be written using an expert approach or a summative approach. An expert approach is the preferred approach in that it is a smoother and more scholarly approach to writing. A literature review takes the classic essay form, consisting of an introduction, the body, and a conclusion. Each component must contribute to an in-depth illustration of interrelated themes and provide an explanation of how the themes are related to the action research. Rubrics may be employed throughout the process in selecting sources, evaluating online sources, and writing the actual review.

KEY TERMS

Concept cluster
Delimiting
Expert approach
Keyword search
Literature review
Metasearch engine (MSE)

Phrase search
Primary source
Search engine (SE)
Secondary source
Summative approach
Tertiary source

DISCUSSION QUESTIONS

1. Compare the literature review process to the cyclical process of action research. How are the two similar? How are they different?

2. Discuss the pros and cons of conducting an onsite literature review versus an online review. Address accuracy, site authenticity, and quality of sources.

3. What are the benefits of using rubrics throughout the literature review? Do they help or hinder the process?

SUGGESTED TOPICS

1. Compare the steps in the literature review process to those involved in action research. List the steps for both processes, and then compare and contrast them.

2. Locate at least three sources for a related action research literature review. Identify the sources as primary, secondary, or tertiary by providing further evidence of each category.

3. Using at least three selected sources, complete Exhibit 3.2. Be prepared to share the completed rubric in groups or research teams.

ONLINE ACTIVITIES

1. Select one or two of the discussion questions provided to set up an online forum. Have students support their ideas with outside sources. Use a rubric for evaluating the postings. (*Note:* This may be completed in small groups or with the entire class.)

2. Conduct an online search using a selected search engine and again with a metasearch engine. Locate a primary, a secondary, and a tertiary source. Evaluate the sources using the rubric. Post findings to a dedicated forum for others to view.

3. Examine the literature review rubric in Table 3.6. In small groups, discuss and dissect the rubric, and identify at least three criteria that could be improved. Design an updated group rubric.

CHAPTER

DESIGNING RESEARCH QUESTIONS

LEARNING OBJECTIVES

After reading Chapter Four, you should be able to:

- Explore action research topics and write a research statement that reflects the focus of the inquiry
- Design a set of overarching questions for a qualitative action research study
- Write a hypothesis for a quantitative action research study
- Identify well-written research questions
- Discuss broad themes and subthemes as related to research questions

WHAT DRIVES A STUDY?

Many graduate students and beginning researchers assume that the research questions that began the inquiry process become the framework of the study. But in fact, that is ordinarily not the case. Most often the inquiry is prompted by identification of a problem, along with several "research questions and ideas" that are then used as the catalyst for the action research. Chances are, however, that the literature review produced additional information on the topic, which in turn sparked additional questions. It is at this point in the action research process that the original research questions be revisited and refined. Revisiting the original focus of the inquiry allows the researcher to develop a set of questions based on the existing body of knowledge. The original research questions and thoughts may be expanded or amended, based on information uncovered during the literature review. Examination of the literature review materials guides revision and design of the research questions. This finalized set of questions becomes the blueprint or framework for the study—which at this point is focused and grounded.

This part of the research task can be difficult for individuals new to the action research process. Refining and revising the original thoughts and questions allows the researcher to identify data sets that will inform the study. Well-written research questions assist in further defining the study and carrying it through. In addition, by expanding the questions as needed, the researcher provides additional focus, which results in a stronger project. The questions guide the researcher in further defining the participants, identifying the data sets, selecting an analysis method, and writing the final action research report. A well-written report follows the questions and inquiry from beginning to end, thus providing a chronology of the action research. Beginners must be careful not to expand the questions so much that the action research becomes all-encompassing and too broad, as this will not only make the study almost impossible to complete but also distract the researcher from the focus, problem, or concern originally identified. Practitioners must trust their judgment as researchers when revising research questions. It is always a good idea to keep a research journal in which to record additional related ideas that may have been uncovered during the literature review. Instead of expanding the questions beyond the scope of the inquiry, the researcher may revisit the ideas recorded in the research journal at a later date in order to extend the inquiry or develop a new action research project.

STARTING POINT FOR GENERATING QUESTIONS

There are a few common starting points in the process of research question design, expansion, and revision. The key to successful research is organization and detail. The materials gathered during the literature review—if organized with detailed notes—become the starting point in revisiting the original research questions and ideas. First, any notes or comments recorded on the literature review gathering instruments (described in Chapter Three) should be reexamined. The notations recorded when the researcher initially examines a source are typically best because first reactions are usually accurate and valuable (see Exhibit 4.1). In addition, the themes recorded when organizing the literature review resources are usually not anticipated. The unanticipated themes and ideas that emerge as a result of a successful literature review create additional interest to the study. Many of these may be relevant to the action research focus, thereby adding to the depth and breadth of the project if pursued. This information becomes integrated into the set of research questions. The information also helps expand and define the questions in a manner that provides a true framework or blueprint for the study—which in itself is critical for the beginning researcher (see Exhibit 4.2). Last, using the unanticipated themes that emerged as a result of the literature review, the researcher is better able to design a tight, concise set of questions.

EXHIBIT 4.1. Initial Anticipated Themes, Findings, and Ideas

Action Research Focus

Implementation of the undergraduate research component in general education classes

Research Idea or Question

What are the perceptions of undergraduate students regarding conducting research?

Themes, Findings, and Ideas	Source Title and Author	Writing Notations	Relevancy to the Action Research Study
High school experiences	*Science inquiry and the high school classroom* (Counts, 2001) *AP English students conduct research on reading preferences* (Roman, 2006)	Many more resources with similar theme and findings. These two are most closely related to the action research. Notes: Similar subjects (age, culture) Similar locations	Highly relevant as perceptions are similar to what was anticipated
Research resources	See files (online articles and inventory of available resources)	Enable research Students seem more confident	Vital to illustrate what's available.

EXHIBIT 4.2. Anticipated and Unanticipated Themes, Findings, and Ideas

Action Research Focus

Implementation of undergraduate research component in general education classes

Research Idea or Question

What are the perceptions of undergraduate students regarding conducting research?

Themes, Findings, and Ideas	Source Title and Author	Writing Notations	Relevancy to the Action Research Study
High school experiences	*Science inquiry and the high school classroom.* (Counts, 2001) *AP English students conduct research on reading preferences* (Roman, 2006)	Many more resources with similar theme and findings. These two are most closely related to the action research. Notes: Similar subjects (age, culture) Similar locations	Highly relevant as perceptions are similar to what was anticipated.
Research resources	See files (online articles and inventory of available resources)	Enable research Students seem more confident	Vital to illustrate what's available.
View of preparation	*Preparation of high school students and the research process* (Jared, 2007) *Preparing for the university* (Connor, 2006) Interviews with high school seniors (HHS)	Unanticipated theme! Studies that examined perceptions of preparation versus actual preparation of high school students and research. Findings indicate that although students took a class on "how to conduct research," most felt unprepared upon entering the university. Similar findings!	Highly relevant to the action research study. Include these resources. Note: Check out list of Web sites.

(Exhibit 4.2 continued)

Structure of research	*The research process—are we teaching it correctly?* (Starrs, 2007) *Introduction to research for high school students* (n.a., n.d.—online) Interviews with content area teachers (HHS, MLKHS, PHS) Interviews with undergraduate students (30 students)	Unanticipated theme! Resources outline the structure of research and what works best for beginners. Studies conducted show that the structure and format of the research project promotes or hinders success. Interviews yield similar findings—high school and undergraduates. Check additional sources.	May be more relevant as the study progress and after interviews with professors.
University mentors	*Working with undergraduates— professors as mentors in the research process* (Caldwell, 2005) *Research mentors and undergraduate research: A successful story!* (online article)	Unanticipated theme! Studies show that undergraduate students preferred university professors as mentors in research over their peers. Although many undergraduate students liked to work in teams, they actually wanted to be assigned a professor as mentor for research. Check additional information in online journal.	May be related as the study progresses. Notes: Add interview question regarding this.
Dissemination	University Scholar's Day Undergraduate Research Symposium Student-Mentor Research Week Online video and PowerPoint presentations	Unanticipated theme! University sites explain how they encourage undergraduate research by setting aside days or weeks for students to present findings. Student comments on sites indicate that ''this is the best part of the process.'' Continue to search and review other university Web sites.	May be very relevant, as this preference comes into play with possible success.

As noted in Exhibit 4.2, several important and unanticipated themes emerged as the researcher gathered and reviewed sources for the literature review. Several themes are highly relevant to the original idea for the action research. If they are to be pursued, the researcher must be able to integrate the new themes into the original research question, making the action research appropriately broader in scope. The unanticipated themes also generate related research subthemes that may later be integrated into the research focus, manifesting themselves into a strong set of research questions.

RESEARCH CONSIDERATIONS

As the researcher examines the themes and subthemes emerging from the literature review, several research issues must be considered. The integration of multiple questions related to emergent themes broadens the scope of the research. This is needed to provide depth to the study. However, in broadening the scope, the researcher must consider the following questions:

- Which themes are most relevant and most important to the action research? The theme should keep the project focused, not fragment it.

- Which themes are critical to the inquiry? Several themes and subthemes may emerge while the literature review is under way. Some will be crucial, while others may be related but can wait to be addressed during a later action research project.

- Which themes are of high interest to the researcher? If interest is high, chances are good that the theme is also relevant to the original research idea or question.

- Which themes are essential to informing and improving practice? Those themes should be pursued as part of the action research.

- Which themes appeal to the widest audience? Wider appeal helps bring about positive change.

- Which themes would require additional time to pursue? Such themes should be put on hold. The researcher must consider how much time the study will take and if the time needed is beyond the hours that can be devoted to a particular project.

- Which themes require access to multiple sites or to sites other than the one originally involved in the research focus? Conducting research at multiple sites will require that the researcher gain permission, revise the IRB proposal, obtain approval letters, and schedule additional visits—all of which may not be within the realm of possibility for the researcher.

The researcher should also consider the cost involved in pursuing additional themes and subthemes. For example, if a subtheme is relevant and interesting, the researcher should weigh the option of integrating the theme into the project against costs that may be involved in traveling to other sites, including additional participants, data collection and storage, and materials and resources.

RESEARCH DESIGN AND RESEARCH QUESTIONS

Although in many instances action research takes a qualitative approach to inquiry, there may be times when a quantitative or mixed-method approach is needed. All approaches require that the researcher develop a research statement and a strong set of research questions. A *research statement* is a sentence that describes the purpose, need, and design of the action research. The *research questions* are designed to elicit what the researcher wants to find out as a result of conducting the action research study.

Depending on the approach, the researcher then develops research objectives and hypothesis statements or overarching questions. Research objectives and hypothesis statements are typically part of quantitative-approach action research, whereas overarching questions become the framework for qualitative-approach action research. Creswell (2005) suggests that a *research objective* is a statement that outlines the goals that the researcher hopes to achieve as a result of a quantitative study. A *hypothesis statement* is the researcher's prediction regarding the outcomes of the inquiry. *Overarching questions*—written in broader terms—act as a guide for a qualitative study. These questions are reviewed and revised throughout the study because a qualitative action research study has no predictive notions at the onset but rather moves in a natural flow while the researcher serves as a participant observer gathering data in a specific environment.

In many instances, action research may employ mixed-method approaches in which all three research components may be present. For example, a mixed-method action research study focusing on improving reading practice may include research objectives, a hypothesis statement, and a few research questions (see Exhibit 4.3). The research objectives, hypotheses statements, and overarching questions are vital to any action research study because these research items provide the blueprint for inquiry.

Remember, the approach is dictated by the focus of the action research. Therefore, only after clearly establishing the focus, problem, topic, or concern to be studied does the researcher determine the best tool for the job. The method chosen then dictates which research components are needed—research objectives, hypothesis statement, or overarching questions.

RESEARCH QUESTIONS AS A BLUEPRINT OR FRAMEWORK

As stated previously, the research questions serve as a guide for the researcher. The questions act as a blueprint or framework and help focus the inquiry. The questions also provide directionality to a study. Many action research projects—due

EXHIBIT 4.3. **Mixed-Method Action Research: An Example**

Focus

Improving reading practice

Research Objectives

■ To describe the overall progress of students who took part in the Early Reading First program

■ To describe improvements in reading comprehension among these students

■ To compare progress of Early Reading First students with students who did not participate in the program

■ To present findings, strategies, and techniques that will better inform practice

Hypothesis Statement

Scores gathered from students who took part in the Early Reading First program will show a significant improvement in reading comprehension over students who did not take part in the program.

Overarching Questions

The following overarching questions will be used for the qualitative portion of the study:

■ Does participation in the Early Reading First program put additional constraints on teaching style and learning style?

■ Are there specific strategies that are part of the program that may be integrated into other subject areas?

to the practicing environment—can grow broader and broader. The practitioner-based environment is rich in data, problems, and concerns. It is easy for a small-scale study to balloon into an undertaking that is far beyond the scope of the practitioner to complete competently. The set of questions is what keeps the study on track. Without the research questions, the study is doomed to fail, for without a blueprint, the job cannot be completed.

Exhibit 4.4 presents a few sample studies. Key research components are missing from each. Remember that a qualitative study includes a set of overarching questions. A quantitative study typically involves research objectives and a hypothesis statement. Mixed methods use several research components as needed and dictated by the methodological approach. Can you determine which methodological approach best suits the inquiry? If so, which research components are missing? In addition,

EXHIBIT 4.4. Sample Studies and Research Components

Sample Study	Research Components
Focus: The use of integrated hands-on science in a middle school Approach: Missing component:	Research objectives: ■ To describe the overall progress of students who took part in the integrated hands-on science program by examining aggregate data ■ To compare scores on science subtests of participating students with those who did not take part in the program
Focus: Perceptions of texting among fifth-grade students as a possible social networking tool for communications Approach:	Missing component:
Focus: Effects of gender bias in university classrooms Approach: Hypothesis statement: Students who take part in classroom activities in which gender-biased materials are used will score lower on university exit tests than students who take part in bias-free classroom activities. Missing component:	Missing component:

the focus of each study is rather broad. Without the required research components in place, the researcher may veer off track and lose sight of the action research focus, wasting both time and resources and possibly jeopardizing the entire action research project. The result is a frustrated researcher who may become very reluctant to engage in action research again.

Exhibit 4.5 illustrates the studies with the methodological approach identified and the missing components supplied (in italics). The questions included in the qualitative study and mixed methods study further focus each study by providing a guide for the researcher. In addition, with the method identified, it is easy to see which components are needed to help the researcher develop a strong action research intent, leaving no question as to which direction the inquiry will follow.

EXHIBIT 4.5. Sample Studies: Quantitative, Qualitative, and Mixed-Method Approaches Identified

Sample Study	Research Components
Focus: The use of integrated hands-on science in a middle school Approach: Quantitative Missing component: Hypothesis statement: Students who participated in the integrated hands-on science program at Harris Middle School will score higher on the state science exam than students who did not participate in the hands-on program.	Research objectives: ■ To describe the overall progress of students who took part in the integrated hands-on science program by examining aggregate data ■ To compare scores on science subtests of participating students with those who did not take part in the program
Focus: Perceptions of texting among fifth-grade students as a possible social networking tool for communications Approach: Qualitative	Missing component: Overarching questions: What are the perceptions held among fifth-grade students in Mrs. X's classroom with regard to using text messaging? Do these perceptions have an effect on social success and popularity, and if so, what effect does this have on school success? What are the implications of text messaging on classroom and social networks, and do these networks hinder or help student success?
Focus: Effects of gender bias in university classrooms Approach: Mixed method Hypothesis statement: Students who take part in classroom activities in which gender-biased materials are used will score lower on university exit tests than students who take part in bias-free classroom activities. Missing component: Overarching questions: Does the use of gender-biased materials have any effect on males? Females? Do students overlook gender-biased materials when used in university classrooms, and if so, what compensations are made to deal with the materials? What other gender-biased experiences have students had on this campus, and how have those experiences affected their academic success?	Missing component: Research objectives: ■ To compare the exit scores of students enrolled in university classrooms that use gender-biased materials to those of students who take part in bias-free classroom activities ■ To compare the rate of retention of students enrolled in university classrooms that use gender-biased materials to that of students who take part in bias-free classroom activities

THE RESEARCH STATEMENT

All action research studies should include a well-developed, well-written research statement. The research statement describes the purpose of the research, establishes the need for the inquiry, and gives a brief overview of the design of the study.

Research statements —also known as *purpose-of-the-study statements* or simply *purpose statements,* are written in terms that are understandable to a wide audience. The research statement offers information regarding why the inquiry is necessary. It is perhaps one of the most important research components in the action research process. Research statements are used in all three approaches—quantitative, qualitative, and mixed-method—because they set the general direction the study will take. The research statement appears in the introduction of the action research report, prior to the literature review. Typically, the research statement consists of a well-written, descriptive sentence (or possibly two or three sentences) explaining the what, why, and how of the action research. Exhibit 4.6 provides several examples of a first try at writing research statements.

Although the research statement can become quite lengthy, the researcher should be sure to include all key points. In addition, the statement should be devoid of technical terms, occupational jargon, and any other expressions that would not be understood by a wide audience of readers. Exhibit 4.7 illustrates well-written research statements.

CHARACTERISTICS OF GOOD RESEARCH QUESTIONS

Once the research statement is written, attention shifts to the research questions. Good research questions can be recognized by several important characteristics:

- *Clear writing style*. Well-written questions are designed with the audience in mind as well as the research itself. The writing style is important because the tone of the question for an action research study should be neither too academic nor too amateur. A clear, concise, descriptive style generally works best.

- *Relevancy*. The research questions should reflect the research statement. By reading the statement, one should be able to see immediately where the questions originated. The questions should be relevant to the focus of the study, themes, and subthemes.

- *Importance*. The research questions should sound important. If, after reading a question, the initial response is "So what?" the question does not seem important enough to be included in the research question set. The research questions should also reflect how the answer to the question will improve practice.

- *Interest*. Research questions should be written in a manner that sparks interest. It should make the outcome seem both interesting and useful in practice and in the field in general.

EXHIBIT 4.6. Getting Started with Research Statements: Some Examples

Quantitative Approach

The purpose of this study is to examine the relationship between after-school jobs and academic success in high school science classes.

This study will examine the effects of large class size on unit tests between students enrolled in 100-enrollment University 1010 classes and those enrolled in 50-enrollment University 1010 classes.

The purpose of this study is to compare rate of retention among high school students enrolled in an after-school tutoring program and their classroom success rate.

Qualitative Approach

This study will examine parental input and student perceptions regarding breakfast and lunch menus at one small, rural elementary school to determine if food choice helps or hinders student choice in other school areas.

The researcher will attempt to examine patterns, views, and perceptions regarding Macs and PCs in order to determine which preferences drive technological literacy among fourth-grade students.

This study will examine perceptions of United States culture, race, and gender held by non-English-speaking kindergarten students enrolled in an urban school.

Mixed-Method Approach

The purpose of this study is to examine student communication patterns in an attempt to identify specific modes of communication that have a direct impact on vocabulary development and writing.

This study will examine the effects of curriculum design on teacher satisfaction and student success.

Remember that any well-written research question should provide focus, illustrate specifics, act as a blueprint, and inform the selection of data sets. The following questions will assist in designing and writing a set of good research questions:

Is the question written in a style that is part academic, part scholar, and part practitioner?

Is the writing style "reader-friendly" to a wide audience?

Is the question devoid of jargon, technical terms, and unusual expressions?

Is the terminology reflective of the target practice?

EXHIBIT 4.7. Well-Written Research Statements

Quantitative Approach

The purpose of this study is to examine the relationship between after-school jobs and academic success in high school science classes. The study is driven by the large number of high school students who hold after-school jobs and who are preparing for the university environment.

This study will examine the effects of large class size on unit tests between students enrolled in 100-enrollment University 1010 classes and those enrolled in 50-enrollment University 1010 classes. University 1010 is offered to students as a means of providing additional information to promote success. The results of this study will be used to prove that class size matters.

The purpose of this study is to compare rate of retention among high school students enrolled in an after-school tutoring program and their classroom success rate. The study will compare test scores and ACT scores of students enrolled in the program with those of students who chose not to participate. Findings will be shared with individuals in decision-making positions to illustrate the need for after-school programs.

Qualitative Approach

This study will examine parental input and student perceptions regarding breakfast and lunch menus at one small rural elementary school to determine if food choice helps or hinders student choice in other school areas. The researcher will focus on six classrooms with fifteen students in each and will gather data in the form of open-ended interview responses, videotaped choice sessions, and student artifacts. Results from the study will be used to inform practice.

The researcher will attempt to examine patterns, views, and perceptions regarding Macs and PCs in order to determine which preferences drive technological literacy among fourth-grade students. Data sets will be collected over one school year. The researcher will examine data for recurring patterns and themes. Findings will be presented at the annual school board meeting in June.

This study will examine perceptions of United States culture, race, and gender held by non-English-speaking kindergarten students enrolled in an urban school. The researcher will conduct one-on-one interviews and group discussions and will record field notes. Data will be analyzed and findings shared with kindergarten teachers in an attempt to provide insight.

Mixed-Method Approach

The purpose of this study is to examine student communication patterns in an attempt to identify specific modes of communication that have a direct impact on vocabulary development and writing. A mixed-method approach will be employed as the researcher collects data, analyzes data, and draws conclusions.

This study will examine the effects of curriculum design on teacher satisfaction and student success. The researcher will take a mixed-method approach in collecting a variety of qualitative and quantitative data. Findings will be shared with school administrators and central office personnel in order to improve current practice.

Does the question reveal the relevancy of the study, theme, or focus?

Is the question relevant to the research statement?

Is the question designed in a manner that commands importance?

Is the degree of importance related directly to improving practice and contributing to the existing body of knowledge?

Does the question spark interest?

Does the question imply relevancy, importance, and interest with regard to current practice?

Note that overarching questions for a qualitative study will be more open-ended and thematic than those written for a quantitative study.

QUESTIONS, QUESTIONS, QUESTIONS: EXAMPLES AND PRACTICE

Perhaps the easiest way to get started writing research questions is to review the focus of the study, reexamine the unanticipated themes, and revisit the research statement. Given the assumption that the focus is front and center and the unanticipated themes have been reviewed, the research statement is the next component that can promote question development. Table 4.1 illustrates the process. The examples reflect all three approaches.

As you can see from the examples in the table, questions that are part of a quantitative-approach study are more aligned with numerical data. Questions that are part of a qualitative-approach study are open-ended and thematic and thus require a variety of data. Data collected to inform the overarching, open-ended questions may consist of numerical data, artifacts, open-ended responses, and other related materials. The questions for mixed-method action research studies consist of a combination of those that generate numerical data and those of a more open-ended nature.

RESEARCH UMBRELLA AS A SOURCE FOR RESEARCH QUESTIONS

Action research may adopt a quantitative, qualitative, or mixed-method approach. The methodological approach is determined by the focus of the study and the heart of the inquiry. However, considering the practitioner-based environment, many researchers determine that the problem at hand is better suited to a qualitative approach due to several factors, including these:

- *Prolonged engagement*. The practitioner is immersed in the practicing environment over a period of time. This sort of prolonged engagement is an advantage in a qualitative study.

TABLE 4.1. Quantitative, Qualitative, and Mixed-Method Research Statements and Questions

Quantitative Approach	Qualitative Approach	Mixed-Method Approach
Research Statement		
The purpose of this study is to compare rate of retention among high school students enrolled in an after-school tutoring program and their classroom success rate. The study will compare test scores and ACT scores of students enrolled in the program with those of students who choose not to participate. Findings will be shared with individuals in decision-making positions to illustrate the need for after-school programs.	This study will examine parental input and student perceptions regarding breakfast and lunch menus at one small rural elementary school to determine if food choice helps or hinders student choice in academic areas. The researcher will focus on six classrooms with fifteen students in each and will gather data in the form of open-ended interview responses, videotaped choice sessions, and student artifacts. Results from the study will be used to inform practice.	The purpose of this study is to examine communication patterns in an attempt to identify modes of communication that have a direct impact on vocabulary development and writing. A mixed-method approach will be employed as the researcher collects data, analyzes data, and draws conclusions.

Research Questions and Overarching Questions

Quantitative Approach	Qualitative Approach	Mixed-Method Approach
Do after-school tutoring programs help students prepare for standardized tests such as the ACT or SAT? How do standardized test scores compare between students enrolled in the after-school program and those who are not?	Do perceptions and views of parental input with regard to menus and menu design have an effect on food choice among students enrolled in a small elementary school, and if so, to what degree can the choices be considered "healthy" and "heart smart"? What patterns of choice emerge as students use opportunities to select their own menus, and do these patterns promote discussion regarding healthy eating? What information may be gleaned from the findings that may improve practice with regard to health programs, lunch programs, and parental involvement?	How do student preferences affect communication patterns and vocabulary use? Does the frequency of vocabulary word use over a period of one month increase or decrease as a result of modes of communication?

- *Multiple sources of relevant data*. The practicing environment is rich with data readily available for collection and analysis. A qualitative approach requires multiple data sets to ensure triangulation.

- *Observation of naturally occurring events*. The events that naturally occur in the practitioner-based environment may be observed on a daily basis, thereby providing more insight during the research. This is another advantage when using the qualitative method.

- *Participant observation*. The practitioner becomes a participant observer while interacting with participants in the setting. A crucial and critical factor involved in qualitative methodology is for the researcher to also take on the role of participant observer.

Due to the fact that action research in many cases requires a qualitative approach, another means for designing and developing research questions is to identify the *research umbrella* that drives the study. The *research umbrella* consists of the general focus of the study aligned with any other information related to the topic and focus uncovered while conducting the literature review. The research umbrella may also consist of the focus matched with other related ideas. Although a researcher begins with a focus or topic, the umbrella opens wider as the literature review is conducted and sources are gathered. The initial idea is refined and expanded as needed. The expertise discovered in the existing body of knowledge helps the researcher identify the research umbrella further.

The importance of the research umbrella in action research is that problems and issues arise out of practice in the practicing environment. Many are unrelated, but more are related in some way. The relationship among problems and issues, when integrated, becomes part of the research umbrella. The research umbrella serves as the focal point. Themes and subthemes uncovered through the literature review are assembled and organized under the research umbrella, providing further depth to the study. In addition, by using the research umbrella to help in the design of overarching questions, the researcher covers all bases, thus promoting inquiry, which leads to informing practice and positive change.

As you can see from the process, the original research focus and question do not have the degree of depth, breadth, and refinement as the end result. The research umbrella broadens the scope of the research and inquiry. Tracing the path from the original research question, one can see that if based on the original question only, the action research would be a bit limiting. The research questions resulting from the research umbrella information may yield much more valuable information. In cases of action research that takes a qualitative approach, the research umbrella should be clearly defined and organized with themes and subthemes selected from the literature review. By doing so, the researcher is better able to refine the research questions.

BROAD THEMES, SUBTHEMES, AND RESEARCH QUESTIONS

After developing the research umbrella, the researcher has a good graphic representation of the overall action research focus along with themes and subthemes. The next means of generating research questions is to explore the broad themes and subthemes. The unanticipated themes uncovered through the literature review should be analyzed for relevancy, importance, and interest. Once a theme is selected to be integrated into the action research, the theme may be further examined to develop overarching research questions. Once themes have been explored, subthemes are reexamined for selection and integration into the study. The subthemes are then reviewed once again as the researcher refines the research questions. Figure 4.1 illustrates how integrated themes are selected for a particular action research study along with possible research questions that may be generated based on those themes.

It should be noted that the questions listed are broad, overarching, and appropriate for an action research study that requires a qualitative approach. The questions are written in a manner that does not demand one correct, preconceived, predicted answer

Action Research Umbrella:
Perceptions, Views, and Design of e-Learning at the University Level

Theme 1: Prior Experience
Student experiences with online learning prior to enrollment
Perceptions based on operating in an information age
Influences of media

Theme 2: Course Design
Charateristics of e-learning
Design elements
Curriculum design
Teaching methods
Integrated resources
Discussion components

Theme 3: Repeat Customers
Number of course taken
Subjects and programs
Study skills
Motivation
Reasons for taking online courses

What perceptions and views do students hold prior to enrolling in e-learning?

Do elements of design (or lack thereof) in an online course prompt students to drop out?

Do perceptions change after completing an online course (repeat customers)?

Note: Initial action research focus: Student enrollment in online classes
Initial action research question: Why are students dropping online classes?

FIGURE 4.1. *Research Umbrella, Themes, and Questions*

but rather in a way that leads the researcher to engage in open-ended, naturalistic inquiry.

Once themes have been selected and organized, the researcher may add sub-themes as needed. As stated previously, the subthemes may provide valuable information to the study and inform the inquiry. Subthemes may also be a good source for generating additional research questions under the broad research umbrella. In addition, the subthemes—although they may not generate different questions—may in fact help the researcher refine the overarching questions in order to promote convergence of ideas within the project (see Figure 4.2).

Action Research Umbrella:
Perceptions, Views, and Design of e-Learning at the University Level

Theme 1: Prior Experience

Student experiences with online learning prior to enrollment
Perceptions based on operating in an information age
Influences of media

Theme 2: Course Design

Charateristics of e-learning
Design elements
Curriculum design

Teaching methods
Integrated resources

Discussion components

Theme 3: Repeat Customers

Number of course taken
Subjects and programs
Study skills
Motivation
Reasons for taking online courses

Subtheme 1: Internal Use for Learning

High school classes taken online or via another distance learning mode

Internet uses—home and school

Subtheme 2: Professor Experiences

Training
Prior teaching experience (online or onsite)
Circumstances of the assignment of online classes

Subtheme 3: Availability

Course offerings available
Online program versus onsite program
Preparation required—if any
Prerequisites

What perceptions and views do students hold prior to enrolling in e-learning, and are these perceptions related to prior experiences or Internet use in the home and school?

Do elements of design (or lack thereof) in an online course prompt students to drop out, and is this caused by factors related directly to the professor?

Do perceptions change after completing an online course (repeat customers), and if so, how are these perceptions driven by availability, program, need, and other related factors?

Note: Initial action research focus: Student enrollment in online classes
Initial action research question: Why are students dropping online classes?

FIGURE 4.2. *Themes, Subthemes, Convergence, and Questions*

The research questions in Figure 4.1 are well written and are based on the research umbrella and themes uncovered during the literature review. However, when compared to the revised overarching questions in Figure 4.2, you can see a convergence of research ideas. The overarching questions in Figure 4.2 provide a solid, broad, and appropriate overall framework for the action research. The questions are well written and integrate the research umbrella, the themes, and subthemes uncovered during the literature review. By giving attention to the subthemes, the researcher is able to concentrate on an in-depth action research study that ideally will yield valuable findings that may be used in improving practice.

RETURNING TO THE LITERATURE REVIEW

In action research, the literature review is critical in the development of the research umbrella and the research questions. The minisearches that are conducted after the initial review are also important in that they help the researcher either expand the subthemes or weed out subthemes that may be related but are not as vital to the action research. The need for multiple minisearches is particularly important to studies that demand a qualitative approach to action research. This is due to the emergence of themes, patterns, and events as the study progresses. As the research is conducted, the researcher may see a particular pattern that is interconnected to the research. When recurring patterns emerge in an action research study that follows a qualitative approach, the research must pursue the pattern in order to explain the phenomenon. The minisearch is the means for further pursuit of an emerging pattern. For example, in the study described in Figure 4.3, as data are collected, an unpredictable pattern of Internet use may emerge among all students who remain enrolled. With further investigation, the researcher may find that students who remain enrolled work online between the hours of 1:00 A.M. and 4:00 A.M. Delving further, the researcher may find that other than online students, the university Web site is minimally used during those hours, resulting in improved speed. Additional investigation may uncover a pattern among those who drop online classes, which shows that most who drop out work online between peak hours and hence are working when the system is sluggish, causing frustration and discouragement with online learning. Finally, a minisearch confirms similar patterns across the country, therefore, substantiating and supporting the emerging pattern and theme.

BLENDING IDEAS TO ACHIEVE REFINED OVERARCHING QUESTIONS

For the most part, once the researcher umbrella has been determined and themes and subthemes have been selected, the questions flow naturally. It is a matter of seeing the blended, holistic picture of ideas that helps the researcher draw questions from the information. Beginning researchers find it somewhat difficult to see the big

Theme and Subtheme: Prior Experience	Theme and Subtheme: Course Design	Theme and Subtheme: Repeat Customers
Overarching Question: What perceptions and views do students hold prior to enrolling in e-learning and are these perceptions related to prior experiences or Internet use in the home and school?	**Overarching Question:** Do elements of design (or lack thereof) in an online course prompt students to drop out, and is this caused by factors related directly to the professor?	**Overarching Question:** Do perceptions change after completing an online course (repeat customers) and if so how are these perceptions driven by availability, program, need, and other related factors?
Data Collection and Analysis Notes: Prior experience is minimal and held to wealthier districts.	**Data Collection and Analysis Notes:** Similar to onsite classes in that "good" professors are popular and bad are avoided.	**Data Collection and Analysis Notes:** Most students enrolled out of need and are forced either to drop out or make the best of it.
Initial Findings: Perceptions based on media (commercial with students sleeping all day. . .)	**Initial Findings:** Many professors are assigned to online classes out of dire need, not preference . . .	**Initial Findings:** Large numbers of "working moms" with no choice . . .

FIGURE 4.3. *Chronology of an Action Research Study*

picture of integrated ideas. In some cases, this is a thinking and learning style in that global thinkers tend to see the integration of ideas a little better than more linear thinkers. However, using diagrams and graphics, any researcher can categorize and group ideas based on the themes uncovered during the literature review. Once this is done, the questions are easily generated and later refined. The key is to read the resources critically and pay close attention to what the existing body of knowledge is saying. In addition, the beginning researcher must build research orientation and trust self as researcher. *Research orientation* is the belief that the practitioner is also a valid researcher. With experience, research orientation becomes second nature as the researcher builds confidence in conducting action research.

The best way to build skills for seeing the blended, holistic picture of ideas surrounding an action research project is to practice. After conducting a literature review and organizing the themes and subthemes, reflect on the following questions:

Which of the themes sparks additional questions that may be of importance to the study?

What do I want to know about these ideas?

How are the ideas related?

What information gleaned from the themes may be vital to improving practice?

How can I convert this information into a data-generating question?

Which ideas may be integrated and combined?

What is the relationship, and is it a sound match?

Are there any original questions that fit two themes or subthemes?

Can these questions be integrated in a more in-depth manner?

How do the questions related to the research umbrella?

Try integrating the themes and subthemes. Then generate at least one refined question based on the blended ideas.

RESEARCH QUESTIONS, CHRONOLOGY, AND WRITING

Well-defined research questions facilitate the writing of the final report. In addition, the questions serve as a guide when identifying data sets and later in data collection. The questions also help guide the researcher through the study. For beginners, the questions become a valuable map for research. Even experienced researchers feel overwhelmed at times when conducting new studies. It is helpful to return to the research questions in order to gather data systematically. For example, moving from question to question in a systematic manner assists in preparing a research schedule, data collection schedule, and data analysis schedule. In addition, if the questions are followed closely, the researcher is able to organize all information based on each question. After data collection and analysis take place, the researcher is better able to write the final report in a chronological manner, following the order of the questions.

By presenting the findings and conclusions in a way that is aligned with each research question, the information is much more understandable to readers of the report. In addition, the task of developing the action plan based on the study flows naturally as each question—which also reflects a component of the study—is addressed. In addition, by using the questions as a guide throughout the study—to collect data, analyze data, and draw conclusions—there is no question that any component of the action research was overlooked. The findings, when written in a chronological order, become the basis for informing practice and effecting change. Researchers find it helpful to record initial information—adding as the data are collected and analyzed. This record comes in handy when drawing conclusions and finally when writing the action research report.

SUMMARY

The general questions that prompt an action research study are typically revealed through problem identification, along with several "research questions and ideas" that are then used as catalysts for the action research. The literature review produces additional information on the topic, which in turn sparks more questions. It is at this point in the action research process that the original research questions are revisited and refined. Reviewing the original focus of the inquiry allows the researcher to develop a set of questions based on the existing body of knowledge. The original research questions and thoughts may be expanded on the basis of information uncovered during the literature review. As literature review materials are examined, the researcher revises and further adds to the design of the research questions. The finalized set of revised questions becomes the blueprint or framework for the study.

Although all research is grounded in a set of research questions, the research umbrella, themes, and subthemes involved in qualitative action research help generate a set of overarching questions that guide the study. As the researcher organizes information according to themes and subthemes, the blended, holistic ideas help develop a refined set of questions. Using these questions as a guide, the researcher collects data, analyzes the data, and draws conclusions. The questions serve as a map when writing the final action research report. Following a chronological order based on the questions, the findings are presented aligned with each research question, ensuring that no aspect of the research is overlooked.

KEY TERMS

Hypothesis statement
Overarching questions
Purpose-of-the-study statement
Purpose statement
Research objectives

Research orientation
Research questions
Research statement
Research umbrella

DISCUSSION QUESTIONS

1. Compare and contrast research questions appropriate for an action research study that requires a quantitative approach, one that requires a qualitative approach, and one that requires a mixed-method approach

2. Discuss the differences between overarching questions, research questions, the research statement, and the research umbrella.

3. What are the benefits of revisiting the literature review, organizing themes, and seeking out subthemes in designing and refining research questions?

4. Discuss possible means for generating questions for action research studies.

5. Explain the role of the overarching question set in writing the final research report.

SUGGESTED TOPICS

1. After developing a possible research umbrella, work in teams of two to generate at least two research questions.

2. Critique the following research statements. Which are effective, and which need improvement? Working in teams, rewrite and revise the statement or statements that fall short.

    a. This study will look at the differences between male and female high school students as they work on computers.

    b. This action research study will examine the views of using literature books across curriculum areas. A qualitative approach will be taken as multiple data sets are collected and analyzed. Findings will be used to inform curriculum design practices.

    c. This study will compare the effects of using wikis and blogs as a tool for instruction. Data will be collected from two classrooms. English test scores will be compared in order to determine the rate of success between students who used the tools and those who did not.

3. After conducting a brief literature review, use the Themes, Subthemes, and Convergence Organizer located with the online resources to map out themes, subthemes, and possible research questions. Be prepared to share your work with others.

ONLINE ACTIVITIES

1. Select one or two of the discussion questions provided to set up an online forum. Have students support their ideas with outside sources. Use a rubric for evaluating the postings. (*Note:* This may be completed in small groups or with the entire class.)

2. Develop a research umbrella, a research statement, and at least three overarching questions for a possible action research project. Post the materials to the designated discussion forum. Select two other postings to critique, and offer suggestions for improving each.

3. Complete the Themes, Subthemes, and Convergence Organizer located with the online resources. Save your work. Share it with others via the designated discussion forum.

4. After conducting a brief literature review, discuss any unanticipated themes or subthemes that were uncovered. How can these be integrated into your study?

CHAPTER

IDENTIFYING DATA SETS TO INFORM INQUIRY

LEARNING OBJECTIVES

After reading Chapter Five, you should be able to:

- Identify different forms of quantitative and qualitative data
- Explore a variety of analysis procedures
- Use a rubric to evaluate primary and secondary source data
- Align overarching questions with possible data sets
- Examine a variety of interviewing techniques
- Discuss data collection procedures and schedules

REVISITING QUESTIONS

The practicing environment is rich in data. For example, the typical classroom contains test scores, writing samples, sources for interviews, student artifacts, and many other data related to the practitioner-based setting. Selection of the multiple forms of data that may be readily available for action research must be based on the research questions and methodological approach. The expertise of the action researcher serves as a guide in selecting appropriate data that will inform the study. The best means of accomplishing this is to return to the research questions. The questions become the basis for selecting data and data sets. The action researcher begins by considering all of the following:

- The research questions or overarching questions, based on the research umbrella
- The selected method—quantitative, qualitative, or mixed-method
- Data analysis—in particular, a means of conducting a statistical analysis for a quantitative study
- Availability of data
- Time involved and set aside for completing the action research

In addition to these considerations, several method-specific aspects must be addressed to determine which data are most appropriate for a specific action research study. For example, a quantitative action research study focusing on a comparison of test scores would involve specific numerical data that would be used in a statistical analysis. A qualitative study focusing on views and perceptions of a particular phenomenon would involve multiple sets of data that would then be analyzed through categorization, coding, defining attributes, and developing grounded theory. Thus the questions matched with the method guide the researcher in determining the best data to inform the inquiry.

QUANTITATIVE, QUALITATIVE, AND MIXED METHODS

Although action research often takes a qualitative approach, many situations require a quantitative approach. The data typically used in quantitative action research is very different from that used in qualitative action research. Keep in mind, however, that while quantitative data consist primarily of numbers, qualitative data are usually a combination of numerical data such as test scores along with other types of data, including writing samples, open-ended interview responses, video and audio recordings, photos, pictures, diagrams, student products, and other *artifacts*. Artifacts collected in a qualitative action research study may include informal notes, diagrams, and drawings. Action research studies that employ a mixed-method approach may include data that combine both numerical and other sources. Action researchers must revisit the research questions and align questions with data that is needed to inform, produce answers, and provide insights.

Because of the accountability demands placed on schools, universities, and other practitioner-based environments—all of which may prompt a quantitative action research study—several key factors must be addressed when determining the data that must be collected. First, data collected as part of a quantitative study must be analyzed appropriately. The analysis procedure typically involves running a statistical analysis test. The test selected is based on the type of numerical data collected, parametric or nonparametric. *Parametric data* represent interval or ratio scales of measurement. *Nonparametric data* represent ordinal or nominal scales of measurement. The main difference between parametric and nonparametric data is what the numbers themselves represent. Use of a Likert scale is a source of nonparametric data. A Likert scale asks respondents to give their opinions on a particular topic using numbers that can later be tabulated to arrive at a meaningful score. Figure 5.1 shows a sample item from a Likert scale survey.

Respondents are presented with a statement and then asked to indicate how closely the statement agrees with their own opinion or feelings. There are often five choices: "strongly agree," "agree," "neither agree nor disagree," "disagree," or "strongly disagree." A number is assigned to each response. For example, "strongly agree" is given a value of 1, "agree" a value of 2, "neither agree nor disagree" a value of 3, "disagree" a value of 4, and "strongly disagree" a value of 5. The researcher can then average the numbers of the responses to get some sense of where the average opinion lies. However, these values are nonparametric because the intervals between the numbers are not equal (or even known) and the numbers themselves do not measure any quantity; they simply express an opinion. Therefore, conclusions cannot be drawn that, say, someone who gives the response "strongly agree" and is arbitrarily assigned the number 1 is in agreement twice as much as someone who selects "agree" and is assigned the number 2. In fact, the researcher does not have to assign numbers in any particular order. For example, the five response could be assigned the numbers 1, 5, 10, 15, and 20 (or any other logical sequence) because each response merely represents an opinion on a continuum, not an actual measurement.

One of the most common mistakes beginning researchers make is to collect nonparametric data from a Likert scale instrument and then use a parametric statistical test such as a *t* test for the analysis. Unlike Likert-style nonparametric data, parametric data do have equal spaces between the numbers on the scale. A parametric test score of 100 is twice as good as a test score of 50. The distance between number 4 and 5 is the same as the distance between 11 and 12. When the temperature is 20 degrees outside, it is twice as cold outside than when it is 40 degrees. When the numbers have equal spacing, they become parametric, and statistical tests designed for these numbers become appropriate.

Nonparametric data can be measured on two types of scales: nominal and ordinal. *Nominal data* are the least stringent, the lowest level of measurement. They are also sometimes called *category data* because all they attempt to do is place persons or items into categories, such as middle school students versus high school students,

Perceptions of Diversity Survey

For each statement, indicate whether you agree or disagree by circling the number that most closely reflects your response, using the following scale:

1 = Strongly Agree 2 = Agree 3 = Disagree 4 = Strongly Disagree 5 = Not Sure

1.	Many of my ideas come from my friends.	1	2	3	4	5
2.	Teachers should treat all students the same.	1	2	3	4	5
3.	If a student is having trouble, teachers should help by doing things differently.	1	2	3	4	5
4.	In my school, all students are treated the same.	1	2	3	4	5
5.	Students should agree with the teacher's ideas.	1	2	3	4	5
6.	All students should be taught in English.	1	2	3	4	5
7.	Students must learn about each other's cultures.	1	2	3	4	5
8.	Differences between people are interesting.	1	2	3	4	5
9.	Teachers must learn about a student's background in order to help them learn.	1	2	3	4	5
10.	There are cliques and in-groups at my school.	1	2	3	4	5
11.	Stereotypes are often used by teachers and students.	1	2	3	4	5
12.	I am comfortable eating lunch with all kinds of students—black, white, Hispanic, Asian, whatever.	1	2	3	4	5
13.	My friends live in a variety of neighborhoods.	1	2	3	4	5
14.	All students are accepted and welcomed at my school.	1	2	3	4	5
15.	It's important to learn about other cultures.	1	2	3	4	5

FIGURE 5.1. *Survey Using a Likert Scale*

students with black hair versus those with brown hair, people who are single versus those who are married, or buildings that are taller than ten stories and those that are shorter. Comparisons can be made based on the number of people or objects that are contained in each group. *Ordinal data* take persons or objects that have been placed into groups (nominal data) and assign numbers ranking them from lowest to highest or highest to lowest. For example, if the group being measured is participants who finished running a race, a researcher could rank the runners starting with the participant who finished first and ending with the participant who finished last, record the time it took for each runner to complete the course, and establish a ranking based on the time. If the first to finish did so in 1 minute and 20 seconds, the second in 2 minutes flat, and the third in 2 minutes and 10 seconds, these results would be ranked 1, 2, and 3. But you can see that the intervals between the runners' finish times are not quantitatively equal; therefore, ordinal data are nonparametric. Likert scales yield ordinal data.

Parametric data also come in two types of scales or variables: interval and ratio. *Interval data* have all the characteristics of nominal and ordinal data but go one step farther. Interval data have equal spaces between the numbers. Ten dollars is equal to twice as much money as five dollars because the space or interval between each dollar is the same. *Ratio data* yield the highest form of measurement because in addition to having equal intervals between the numbers, they use a scale that has a true zero point. A student who earns a score of 80 on a test has twice as many points as a student who earns 40 because it was possible to score 0 on the test. Scores, distances, weights, speeds, and time are all examples of scales that start at zero with the spaces between the numbers thereafter being equal (see Figure 5.2).

The statistical test is selected based on the type of data, parametric or non-parametric. Although it is not the intent of this book to provide in-depth coverage regarding statistics and statistical tests, the following general information is provided to assist beginning researchers. If a quantitative approach is determined to meet the needs of the action research, the researcher should consult a text devoted entirely to statistics, an advanced statistical software package, or Microsoft Excel for simple statistical analysis tests. The following statistical tests are commonly used with parametric data:

t test—used to test differences between the mean scores of two independent groups

t test for dependent samples—used to test differences between the means of two dependent groups

ANOVA (analysis of variance)—used to test differences among three or more independent groups

MANCOVA (analysis of covariance)—used as a technique for controlling extraneous variables

Pearson product correlation—used to test whether a correlation differs from zero

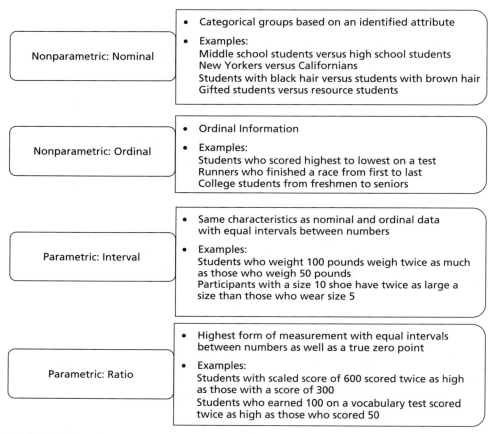

FIGURE 5.2. *Parametric and Nonparametric Data*

Common statistical tests used with nonparametric data include the following:

chi square—used to test the difference in proportions of two or more groups

median test—used to test the differences of medians of two independent groups

Mann-Whitney U—used to test the difference of the medians of two independent groups

Wilcoxon signed rank test—used to test the difference in the ranks of two related groups

Kruskal-Wallis test—used to test the difference in the ranks of three or more independent groups

Spearman rho—used to correlate ranked data

EXHIBIT 5.1. Types of Validity

Conclusion validity: Validity of the statistical conclusions. Indicates that interpretation of the results of the statistical analysis test are accurate.

Construct validity: Accuracy of the instrument used to gather data (standardized test scores, classroom scores, survey instrument, and so on) as well as the test used to conduct the statistical analysis.

External validity: Whether the study and findings can be generalized to larger groups and produce similar results. Factors to consider include similar populations, interaction of subjects and action research, the environment, data, and time involved to conduct the study.

Internal validity: Absence of flaws in the study itself, such as insufficient number of subjects, attrition, or lack of time to complete the study.

It is important that the test match the data because of validity factors in quantitative studies. *Validity* is the notion that the test measures what it says it will measure. Validity also infers the soundness of the research design. Several important types of validity that should be considered are conclusion, construct, external, and internal. Exhibit 5.1 provides further explanation.

In addition to validity factors, action research that requires a quantitative approach must also address reliability concerns. *Reliability* relates to the consistency of the instruments used in the study. In action research, these instruments may include standardized tests, interview instruments, questionnaires, classroom test scores, writing test results, and survey instruments. The following questions should be asked:

Did this instrument yield the same results repeatedly?

Has the instrument been used effectively with a variety of groups and populations?

Who were the subjects, and are they similar to those involved in the action research?

Several means of determining reliability are to conduct a retest or to use an alternative form of the original test. If the results are similar, reliability is established. If data collected will be scored or evaluated by multiple researchers, *interrater reliability* must also be established as well. *Interrater reliability* is established when multiple researchers all arrive at similar conclusions when analyzing and evaluating data. This happens in cases where a rubric is applied to writing samples or student projects that are then collected as data for an action research study. Similar to how standardized writing tests, advanced placement exams, and ACT writing subtests are scored, interrater reliability is established by identifying an anchor. The anchor is the product that—when evaluated by multiple people—all evaluators arrive at the same score or conclusion. Establishing interrater reliability reinforces the overall reliability of an action research study.

Selecting data for quantitative studies is less time-consuming than selecting data for qualitative studies. For example, the hypothesis component of a quantitative action research project is typically designed with data in mind. Therefore, the data are already identified and determined.

Due to the nature of action research, many of the research factors typically considered in an action research study employing a quantitative approach are dealt with differently in a qualitative study. Reliability and validity factors—although important—are not as significant to quantitative research as they are to qualitative research. Instead, *generalizability,* the idea that the study may be applicable to or duplicated in larger situations with larger numbers of participants, is critical. The generalizability factor involved in quantitative studies does not come into play in qualitative research because the nature of the method requires an in-depth study of particular phenomena in a specific situation at a given point in time. Typically, qualitative action research is not intended to provide results that may be applied to larger groups in other situations. Rather, the intent of qualitative research is to gain insight into a particular situation in order to improve practice. In addition, the action researcher takes on the role of researcher-as-instrument in many situations. The practitioner, drawing on personal expertise, learns to become comfortable in the role of researcher-as-instrument. In addition, the nature of action research requires research to be conducted in the practicing environment. The participants in any given study are also participants in the environment that is being studied. Therefore, the environment and interaction in that environment really can't become a defining factor that hinders validity. The environment, interactions, and practicing expert are all vital to the action research process. However, in the event that an action research study requires a quantitative approach, the researcher should follow guidelines determined by the research umbrella, research hypothesis, research questions, data, and statistical analysis involved.

DATA VERSUS DATA SETS

The terms *data* and *data sets* both refer to the information collected to answer and inform the research questions. Research reports may use both terms; however, the term *data* is commonly used when referring to quantitative studies and *data sets* when referring to qualitative studies. As noted earlier, data may consist of many types of information. Quantitative data are usually numerical, while qualitative data are a combination of numerical and nonnumerical items. The data in a qualitative action research study are usually grouped into categories based on the overarching questions. Therefore, data collected to inform a particular overarching question may consist of three different types. When the data are grouped together to inform the

TABLE 5.1. **Types of Quantitative and Qualitative Data**

Quantitative Data	Qualitative Data and Data Sets
Numerical data in nominal, ordinal, interval, or ratio form	Primary and secondary sources providing information on naturally occurring events, interactions, and other activities
Examples Standardized test scores Classroom test scores Raw scores Scale scores Statistical information Percentile scores Percentages	Primary Source Examples (Naturally Occurring) Audiotapes and videotapes and transcripts Researcher field notes Participant journals Photos Responses to open-ended interviews Recordings of discussions and dialogues Conversations and interactions
	Secondary Source Examples (Artifacts and Related Items) Personal documents (family records) Cued responses Survey responses Projects Participant products Cued journal responses Questionnaires Memos and notes Diagrams, drawings, and charts E-mail, participant Web sites, and blogs

overarching question, they become part of a data set. A comparison of examples of data typically collected in a quantitative action research study and a qualitative action research study is provided in Table 5.1.

When selecting data sets for an action research study using a qualitative approach, the process involves several steps. The researcher should approach data selection with an open mind, carefully considering all types of data available in the practicing environment. The first step in the process is to reexamine the overarching questions. Working systematically, select one overarching question and then list data sources needed to inform the inquiry. Each overarching question should be matched with at least three forms of data. The data sets should then be examined again to ensure that each set is well matched to the overarching question.

The key step in the process is to conduct a brainstorming session to list as many data sets as possible for each overarching question. Begin with one question, and exhaust the list of possible data sets for that one before moving on to the next question. Because the action research process is recursive, the researcher does not have to begin with the first overarching question; any one of them will work. After listing the possible data sources, the researcher should return to the focus of the action research and list additional data, if any, that may be helpful in informing the inquiry. Finally, the possible data sources should be examined to ensure a well-balanced variety. A combination of primary and secondary data sources will cover all questions and provide a wealth of information.

As your lists of possible sources are developed, several sources may appear for more than one question. This is typical in action research studies that employ a qualitative approach. When determining which source will yield the best information, the researcher should match the source with the question, weeding out sources that may be better matched with a different question.

DATA SETS THAT INFORM

When selecting data sets for a qualitative action research study, the researcher, working in the practicing environment, has multiple sources of data readily available. The researcher must therefore critically select the type of data that will yield appropriate information that will best inform the study. Selection criteria should guide the compilation of a well-matched set of data for each question. Selection criteria may include the following:

Alignment: Data that are closely aligned with the overarching question. *Ask:* Are the data closely aligned to the overarching question? Can the data be aligned with more than one question in order to yield appropriate results?

Relationship: Data directly related to the question, setting, and participants. *Ask:* How are the data related to the question, setting, and participants? Are the data readily available in the research setting?

Primary sources: Data gleaned from naturally occurring events such as student presentations, conversations, interactions, informal activities, and formal classroom activities, as well as transcripts of those events. *Ask:* Are the data representative of naturally occurring events? Do the data provide a wide range of events that take place as normal activities in the research setting? Can the data be converted into transcripts? Will the transcripts accurately represent the events that took place?

Secondary sources: Student artifacts such as memos, notes, drawings, and diagrams. *Ask:* Do the artifacts provide information valuable to the action research study? Are the artifacts representative of the participants? Do the artifacts provide further insight that may inform the study?

Some researchers find it helpful to employ a simple selection rubric when examining data for action research studies that follow a qualitative approach. Exhibit 5.2 illustrates a selection rubric.

The checklist in Exhibit 5.3 is helpful when selecting data for qualitative action research. With experience, the process of selecting data flows naturally. In addition, one characteristic of qualitative methods is that as the study progresses, unanticipated data sets may be added to explain particular phenomena that emerge during the inquiry. The initial lists of possible data should be recorded and filed so that the researcher may return to the list if needed during the study.

ALIGNING MULTIPLE FORMS OF DATA WITH OVERARCHING QUESTIONS

Once each overarching question has been reexamined and matched with lists of possible data sources, it's time to complete the selection process and line up sources that will actually be collected during the action research study. The rubric (Exhibit 5.2) and checklist (Exhibit 5.3) assist the process. A simple graphic organizer helps align the overarching questions with the selected data sources (see Exhibit 5.4). The data sources are grouped with each overarching question, making small groups of three or more data sets per question. For each overarching question, the researcher conducts a brainstorming session to list possible data sources that may be collected. The exhibit shows possible sources resulting from the brainstorming session and lists possible sources generated for each particular overarching question.

In this example, several data sources would best inform question 1 while others are more closely related to question 2. At this point, the researcher would examine the generated lists, group the sources, and make final selections. The end result would be a variety of closely aligned data sets for each question, as shown in Exhibit 5.5.

Keep in mind that several data sources may be used to inform more than one question. For example, qualitative methods recommend that the researcher keep a field journal in which to record entries describing, in a nonbiased manner, the naturally occurring events in the action research environment. Since field journal notes are a vital component of qualitative methods, it is appropriate to use the notes to inform multiple overarching questions. As a rule, however, the researcher should use a variety of sources to glean the best information to improve practice. Remember that a combination of primary and secondary data sources gives the best result.

EXHIBIT 5.2. Rubric for Selecting Data

Primary Source Data:

Secondary Source Data:

Selection Criterion	Appropriate for the Study	Possibly Inappropriate for the Study
Alignment	Data are closely aligned with the overarching question. Data may be used to inform one or more overarching questions. Data are closely aligned with the action research focus. Data are vital to providing insight and informing the overarching question. Data are critical to providing insight and informing the overall study.	Data are somewhat aligned with one overarching question. Data are aligned with the action research focus. Data may provide insight to this particular study. Although the data are interesting, the researcher is somewhat unclear regarding the information that may result from analysis.
Relationship	Data are directly related to the research environment. Data are unique to this particular setting. Data are directly related to the participants. Data are readily available in the selected research setting. Data accurately and appropriate represent the setting and participants.	Data are somewhat related to the research environment. Data are similar in similar settings. Data are somewhat related to the participants. Data are available in the selected research setting. Data somewhat represent the setting and participants.

Primary sources (naturally occurring events)	Data are representative of the naturally occurring events in the setting. Data provide a wide range of information regarding events. Data provide an accurate illustration of the environment. Data may be easily collected in this environment. Cameras and other equipment may be set up in a nonobtrusive manner. Equipment can be integrated naturally at the site. Information may be easily converted into transcripts. Participants are willing to keep accurate field journals. Co-researchers, if any, are willing to keep accurate field journals. Instruments (open-ended interview instruments) are available. Participants are willing to discuss aspects and information openly.	Data are somewhat representative of the naturally occurring events in the setting. Data provide a range of information regarding events. Data provide an illustration of the environment. Data may be collected in this environment, but space is limited. Participants are somewhat willing to keep accurate field journals. Co-researchers, if any, are hesitant regarding field journals. Instruments (open-ended interview instruments) may be available.
Secondary sources (artifacts and related information)	Records are readily available for research purposes. Artifacts are representative of the participants and the environment. Selected artifacts (products, projects, and the like) are vital to the study. Selected artifacts are readily available for research purposes. Memos, notes, drawing, diagrams, and other materials can be easily obtained.	Records are available for research purposes. Artifacts are somewhat representative of the participants and the environment. Selected artifacts (products, projects, and the like) are somewhat important to the study. Selected artifacts are available for research purposes. Memos, notes, drawing, diagrams, and other materials may be obtained.

EXHIBIT 5.3. Data Selection Checklist

Action Research Focus:
Primary Source Data:
Secondary Source Data:
Alignment

❑ Data are closely aligned with the overarching question.

❑ Data may be used to inform one or more overarching questions.

❑ Data are closely aligned with the action research focus.

❑ Data are vital to providing insight and informing the overarching question.

❑ Data are critical to providing insight and informing the overall study.

Relationship

❑ Data are directly related to the research environment.

❑ Data are unique to this particular setting.

❑ Data are directly related to the participants.

❑ Data are readily available in the selected research setting.

❑ Data accurately and appropriate represent the setting and participants.

Primary Sources (Naturally Occurring Events)

❑ Data are representative of the naturally occurring events in the setting.

❑ Data provide a wide range of information regarding events.

❑ Data provide an accurate illustration of the environment.

❑ Data may be easily collected in this environment.

❑ Cameras and other equipment may be set up in a nonobtrusive manner.

❑ Equipment can be integrated naturally at the site.

❑ Information may be easily converted into transcripts.

❑ Participants are willing to keep accurate field journals.

❑ Co-researchers, if any, are willing to keep accurate field journals.

❑ Instruments (open-ended interview instruments) are available.

❑ Participants are willing to discuss aspects and information openly.

Secondary Sources (Artifacts and Related Information)

❑ Records are readily available for research purposes.

❑ Artifacts are representative of the participants and the environment.

❑ Selected artifacts (products, projects, and the like) are vital to the study.

❑ Selected artifacts are readily available for research purposes.

❑ Memos, notes, drawing, diagrams, and other materials can be easily obtained.

EXHIBIT 5.4. Aligning Data Sources with Overarching Questions

Overarching Question	Possible Data Sources
Question 1: What perceptions and views of adjunct professors are held by university seniors, and how do these perceptions and views affect instruction and academic success?	Open-ended interview responses Researcher field notes Interviews with adjunct professors Small group open-discussion sessions with students Online chat Online discussion board responses Student records Student transcripts Participant field journals Videos (classroom) Audio recordings of classroom sessions Student artifacts (projects)
Question 2: To what degree does the status of "adjunct" affect general departmental enrollment, program success, and overall student satisfaction with the university?	Enrollment information Adjuncts per department Faculty evaluations Exit interviews (end of semester) with students Researcher field notes Interviews with department chairs Interviews with administrators Online discussion board responses Online chat

TRIANGULATION AND THE TRIANGULATION MATRIX

When selecting data sources, the researcher should select at least three types of data aligned with each overarching question, the rationale being that qualitative methods demand triangulation of data. *Triangulation* occurs when multiple forms of data—when analyzed—show similar results, thereby confirming the researcher's findings. Triangulation of data is critical in an action research study that follows a qualitative methodology. As the study progresses and data are collected, triangulation enables the researcher to validate findings based on data sources. For example, field notes may reveal a certain pattern. As the researcher collects additional data sets, the pattern may emerge within an open-ended interview, video transcript, or artifact, thereby validating the findings. No single data source should ever be used unless it can be validated or triangulated by at least two other sources (Lincoln & Guba, 1985).

EXHIBIT 5.5. Final Selection of Data Sources

Overarching Question	Possible Data Sources
Question 1: What perceptions and views of adjunct professors are held by university seniors, and how do these perceptions and views affect instruction and academic success?	Open-ended interview responses Researcher field notes ~~Interviews with adjunct professors~~ *(better suited to a different question)* Small group open-discussion sessions with students ~~Online chat~~ *(may turn into a "gripe" session)* Online discussion board responses ~~Student records~~ Student transcripts ~~Participant field journals~~ *(more feasible to set up a discussion forum)* Videos (classroom) ~~Audio recordings of classroom sessions~~ *(schedule of videotapings would work better)* ~~Student artifacts (projects)~~ *(assignments do not allow for artifact collection)*
Question 2: To what degree does the status of "adjunct" affect general departmental enrollment, program success, and overall student satisfaction with the university?	Enrollment information Adjuncts per department Adjunct faculty evaluations Exit interviews (end of semester) with students ~~Researcher field notes~~ *(will not be used for this question)* Interviews with department chairs ~~Interviews with administrators~~ *(determined that this source would not yield appropriate information)* ~~Online Discussion Board responses~~ *(better suited to question 1)* ~~Online chat~~ *(ruled out—see question 1)*

Thus triangulation reinforces the validity and trustworthiness of the action research. This type of triangulation is referred to as data triangulation (Patton, 1990).

Patton (1990) suggests that triangulation may also be established through researcher triangulation. Action research is often collaborative. Teachers and other practitioners work together conducting action research in order to improve practice. Researcher triangulation is established when two or more researchers engaged in action research arrive at the same findings. For example, researcher field notes recorded and compared may yield the same information. After examining video transcripts, three researchers working collaboratively on the same action research study identify similar patterns.

One means of illustrating triangulation is to use a triangulation matrix. The matrix serves as a recording device for the researcher and comes in handy when writing the final action research report. The matrix is a graphic representation of overarching questions, data sets, and general findings. It helps establish validity and trustworthiness and may be integrated into the final action research report. In addition, the triangulation matrix helps in structuring the framework for the action research study. It is strongly recommended that beginning researchers use a matrix, as it also helps when designing the data collection schedule. Exhibits 5.6, 5.7, and 5.8 provide examples of completed triangulation matrices.

Information on the triangulation matrix provides a map for collecting data during the action research study. As data are collected, an extra "Notes" column may be added so that the researcher can record additional details for data analysis purposes. This helps in identifying emerging patterns, unanticipated events, and general findings. Finally, the matrix helps organize the data, which makes it easier when analyzing each data set and later when reporting findings in the final action research report.

QUALITATIVE DATA INSTRUMENTS AND SCHEDULES

Qualitative methods rely heavily on the interaction between the researcher as participant observer, the participants, and the environment. Action research that takes a qualitative approach typically involves a number of instruments and techniques appropriate when conducting research in the practitioner-based environment. The instruments are used to collect data gathered as part of the study. Various techniques, like research instruments, assist the researcher in conducting systematic inquiry based on the action research process. One such technique is the open-ended interview. The open-ended interview may be an in-depth, one-on-one interview or an informal interview in a small group setting in the research environment. Lincoln and Guba (1985) describe an interview as a "conversation with a purpose." Such interviews are typically conducted by a researcher who is also a participant observer. This is important because by serving in the capacity of participant observer, the researcher is able to work in the action research setting, thereby gaining the trust of participants. This

EXHIBIT 5.6. Triangulation Matrix: Example 1

Focus of the Action Research Study

Homework in high school

Overarching Question	Data Source 1	Data Source 2	Data Source 3
What views and perceptions regarding homework are held by sophomores and juniors enrolled in a suburban high school, and how do these views and perceptions affect academic success?	Open-ended interviews with students and teachers	Homework grades collected from subject area teachers	Researcher field notes
What views and perceptions regarding homework are held by parents and, if applicable, employers of students enrolled in a suburban high school, and how do these views and perceptions affect academic success?	Open-ended interviews conducted via e-mail and phone with parents and employers	Discussion forum set up for parents to post comments	PTA meeting dedicated to "attacking the homework problem"
Do the design and structure of the homework assignment promote knowledge retention, application, and skill development, and if so, which designs and assignments are most effective in promoting success?	Homework assignments collected from subject area teachers	Researcher field notes recorded from classroom observations	Information recorded from teachers who supervise the "homework hotline"

trust encourages honest responses, which provide valuable information in informing inquiry. Open-ended interviews may be unstructured and informal or may follow the format dictated by an interview instrument. The questions—worded in a manner to elicit a variety of responses—are developed using a framework that may be added to, revised, and edited as the study progresses.

EXHIBIT 5.7. **Triangulation Matrix: Example 2**

Focus of the Action Research Study

Student choice of group members in literature circles

Overarching Question	Data Source 1	Data Source 2	Data Source 3
How does student choice affect the success of student comprehension when working in literature groups?	Flowcharts of student choice of group members	Video transcripts of student literature circle sessions	Researcher field notes
What patterns emerge as students engage in self-grouping choice with regard to group makeup, book selection, degree of discussion, and literature-based writing?	Lists of group members with descriptors (female, male, number, cultural diversity, and so on)	Student writing journal entries describing selected literature books for literature circle sessions	Writing samples collected for one marking period
What information may be gleaned from the study that can be used to provide insight to teachers when using literature circles in the classroom setting?	Student comprehension test scores and samples of essay questions based on literature books	Researcher field notes	Student literature projects— group and individual

Informal, *unstructured interviews* may be guided by a set of questions—generally, open-ended questions (see Exhibit 5.9). Additional questions may be asked, depending on the participant's responses. Conducted by the researcher, the informal, unstructured interview is more like a conversation than an interview in that the questions are posed in a conversational manner. Again, this type of interview may be conducted individually or with a small group of participants. The responses may be recorded in a researcher's field journal. However, due to the openness of the interview, audiotapes are recommended. Once the interview is complete, the researcher may listen to the tapes and transcribe the information for analysis purposes. The formal, *structured interview* is typically conducted individually. The structured interview consists of a list of questions that are used to gather information from a series of participants (see Exhibit 5.10). Although the questions are typically open-ended, the list of questions is strictly followed without any deviation. An interview guide is

EXHIBIT 5.8. Triangulation Matrix: Example 3

Focus of the Action Research Study

Peer leadership, perceptions, and views among female college basketball players

Overarching Question	Data Source 1	Data Source 2	Data Source 3
What perceptions of peer leadership are held by members of a university women's basketball team, and do these perceptions promote or hinder success on the court?	Open-ended interview sessions with team members individually and in small groups	Leadership survey responses	Researcher field notes
What is the effect of peer-led sessions on skill, performance, and team spirit?	Game film	Debriefing sessions after games	Team statistics
What information can be gleaned from the study that might improve teamwork and athletics in general among all collegiate team sports?	Team statistics	Researcher field notes	Interviews with coaches

EXHIBIT 5.9. Excerpt from an Informal, Unstructured Interview Instrument

1. What are your feelings on using information taken from Wikipedia when conducting research for school assignments?

2. How accurate do you feel Wikipedia information is?

3. Do you believe that "experts" contribute to this online source?

[Ask related follow-up questions as appropriate.]

EXHIBIT 5.10. **Excerpt from a Formal, Structured Interview Instrument**

Category: **Using Online Technology Tools for Research**

1. Do you feel that online tools (such as Wikipedia, blogs, and Web sites) should be used when conducting research for school assignments?

2. What are your thoughts on the types of assignments that work best with online sources?

3. What are your opinions of information that is typically available online?

Category: **Accuracy and Reliability of Sources**

4. What are your opinions of the accuracy of the sources?

5. Do you feel that "experts" contribute to the sources? Please explain your answer.

Category: **Process and Behaviors**

6. Describe the process that you use to locate information online.

7. In your opinion, when is the best time of the day to use the Internet to locate online sources? Please explain your answer.

---

prepared before the interview is conducted. The questions are followed and recorded for later transcription and coding.

Maykut and Morehouse (1994) suggest that prior to the interview, the researcher should develop the set of open-ended questions, develop categories for the question items, and decide on an interviewing format. When developing questions for the interview, keep in mind that open-ended questions typically incorporate phrases such as these:

"What are your thoughts regarding . . . ?"

"How do you feel about . . . ?"

"What are your views on this topic?"

"In what ways do you think . . . ?"

"What is your opinion on . . . ?"

The questions are written such that the answer cannot be "yes" or "no." Once the questions are drafted, the researcher can develop categories in which to group them. This technique helps the researcher in the analysis stage of the research. For example, an open-ended instrument focusing on views and perceptions of teacher education preparation may reflect the following categories:

Diversity: Preparation in working with diverse populations of students

Methods: Preparation in using a variety of methods

Technology: Preparation in integrating technology into lesson planning

Collegiality: Preparation in working collaboratively with colleagues

In addition, the researcher may further group the questions around perceptions, opinions, feelings, experience, behaviors, and knowledge (as in Exhibit 5.10).

The prepared interview instruments help the researcher focus on key information. However, every researcher, no matter how experienced or inexperienced, will meet a reluctant interviewee. In the event that a participant is hesitant to provide responses, Patton (1990) suggests using interview probes. Interview probes enable the researcher to prompt the participant for responses. There are three types of interview probes: detail probes, explanation probes, and clarifying probes.

Detail probes prompt the interviewee to offer details regarding opinions, feelings, ideas, and thoughts. Detail probes may consist of questions such as these:

"What colors?"

"Who were you with?"

"Where were you?"

"When did this take place?"

"How did this happen?"

Explanation probes prompt the interviewee to provide further explanation and elaborate on a response. Explanation probes may consist of comments such as these:

"That's interesting. Please tell me more."

"Can you give me a few examples?"

"That information is very helpful. Please explain that a little more."

"Go on; I'd like to hear more about that."

Clarifying probes encourage the interviewee to refine thoughts and ideas to aid understanding on the part of the interviewer. Clarifying probes may be formulated like these:

"I'm having a hard time understanding that. Can you explain what you mean by 'dead linking'?"

"I want to be sure that I completely understand what you're telling me. Please describe that situation again."

"I'm unfamiliar with that term. What does it mean?"

Once the researcher is satisfied with the interview instrument and structure, a schedule for conducting the interviews should be established. Typically, an interview schedule consists of a day-by-day, weekly, or monthly timeline (see Exhibit 5.11). The schedule should be set up and agreed to by the participants. The interviewees should be contacted prior to the interview. In some cases, the researcher may inform the interviewees regarding the overall, general focus of the interview. Any materials needed to conduct the interview should be assembled and

EXHIBIT 5.11. Sample Interview Schedule

Interviewee Type		Interview Date	Reminder Date			Interview Completed as Scheduled	Notes
			E-Mail	Mail	Phone		
JD	Structured Individual	May 20, 2009	✓			✓	Sent out e-mail reminder 48 hours prior to interview. Note probes, if needed.
PC	Unstructured Group	June 18, 2009	✓		✓	✓	Transcription on two tapes.
ACC	Unstructured Group	June 18, 2009	✓		✓	✓	Transcription on two tapes.

ready. For example, copies of the instrument should be available for all participants. Recording equipment—audio or video—should be set up prior to the interview. In addition, the researcher should bring the field journal to record additional notes as needed. Interview times must be strictly adhered to in order to encourage interaction and response. Last, after the interview takes place, it is a good idea to reflect on the interview and record notes in the field journal as needed.

Structured interviews are the easiest to conduct because the researcher adheres to the scripted questions. A structured interview should generally be kept to around thirty to forty-five minutes. Unstructured interviews are a bit more difficult because although the researcher has a framework, the interview may go in unanticipated directions. In addition, open-ended unstructured interviews are often conducted in small groups, requiring the researcher to record the responses.

Once the interviews have been conducted, the researcher must transcribe the audio or video recordings. With technology readily available, the best way to transcribe is to enter the information in a word processing document. As the recordings are examined, the researcher types each question and response. This process works well for transcribing structured interviews, open-ended interviews, recorded conversations, and discussions. To ensure participant anonymity, each interviewee should be assigned a code. For example, initials may be used. Another technique is to assign each participant a number. When transcribing responses, each participant response is indicated by the number assigned. Each line of the transcript must be numbered.

EXHIBIT 5.12. **Transcript of an Unstructured Interview**

Date: June 18, 2009

Interviewees: JN, PC, ACC, AJV

Q#1. What are your feelings on using information taken from Wikipedia when conducting research for school assignments?

1. JN: I think that taking information from Wikipedia is perfectly fine. It's an easy way to
2. locate the information, and it makes it easier when you're working on a schedule.
3. PC: Yeah, I agree. I do my schoolwork at night after I come home from work. I don't
4. have time to look at books or go to the library.
5. ACC: I'm the same way. After school I go straight to work and then when I get
6. off—usually around 11:00—I then have to do papers and stuff. So, yeah, it is just easier
7. for me, too.
8. AJV: I use Wikipedia and don't think there's anything wrong with it. But I do have to try
9. to use other online stuff just to keep the teacher off my back.
10. PC: I don't see why teachers have a fit about using Wikipedia. If they had it when they
11. were in high school, you know they would be using it.

The number is used later when reporting findings or when referencing responses. Although the transcription can get tedious at times, it is a critical element in qualitative action research because the transcripts may later be used in the triangulation process (see Exhibit 5.12 and Exhibit 5.13).

RESEARCH AND DATA COLLECTION SCHEDULES

The flow of activities in the practicing environment is steady and dynamic. To integrate action research, the practitioner must be sure that the study is well structured and that the design and methods are sound. In addition, several tools are helpful in keeping the research on track. These may be easily developed by the individual researcher and are in fact best when designed to meet the needs of the environment. A research schedule is a simple tool that outlines the progression of the action research. The schedule may be developed in a linear manner following a calendar or timeline. A data collection schedule is similar; however, the data collection schedule provides more detail for the researcher in terms of when, where, and how the data sets will be collected and when the analysis will be conducted.

Research schedules and data collection schedules are specific to the researcher, the study, and the environment. One researcher may prefer to use a calendar; another may opt for a checklist or chart. Typically, the research schedule is developed first. The researcher charts the projected progress of the action research. Next, the data

EXHIBIT 5.13. **Transcript of a Structured Interview**

Date: May 20, 2009

Interviewee: JD

Researcher: R

Category: **Using Online Technology Tools for Research**

Q#1: Do you feel that online tools (such as Wikipedia, blogs, and Web sites) should be used when conducting research for school assignments?

1. JD: I think that the things you can access online like Wikipedia, blogs, podcasts, even
2. videos on YouTube, are OK for doing school assignments because most of us work on
3. assignments when we can. We can access these things at any time. We can work our
4. assignments into our schedules.

Q#2: What are your thoughts on the types of assignments that work best with online sources?

1. JD: I think just about anything. I wish all my assignments could be done with online
2. sources.
3. R: I'm not sure what you mean. It seems like you enjoy using online sources for
4. assignments. I'm not sure what kinds of assignments work best, though. Can you explain
5. or give me an example?
6. JD: Sure, like, if you have to do a paper. That works well when you use online sources.
7. And projects where you have to look stuff up and put together a presentation. You can
8. get information, pictures, you know, just about anything.

collection schedule is developed. Information and dates listed on the researcher schedule are double-checked and entered on the data collection schedule. Additional details are added to create a clear, descriptive picture of the collection process. The schedules serve two important roles in the action research process. First, the schedules map out the study in detail. It is much easier to complete a study with a road map. Second, the schedules provide additional information when reporting findings.

When designing the research schedule and the data collection schedule, the researcher should keep the following factors in mind:

■ The schedules—for research and data collection—should reflect the personal preferences of the researcher. Calendars, checklists, charts, and tables all work well; however, if the researcher is not comfortable with a particular format, progress of the study may be halted.

■ The schedules must reflect the practicing environment and any time constraints involved as part of the setting. For example, if the action research is scheduled to be conducted in a public school environment, be sure that any school calendar dates are worked into the schedule.

■ The schedules must also reflect the scope of the action research and must be as detailed as possible. Brief descriptions, overviews, short summaries, and notes help the researcher as the study progresses.

■ The research schedule should illustrate a day-by-day, week-by-week, or month-by-month account of all activities related to the action research study, from beginning to end. These activities include designing the proposal, designing the consent form or assent form, IRB approval, contacting participants, and setting up interview schedules.

■ The data collection schedule should also illustrate a day-by-day, week-by-week, or month-by-month account of data sets collected, described in detail, in addition to a summary of when, where, and how data will be analyzed.

A research schedule is shown in Exhibit 5.14 and a data collection schedule in Exhibit 5.15.

SUMMARY

The practicing environment is rich in data, with multiple forms available. Selection of data for action research must therefore be based on the research questions and the methodological approach. The expertise of the action researcher serves as a guide in selecting the most appropriate data to inform the study. The best means of accomplishing this is to return to the research questions. The questions become the basis for selecting data (and data sets, if needed). Quantitative action research studies typically consist of data that would be used in a statistical analysis. A qualitative study would involve multiple sets of data that would then be analyzed through categorization, coding, defining attributes, and developing grounded theory.

There are two types of numerical data, parametric and nonparametric. Nonparametric data are of two types: nominal and ordinal. It is important that the statistical analysis test match the data because of validity factors in quantitative studies. Test results determine validity, evidence that the test measures what it says it will measure. Validity also infers the soundness of the research design. Due to the nature of qualitative action research, many of the research factors typically considered in an action research study employing a quantitative approach are dealt with differently in a qualitative action research study. Reliability and validity factors—although important to the study—are not as much of an issue in qualitative action research studies. Triangulation involves multiple confirmation of results. One means of demonstrating triangulation is to use a triangulation matrix. It helps establish validity and trustworthiness and may be integrated into the final action research report. In addition, the triangulation matrix helps in structuring the framework for the action research study.

EXHIBIT 5.14. Sample Research Schedule

Research Task	Description	Completion Deadline	Date Completed
Research proposal	Final draft and edits of proposal (sections 1, 2, and 3)	January 15, 2009	January 15, 2009
Consent forms and assent forms	Design consent and assent forms	January 16, 2009	January 17, 2009
	Prepare cover letter	January 16, 2009	
Human subjects training	Study online sources	Week of January 15, 2009	January 20, 2009
	Complete training modules	January 20, 2009	
Open-ended interview instruments	Design instrument for structured and unstructured interviews	January 21, 2009	January 23, 2009
Meetings with administrators	Meet with school administrators at two sites (see dates)	Meeting scheduled for January 22, 2009	January 22, 2009
	Prepare overview of action research		
	Share sample letter approving the study, which will later be submitted to the IRB	Prior to January 22 meeting At meeting	
Submit to IRB	Make copies	January 24, 2009	Approval received February 10, 2009
	Submit proposal for IRB approval	January 25, 2009	
Contact participants	Draft invitation letter	February 15, 2009	February 15, 2009
	Send letter to potential participants	February 20, 2009	February 21, 2009
	Schedule onsite informational meeting	Meeting scheduled for March 1, 2009	March 1, 2009
	Secure location for meeting		February 15, 2009
	Make copies of consent forms, assent forms, and cover letters	February 17–18, 2009	February 28, 2009
	Prepare flyer for participants (overview of study)	Prior to meeting	February 28, 2009
	Assemble packets for distribution	Prior to meeting	February 28, 2009
Collect signed consent and assent forms	Distribute consent and assent forms at meeting; encourage potential participants to submit forms at the end of the meeting	March 1–5, 2009	All forms collected by March 4, 2009

133

EXHIBIT 5.15. **Sample Data Collection Schedule**

Research Question	Data Set	Data Collection Deadline	Date Collection Completed	Analysis	Date Analysis Completed
Question 1 What views and perceptions regarding homework are held by sophomores and juniors enrolled in a suburban high school, and how do these views and perceptions affect academic success?	Open-ended interviews with students (unstructured) Open-ended interviews with teachers (unstructured)	Interviews scheduled for 3/3/09 Participants: ZJC, GB, SD, DD Interview scheduled for 3/4/09	3/3/09	Transcripts complete and coded Analysis for recurring themes Transcripts complete and coded Analysis for recurring themes	3/5/09 3/8/09 3/6/09 3/8/09
Question 1	Homework grades collected from subject area teachers	Meetings scheduled for 3/10/09 through 3/12/09	3/12/09	Grades coded and matched with participant codes Analysis of trends	3/15/09 3/20/09
Question 1	Researcher field notes recorded during classroom observations	Observations 3/11/09 through 3/12/09	3/12/09	Ongoing coding of themes	Ongoing

KEY TERMS

Artifacts
Category data
Data
Data set
Generalizability
Interrater reliability
Interval data
Nominal data
Nonparametric data

Ordinal data
Parametric data
Ratio data
Reliability
Structured interview
Triangulation
Unstructured interview
Validity

DISCUSSION QUESTIONS

1. Compare and contrast the types of data and data sets appropriate for quantitative, qualitative, and mixed-method approaches to action research.

2. Discuss the differences between parametric and nonparametric data. Provide examples of each.

3. Describe nominal, ordinal, interval, and ratio data. Provide examples of each.

4. Discuss statistical tests that are appropriate to use with parametric data and nonparametric data.

5. Explore the relationship between a hypothesis and the type of data typically present in a quantitative action research study.

6. Identify possible qualitative data sets, and explain how these data relate to the overarching questions.

7. Discuss validity, reliability, generalizability, and triangulation as related to quantitative and qualitative action research.

8. Describe the rationale behind developing a research schedule and a data collection schedule. Provide an explanation regarding use of the schedules.

SUGGESTED TOPICS

1. After brainstorming in small groups, identify a simple action research focus. Develop a ten-item survey instrument that uses a Likert scale.

2. Working in pairs, examine the following research hypotheses and overarching questions. Identify the appropriate data for each.

   a. *Hypothesis:* University students who take part in a series of workshops focusing on study skills will score higher on major exams than students who did not take part in the workshops.

   b. *Hypothesis:* Kindergarten students who take part in a fully balanced breakfast and lunch program will score higher on the DIAL test and maintain steady progress in both reading and math than kindergarten students who only took part in the lunch program.

c. *Overarching Question:* What views and perceptions regarding natural childbirth are held by female university seniors who are in the first trimester of pregnancy, and how do these views and perceptions affect their choice of birthing situation?

d. *Overarching Question:* What preferences regarding student-led scheduling sessions are held by high school sophomores, and how do these perceptions affect class and instructor selection?

3. Design a structured interview instrument and an unstructured interview instrument. Be prepared to share your work in small groups.

4. Design a one-month research schedule and data collection schedule.

ONLINE ACTIVITIES

1. Select one or two of the discussion questions provided to set up an online forum. Have students support their ideas with outside sources. Use a rubric for evaluating the postings. (*Note:* This may be completed in small groups or with the entire class.)

2. Develop a simple ten-item survey based on a Likert scale. Post it to the designated forum. Critique at least two other surveys posted by classmates. Provide feedback for improving the survey.

3. Design a structured interview instrument and an unstructured interview instrument. Post your instruments to the designated forum for sharing.

4. Using Exhibit 5.6, list at least three overarching questions. Complete the triangulation matrix by identifying appropriate data sets. Post the completed matrix to the designated forum for small group sharing.

5. Examine the research schedule presented in Exhibit 5.14. What questions would you have for the researcher regarding the progress of research tasks?

CHAPTER

6

THE ACTION RESEARCHER'S TOOLS

LEARNING OBJECTIVES

After reading Chapter Six, you should be able to:

- Examine specific tools that enable effective research
- Discuss the difference between the field journal and the participant field journal
- Identify types of field journal entries and their purposes
- Examine elements of entries
- Explore purposes and types of reflection as related to action research

TOOLS FOR CONDUCTING RESEARCH

In thinking about the practicing environment, we have already established that the setting is rich in data—readily available for research purposes. The data are collected, analyzed, and used to improve practice. However, as the action research study progresses, the researcher must also identify the research tools needed to complete the study and develop the action plan. Just as data are readily available in the practicing environment, so are the tools needed for conducting action research. In many instances, the data are also the tools. This is especially true if the action research requires a qualitative approach. For example, an action research study may demand that the researcher keep a field journal in which notes are recorded while observing or interacting. The *field journal* is a research tool. The field journal is the researcher's personal journal in which daily entries are recorded. The entries may consist of reflections of observations, notes regarding the research, and related information in the form of comments and memos. The researcher's field notes, recorded in the journal, are also part of the data collected to inform the inquiry. It should be noted that whether the selected approach is quantitative or qualitative, there are certain research tools that are identified as part of the research process and the practicing environment. Several research tools that are vital to action research include field journals, artifacts, electronic materials, and—if appropriate—photos.

Action research—as part of the practitioner-based environment—takes place in the natural setting. Although qualitative researchers typically keep field journals and field notes, the field journal is not usually part of quantitative studies. When conducting action research, however, the field journal is critical because the research is taking place in the practicing environment. Even if the study takes a quantitative approach, a field journal is highly recommended. In addition, the field journal or research journal assists the beginning researcher in carrying out the inquiry through the practice of recording thoughts, ideas, notes, and other details related to the action research study.

The Researcher's Field Journal

The *researcher's field journal* is the first critical tool needed when conducting action research. The researcher's field journal may consist of a notebook, a decorative journal, or a running log entered electronically via a word processing program. The field journal helps the researcher carry out the inquiry through the physical act of recording notations. The journal serves many purposes. In a strictly qualitative action research study, the field journal would be used when recording naturally occurring events, during observations, or when conducting interviews. The field journal entries become actual sources of data that are later coded and analyzed for emerging themes and patterns. However, in any action research study—whether the approach is quantitative or qualitative—the researcher uses the field journal to record details such as the following:

■ Thought processes

■ Problem identification and related notes

- Information regarding the participants
- Notes regarding IRB procedures
- Memos dealing with logistics, plans, and schedules
- Related ideas
- Drawings, diagrams, charts, and the like
- Questions and concerns
- "To do" lists
- Notes regarding progress of the study
- Information recorded during interviews
- Planning notes
- Observational notes
- Reminders
- Questions regarding the study
- General "wonderings" that the researcher has as a result of the inquiry

The researcher's field journal guides the process in that the act of writing and recording encourages the researcher to think through the acts of inquiry. In reality, a practitioner researcher should get in the habit of keeping some type of journal set aside for recording ideas regarding possible research. As notes and ideas are preserved, the journal acts as a record for future research.

Think of the early brainstorming sessions that typically take place as part of the action research process. Information from the beginning stages of the action research study, when recorded in a field journal, may be revisited at any time. There is much value in keeping detailed notes throughout the process, as the notes are informative and thought-provoking. The process of keeping a field journal is similar to a technique regularly used to promote literacy. Early literacy teachers usually encourage students to draw pictures. Once the picture is complete, the teacher asks, "Tell me about your drawing." As the student provides an explanation, the teacher records the words so that the picture is now narrated. This is repeated until the student can draw and record thoughts in the form of a word or two, a sentence, several sentences, and paragraphs. The act of writing helps the early learner make the connection between sound, symbol, and graphic—leading to literacy.

Going a step further, Blumer (1969) suggests that in any given situation, we view life through symbols that have already been established, internalized, and given meaning. Therefore, when interacting in a new environment, we base those interactions on the previously established symbolic meanings. Blumer's *theory of symbolic interaction* implies that communication is the most natural and humanizing activity in which people can engage; communication consists of three core principles: meaning, language, and thought; and interactions and communication lead to conclusions about self and the environment in which the interactions take place.

Because language is a tool for interaction and communication, the field journal becomes vital to the research process. Language is used to make meaning and provide explanation. In terms of research, consider the following key factors:

■ Interactions are based on previously established meanings.

■ Meanings are influenced by a number of outside variables, such as society, culture, ethnicity, and prior experiences.

■ We establish new meanings through interactions in new environments and settings.

■ New meanings are internalized and then later revisited and checked through additional interactions and communication.

Considering how this information applies to action research, the role of language is extremely important because language enables interaction among the researcher, the environment, and the participants. Researchers typically interact with people and environments based on the meanings they assign. Once a researcher determines what is taking place in a specific practicing environment, meaning may be assigned. The action researcher is able to make sense of what is taking place and use that information to gain insights that will improve practice. Figure 6.1 illustrates the concept further.

Newcomers to the action research process—or any research process—are in the early stages of research literacy. The act of recording thoughts and ideas leads to competency and understanding of research, thereby bringing about research literacy

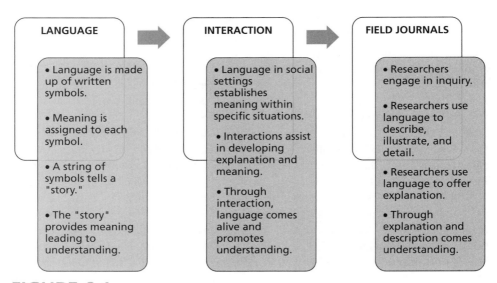

FIGURE 6.1. *Language, Interaction, and the Role of Field Journals*

or *research orientation*. Research orientation develops as a result of thinking through a study from beginning to end and combining that thought process with the actual act of implementation. The field journal or research journal is one tool that enables the development of research orientation and research literacy. It promotes the knowledge needed to conduct research successfully. This in itself is important due to the fact that the action researcher must build skills, knowledge, and confidence in the concept of researcher-as-instrument as well as practitioner-as-researcher. Last, just as the early learner draws and then writes, the beginning researcher is encouraged to record not only words but also illustrations, pictures, diagrams, and drawings. Research journals are wonderful resources to examine because they are rich with ideas, notes, color, and thoughts. The research journal is as individual as the researcher.

Generally, a researcher's field journal will contain three types of information:

- *Ideas and wonderings.* These are notations that reflect the researcher's thought process. This type of information is useful to the researcher alone and is more personal than the other two types of information. These are notes to oneself as well as any other information that is meaningful to the researcher.

- *General research information.* This consists of notes, memos, and other details related to the study in general. Information in this category may consist of procedural notes, reminders, scheduling notations, memos regarding materials needed, and the like.

- *Environment and participant-based information.* This includes notes regarding observations and naturally occurring events, interview notes, and information recorded regarding specific participants, the environment, and other aspects of the study.

Typically, the field journal is used throughout the action research process. Some researchers find it helpful to engage in ongoing recording while others prefer removed recording. *Ongoing recording* consists of notes entered as events occur. *Removed recording* (also known as *reflective recording*) consists of entering reflective entries after observing or interacting. A balanced combination of ongoing and reflective recordings works best and provides a good continuum for the study.

Although field journals are usually handwritten, technology enables researchers to record notes electronically. Electronic notes serve the same purpose as handwritten field notes. However, unless a computer is available during observations, it is strongly recommended that the notes be handwritten. Many physicians' offices use electronic notebooks. Electronic notebooks enable the nurse, physician's assistant, or physician to enter information immediately. The computers are usually small, lightweight, and portable. Many allow for handwritten notes to be converted to print, but this depends on the capabilities of the particular computer. If an electronic notebook is available, the researcher should make use of it as the technology provides a shortcut. Otherwise, the researcher should handwrite notes in the journal or engage in reflective recording. Note that if the action research is being conducted by two or more researchers, all should keep field journals, as the information recorded may assist in triangulation of data during data analysis.

The Participant Field Journal

In action research studies that adopt a qualitative approach, it is often necessary to ask participants to keep participant field journals. The purpose of the *participant field journal* is a little different from that of the researcher's journal. When working with small groups of participants, a researcher may require each participant to keep a journal to record information regarding views, perceptions, and ideas surrounding the study. Researchers also make use of the participant field journal when asking participants to respond to a prompted question or to record reflections after taking part in research activities. For example, after conducting an open-ended unstructured group interview, the researcher may ask or prompt participants to reflect on what they discussed and record reflections in a participant field journal. For instance, an action research study focusing on student perceptions of science lab activities may include the following prompts:

> "Think about the science lab activity we just completed. What did you like about it? What did you dislike?"

> "What did you think about your partner? Was he or she bossy, friendly, or helpful? What other adjectives describe your partner?"

> "What did you think of today's task and the equipment?"

> "How can we improve this science lab activity? What will help make the task better?"

The researcher may ask participants to record responses in the participant field journal. Later the information is used as a data set for analysis purposes or for triangulation. The participant field journals are usually a rich source of data. They are as individual as each participant and provide insight for the researcher—especially one who is working with minors. One word of caution is that if information recorded in participant field journals will be used as data, be sure to remove all personal information to ensure that the identity of the participant is protected. Depending on the study, participant field journals may be used in the following ways:

- As participant daily reflection logs to record thoughts after taking part in research tasks and activities

- As planning logs to record "how to" information and "to do" information

- As participant response journals to record responses to prompted or cued interviews and questions

- As participant research journals to record views and perceptions regarding the actual action research study

- As wonderings journals to record general ideas, thoughts, notes, diagrams, drawings, and other musings

Before asking participants to keep participant journals, it is strongly recommended that the researcher provide the following information:

- How the journals will be used throughout the study
- What information will be recorded in the journals
- What options a participant has if he or she does not agree to keep a field journal
- The procedure for storing the journals after the study ends or the procedure for returning the journals to participants

In addition, participant consent must be secured before any information recorded in the participant journals may be used as data. Many minor participants will agree to keep participant field journals; however, they want to know when and how the journals will be returned. In the event that the information recorded in the journals will be used as a data set and if the researcher agrees to return the journals, copies should be made and kept on file, thereby securing the information for triangulation purposes. It is recommended that procedures for storing data used in an action research study as outlined in IRB guidelines be referred to for individual studies. The IRB guidelines prepared by institutions usually outline how data must be stored after the study ends, where the data must be stored, and procedures for returning materials to participants.

Elements of Recording

Because they originate in the practitioner-based setting, field notes become a record of the researcher's understanding of the participants, events, and environment that are the focus of the research. Based on this premise, an unbroken link between field notes recorded in the researcher's field journal and the actual action research is formed. The researcher must then consider and remember that any events, activities, tasks, and interactions recorded are ultimately collected and analyzed as data collected as part of the inquiry and that any field notes recorded should focus on the meanings, concerns, and interactions of the participants studied as well as the environment.

In addition, any field notes recorded during an action research study are essential in providing a coherent account of what takes place in the practicing environment. The detail provided offers insight into the social and interactional processes of the participants in the specific environment being studied (Emerson, Fretz, & Shaw, 1995).

Since field notes are viewed and valued as a form of data, they must be recorded in a nonbiased, informative, and reportlike manner. The researcher—returning to the notion of researcher-as-instrument—must rely on professionalism and record accurately what takes place during observations, interviews, and other research-related activities.

Basically, there are two types of field note entries: descriptive entries and reflective entries. *Descriptive entries* provide a detailed description of an event or activity observed by the researcher. A descriptive entry attempts to paint a picture of what took place on any given day during the action research study. The notes are written in a detailed manner to preserve a vivid illustration of the event, the interview response, or an interaction. By contrast, *reflective entries* record the researcher's personal reflections. These may consist of a variety of items, thoughts, or ideas related to the action research or additional questions related to the focus of the inquiry. In action research, both descriptive and reflective field notes are unbiased and grounded in inquiry—with the purpose of gathering information in order to improve practice.

Delving further into descriptive field note entries, the following questions provide a guide for recording. Think in terms of who, what, when, where, and how when recording descriptive entries. Just as a reporter records notes for a news story, the action researcher records descriptive field note entries that are later treated as data.

- *Who:* Who is being observed? Who are the participants—male, female, cultural background, ethnicity, language, and so on. Who is being interviewed?

- *What:* What activities or tasks are the participants engaged in? What types of interactions are occurring? What is the makeup of groups? What questions are being asked? What type of interview is being conducted?

- *When:* What day, month, year, time of day?

- *Where:* Where is the observation taking place? Where is the interview? Where is the actual research site?

- *How:* How are the participants interacting with each other? How are participants interacting with the environment?

For beginning researchers, the job of recording descriptive field notes may seem tedious and time-consuming. Some researchers feel that the act of recording takes away from valuable time actually observing. With experience, the task of recording descriptive entries becomes easier. The researcher, using instinct and research experience, is eventually able to record descriptive entries that preserve key information without having to write verbatim what is taking place. In addition, by videotaping observations, the researcher is better able to home in on critical interactions and factors. These are recorded as descriptive entries. Later, the videotapes of the same interactions are viewed in order to verify what took place and to confirm what was recorded in the field journal.

Here are some tips for recording descriptive field journal entries:

- Enter the observation with no preconceptions. The practitioner researcher knows the environment as well as the participants. Using expertise in the practitioner setting, the researcher is able to record descriptive entries in an unbiased, objective manner.

- Record notes while at the site. Descriptive entries must be recorded at the time of the observation while interacting in the action research environment.

- Transcribe (if needed) as soon as possible. Descriptive field note entries should be transcribed shortly after the observation or interview takes place. If the notes were recorded in a manner that doesn't need transcription, the researcher may set them aside for later analysis or transcribe videotapes of the same observation or interview and verify the notes for later analysis.

■   Include the date, time, and topic or focus. Be sure to record the "vitals" accurately for each descriptive field note entry.

■   Include descriptive information regarding all observations, such as participants being observed and their interactions.

■   List key words and outlines. Some action researchers find it helpful to list key words or record notes in outline format. Others record descriptive entries as a narrative. Either way is fine as long as the information is accurate, detailed, and nonbiased.

Graduate students and beginning researchers are encouraged to practice recording descriptive field journal entries before beginning an action research study. The practice helps in determining what information is important to record, learning how to record the information, and keeping the entry devoid of bias and rich in detail. Exhibit 6.1 contrasts inappropriate and appropriate descriptive entries in a field journal. Both examples are taken from field notes recorded in a seventh-grade language arts class at the same time during the same activity. The action research focus in this particular setting examined the effects of student-selected groups on writing development and writing production.

You can see that the second example provides a nonbiased picture of what took place. The appropriate example illustrates a clear, concise, descriptive picture of the setting as well as the participants observed. The notes recorded are devoid of any preconceived notions and report the events clearly.

REFLECTIVE PRACTICE

The researcher's field journal provides a vehicle for self-reflection and encourages the researcher to engage in reflective practice. The act of recording reflective entries assists the researcher in thinking about research. For example, metacognition is sometimes considered "thinking about thinking." Research reflection that results from recording reflective entries allows the action researcher to take time to think about the researcher being conducted. This process is vital to action research due to the fact that the research is being conducted in the practitioner's work-based environment. To understand the role of reflection and its relationship to the action research process, consider the actual act of reflection.

Reflection may be defined as a mental process during which events, experiences, problems, or situations are revisited and examined in order to promote further understanding. The understanding leads to solutions, ideas, improvement, and change. Reflection may also be defined as a process of viewing an individual or personal experience in order to conduct a close examination that may lead to in-depth understanding. The reexamination and revisiting of specific experiences enables the researcher to take a closer look with "new eyes." The familiarity of the

EXHIBIT 6.1. Field Note Examples, Good and Bad

Inappropriate Entry

I observed two students talking together. It looked to me like they were gossiping about the teacher. I can't believe how stupid these kids are! And the teacher had no clue! Now one just said she hated the science teacher! (Note: Tell teachers later.)

Appropriate Entry

Date: June 20

Time: 8:45–10:15 a.m.

Participants: SS (female, Caucasian seventh grader), AB (female, Caucasian seventh grader)

Nature of observation: Small group writing project in seventh-grade language arts class (Ms. J.). Ms. J. directed students to assemble into small groups. She distributed the writing assignment and went over the directions and guidelines. Then students were given an opportunity to ask questions—no one did. Ms. J. put in a CD with soft music and then began monitoring the students. She stopped at each desk.

Entry: Observation of SS & AB

10:05: SS & AB worked together on the assignment. SS read the directions again (out loud).

SS: How do you want to get started? I think I would rather write the opening sentence—what about you?

AB: Forget the assignment, what about that new science teacher? I hate him!

SS: Whatever. I think we need to get going on this assignment. I don't want to mess up my grade because you hate the science teacher. Here—I already wrote the opening sentence. Proofread it. I'll work on the first part of the body.

10:21: SS and AB exchange sections of the paper.

AB: This part is OK. What's next?

---

researcher allows for a critical reexamination. The reexamination—matched with the expertise of the practitioner—establishes a connection that leads to insight and understanding of the situation. The relationship between reflection, action research, and the researcher's field journal is similar to the relationship between reflection, teaching, and learning. Reflection—as related to teaching and learning—is a process through which practice may be examined in order to effect change and improvement. Reflecting on teaching and learning allows a teacher to examine practice in order to determine what techniques, strategies, or methods are working effectively; what techniques, strategies, or methods need further examination; what changes are needed, what changes are critical, and what plan of action needs to be implemented in order to improve practice.

Reflection, action research, and the field journal are blended and integrated in a similar manner. Reflective entries—recorded during an action research study—enable the researcher to determine what patterns emerge from the interactions between the participants and environment, what techniques and strategies are working effectively, what changes in the study are needed, what changes in the study are vital, what additional data are needed to inform, and what plan of action needs to be implemented as a result of the research.

Elements of Reflective Practice

As with all other processes involved in action research, the reflective process involves several elements. The elements promote deep thinking through reflection, which leads to a deeper examination of the inquiry. In essence, reflective practice encourages the action researcher to engage in a critical analysis of practice in a way that helps connect the researcher's experience to the actual act of practice. Schön (1987) suggests that reflection is a "dialogue of thinking." It is through the dialogue of thinking that the practitioner becomes more skilled. The reflective process enables the researcher to glean important information from the action research experience, thus building the skills and knowledge needed to apply the information in new situations and contexts. This "learning from experience" is truly at the heart of reflection as well as the action research process itself.

Several important elements of reflection and reflective practice apply to the action research process, including the following:

- *Critical analysis.* The reflective process requires the action researcher to think critically about the inquiry and to reflect on the events, observations, data, participants, and interactions in the practicing environment.

- *Problem solving.* The reflective process—as part of action research—allows the researcher to expound on thoughts, ideas, and inquiry through reflective entries in the field journal. As a result, the action researcher is able to think about the study in order to generate solutions and plans for improvement.

- *Self-analysis and professional growth.* The reflective process helps the researcher-as-practitioner identify professional development goals related to the practicing environment and improvement. For example, after conducting an action research study, the researcher may determine that additional information and training are needed to implement a new program successfully. The researcher identifies the need and sets professional goals related to self as well as environment. The process also requires the researcher to engage in continuous self-analysis as related to practice, the result being improvement and change.

- *Application.* The reflective process encourages the action researcher to think about research as it relates to the practicing environment in order to use new information applied to new situations. The application of information gained through reflection and action research assist in enabling understanding, developing skills as a practitioner, and making informed decisions based on inquiry.

As the action researcher thinks about research, makes reflective journal entries, and engages in continuous reflection, deep learning takes place. The deep learning brings about a connection between the act of inquiry, action research, and practice and allows the action researcher to learn from experience.

Reflection also involves retrothinking and prospect thinking. *Retrothinking* occurs as the action researcher thinks about the research events that took place before making reflective entries. Retrothinking prompts the researcher to ask questions such as these:

What happened during the event?

What were the participant reactions?

Did the interview go well?

Were the interview instrument and structure appropriate?

Did any new patterns emerge?

What interactions took place?

Prospect thinking prompts the action researcher to ask questions in advance of a research event or activity. Prospect thinking may generate questions such as these:

How will the participants react to this interview?

What types of interactions may take place?

What materials will I need to conduct this interview or observation successfully?

What data will be needed?

What things should I focus on during the observation?

In addition, Schön (1987) suggests that reflective practice includes reflection-in-action and reflection-on-action. *Reflection-in-action* involves engaging in reflection in the present. *Reflection-on-action* involves reflection after an event takes place. In terms of action research, reflection-in-action would consist of recording reflective entries during an event, observation, interview, or related research activity. Similar to the teacher who records notes during a lesson, reflection-in-action would require the action researcher to jot reflective entries during the actual research, such as noting any interesting, creative, or unusual responses during an interview that could be reexamined later; jotting down questions that may arise out of a research event, interaction, or observation; or making note of any new patterns when they are first noticed. Reflection-in-action may be considered a combination or joint act of entering a reflective entry paired with the actual observation or interview being conducted.

Reflection-on action—which takes place after a research event or activity—allows the researcher to engage in a deeper self-analysis. Reflection-on-action allows the researcher to delve further into personal experiences as a practitioner. It involves the researcher entering the reflective entry while thinking about personal ideas, actions, theories, or goals as related to the inquiry.

Imagery in Reflection and Research

A discussion about the act of recording reflective entries must also include two important issues: imagery and accuracy. The practitioner researcher who engages in action research extends expertise beyond the practicing environment and becomes part of the larger research community. This takes place the moment the practitioner begins the first action research study and continues as the action researcher develops the action plan and shares findings. In making the extension into the research community, the practitioner researcher develops *reflective self.* Reflective self develops as the researcher actualizes the process of research and progresses through the inquiry to the point of implementing the action plan and sharing findings to improve practice.

Reflective self empowers the researcher with the ability to develop *research imagery* of others in the research setting. Research imagery helps the researcher see the setting from the participant's perspective. Research imagery may be accurate or negative. Accurate research imagery created through reflective entries helps the researcher understand the research setting, interactions, participants, and overall phenomena being studied. The reflective field entries provide a vehicle for the researcher in developing research imagery.

Accurate research imagery is a direct result of the researcher's blending and integrating personal experience and expertise, accurate visual images of the participants and the research setting (digital, photo, or descriptive), and additional background information gathered in the literature review. Accurate research imagery prompts research-based ideas and encourages ongoing inquiry-based thought as the study progresses. As a result, the information recorded as reflective entries is vital to the study and part of the data collected.

Negative research imagery reveals the researcher's personal beliefs and biases. Negative research imagery is a result of preconceived notions regarding the action research, participants, or setting; participants matched with stereotypes commonly portrayed by the media; biased, stereotypical information regarding the setting or the participants held by the researcher; and personal preferences, views, ideas, and theories held by the researcher that are allowed to rise to the surface and influence the study. Negative research imagery influences the study in a way that taints any information recorded in the reflective entries. For example, one of the participants taking part in an action research study focusing on the views and perceptions of high school students regarding teaching and learning happens also to be a dance team member. The action researcher—with preconceived notions and stereotypical beliefs regarding dance team members—discounts any response given by the participant. In fact, the researcher may go so far as to ignore any interactions with the

EXHIBIT 6.2. Three Examples of Negative Research Imagery

Negative Image of Setting

Setting: Rural school

Although the practitioner researcher teaches in a rural school setting, she feels that rural schools are below standard. In fact, the researcher holds the following stereotypical beliefs:

■ No rural schools are new.

■ Rural schools serve only poor children who live in trailer parks.

■ Rural schools never have any materials or resources.

Negative Image of Participants

Participants: University freshmen

The practitioner researcher is a university professor who typically works with freshmen and sophomores. However, he holds the following stereotypical beliefs:

■ All university freshmen are getting a "free ride."

■ University freshmen are all drunks.

■ All university freshmen belong to fraternities or sororities.

Negative Image of Method

Method: Quantitative

Although the action research study calls for a quantitative approach, the researcher holds the following beliefs:

■ Quantitative research is dull and boring.

■ Quantitative research is bogged down with too many numbers and statistics.

■ Quantitative research findings are useless.

dance team participants. When recording reflective entries in the field journal, the researcher describes the dance team participant with words such as *airhead*, *floozy*, and *ditz*. In addition, the reflective entries include the participant's responses to interviews followed by comments regarding lack of intelligence. Reflective entries recorded with a negative research imagery bias must be discarded and cannot be used as a source of data. In this case, the researcher may be throwing out valuable information based on negative research imagery regarding a specific participant. Exhibit 6.2 provides several examples of negative research imagery. Any reflective entries recorded by the researchers described in the exhibit would not be valid because the researcher's bias taints the information, and so the data would have to be discarded.

Accuracy in Reflection

Becker (1998) notes that because imagery influences practice, researchers should be sure that it is accurate. When recording ongoing entries in the field journal, the researcher pays close attention to the actual research event, making sure to record unbiased, factual entries. The same is true when recording reflective entries. The researcher must once again rely on expertise when serving as researcher-as-instrument. The task is more difficult when recording reflective entries because reflection by its very nature requires a blending of personal beliefs, theories, and ideas. Drawing on the practitioner as expert in the field, the action researcher must take precautions to ensure that the reflective entries present an accurate account of the observation, interview, or other related research event in an unbiased manner; blend the accuracy of information with the experience of the action researcher; integrate the researcher's personal background and expertise as related to the inquiry; and reflect the process of deep learning and deep thought through self-analysis.

The action researcher must be sure to balance personal ideas and theories with accuracy in recording reflective entries. If a reflective entry reveals a great deal of the researcher's personal ideas and theories, the entry should not be used as data because the information is not unbiased and may take the study in an inappropriate or misleading direction. Figures 6.2 and 6.3 illustrate the dramatic importance of accuracy to an action research study.

Although the entry in Figure 6.2 begins with what seems to be an accurate account of the high school students' responses, the researcher interjects a lot of personal experience and ideas in the reflective entry. By doing so, the researcher misses what the high school students are really saying. For example, the comment regarding the teachers' being too friendly and showing disappointment may indicate emerging patterns. However, by disregarding the high school students' responses and relying heavily on personal experience, the researcher misses key information. Other than the information recorded at the beginning of the field journal entry, the data recorded through the reflective entry are useless to the study.

The example in Figure 6.3 begins with an accurate account of the high school students' responses. However, the researcher is able to focus on the responses in the context of inquiry. The reflective entries are devoid of bias and do not reveal the personal ideas, theories, or beliefs of the researcher. The researcher uses the information gleaned from the student responses to delve further into the inquiry. The information recorded in the reflective entry notations help keep the focus on key information provided by the high school participants. The researcher uses expertise as a practitioner and researcher while attempting to understand the views and preferences of the participants.

Field Journal / Reflective Entry

Observation: Preservice students taking part in a videoconference with high school students at a remote location. The preservice students generated a list of questions to ask in an informal, unstructured group session. Today's session began with the question "What makes a 'good' teacher?"

Date: 10/17
Time: 1:30–2:45 (video conference)

Action research:
Views and perceptions of teaching and learning held by university students and high school juniors and seniors

Participants:

Ten preservice students (secondary education with majors in history, math, English, and biology)

Ten high school participants representing PHS / PDS

Videoconference Session

Preservice #1: What makes a "good" teacher?

Preservice #2: We want you to tell us what you think. What are your thoughts—you know, what do you think makes a teacher "good"?

HS #3: I think teachers who get on the student's level are the best kind. But they have to be careful not to become the student's friend. That makes me sick. You know—when they cross the line.

HS #1: They need to relate to the problems we have as seniors.

HS #2: I don't like teachers who show that they are disappointed in something I do—like not getting a good grade. Instead, they should help us. The ones who show concern and try to help are much better.

Researcher: I'm not sure the high school kids have enough experience to offer this advice. They seem to like being on the videoconferencing screen—with all the primping and makeup. When I was in high school we were not ever allowed to dress like these kids. How can we take them seriously? . . . and here we are listening to them talk and talk and talk . . .

FIGURE 6.2. *Reflective Field Note Entry: Example 1*

Field Journal / Reflective Entry

Observation: Preservice students taking part in a videoconference with high school students at a remote location. The preservice students generated a list of questions to ask in an informal, unstructured group session. Today's session began with the question, "What makes a 'good' teacher?"

Date: 10/17
Time: 1:30-2:45 (video conference)

Action research:

Views and perceptions of teaching and learning held by university students and high school juniors and seniors

Participants:

Ten preservice students (secondary education with majors in history, math, English, and biology)

Ten high school participants representing PHS/PDS

Videoconference Session

Preservice #1: What makes a "good" teacher?

Preservice #2: We want you to tell us what you think. What are your thoughts—you know, what do you think makes a teacher "good"?

HS #3: I think teachers who get on the student's level are the best kind. But they have to be careful not to become the student's friend. That makes me sick. You know—when they cross the line.

Researcher: Interesting to hear that students still want what sounds like traditional roles between the student and teacher. Note: check reference on this.

HS #1: They need to relate to the problems we have as seniors.

Researcher: Follow up—what types of problems are "senior problems"?

HS #2: I don't like teachers who show that they are disappointed in something I do—like not getting a good grade. Instead, they should help us. The ones who show concern and try to help are much better.

Researcher: Follow up—Is the display of disappointment typical for one subject or is it experienced in a variety of content areas? Note: Conference went well—all participants discussed naturally—prompt helped at the beginning. Check: May be time to schedule onsite visit for all preservice.

FIGURE 6.3. *Reflective Field Note Entry: Example 2*

IDENTIFYING AND COLLECTING ARTIFACTS

Artifacts—when collected as part of an action research study—are valuable research tools. Although not typically part of an action research study that employs a quantitative approach, artifacts may be collected as data in a qualitative action research study. Artifacts usually consist of items that are readily available in the research setting, relate to the focus of the action research, and inform the inquiry and provide insight into the situational milieu. In structuring an action research study, the researcher identifies specific data sets that are aligned with the overarching questions. However, as the study progresses, the need to collect additional data sets in the form of artifacts may arise. This is not unusual in action research that takes a qualitative approach. In addition, the reflective entries recorded as part of the study may prompt new ideas and thoughts related to the action research that may lead the researcher to new artifacts and other possible sources of data.

If the need to collect additional artifacts arises after the study is under way, the researcher should consider the following questions:

Is the need to collect additional artifacts a result of a reflective entry, a research event, or an emerging pattern or theme?

What type of artifact would best inform the inquiry at this point in the study?

How relevant is the artifact, and is it worth the time to collect and analyze at this point in the study?

How does the artifact relate to the existing set of overarching questions?

Is the artifact related to other data sets, and if so, how?

The researcher may decide that additional artifacts are needed as a result of an emerging question, theme, or pattern. If this is the case, a new research question should be developed and added to the existing set of overarching questions originally recorded on the triangulation matrix. Doing so allows the researcher to determine how the new question fits and whether there are other data sets that—when aligned with the new question and artifacts—can ensure triangulation. Many times an emerging question is the result of a reflective entry or a research event. The question may help the researcher delve further into the inquiry and if pursued may yield results that provide valuable insight.

MAKING USE OF ELECTRONIC SOURCES AND TECHNOLOGY

Action researchers often have technology tools available at the research site. Technology in research may consist of computers as well as other electronic equipment such as digital cameras and video recorders. In addition, electronic sources—available via the Internet—may be used as a data source. Electronic sources typically used as data sets or sources include information gleaned from blogs, Web sites, online discussion forums, and other online resources. Considering that action research takes place in the practicing environment, it is quite normal for computers, Web access, and related software to be part of the setting. Researcher should make use of any appropriate technology available. Technology usually helps the research progress smoothly and also assists in data analysis in the case of action research using a quantitative approach that requires statistical analysis. Before beginning a study, the practicing researcher should conduct an informal inventory of available technology. For example, a computer with Internet access comes in handy when conducting ongoing literature reviews. A simple word processing program may assist in recording electronic field notes. If the researcher plans to rely on any sources of funding for research materials and equipment, the informal inventory provides the information needed to support any requests for funding. The informal inventory also provides information regarding the availability of digital cameras and video recorders that may be needed to conduct a qualitative action research study. In addition to the typical technology and electronic tools, the action researcher may determine that electronic resources such as information recorded on blogs, online journals, or discussion forums may be appropriate data sources that have great potential in informing the inquiry.

Electronic Resources

Action researchers may consider electronic sources as part of the data collected during a study. Depending on the nature and focus of the action research, information recorded on blogs may be appropriately collected as a data set. Of course, accuracy in the recordings must be addressed and evaluated. However, depending on the study, research questions, or overarching questions, a researcher may determine that blog information best suits the study as a form of data. There are many notable sites where reporters, researchers, and experts record entries on daily blogs. A *blog* (short for *Web log*) is an online journal in which a person (the *blogger*) makes public entries regarding a variety of topics. Typically, the expertise of the blogger can be verified, as can the authenticity of the site itself. It is strongly suggested that if blog information is used as a source of data for action research, the researcher should verify the site as well as the blogger.

Action researchers who are knowledgeable regarding Web design and blogging may decide that an online blog would facilitate the study and would work well for recording notes and thoughts. When working at multiple sites or with co-researchers, an online research blog may be appropriate because it can be accessed at any time and is viewable by multiple researchers simultaneously. However, the blog information must meet certain criteria:

- It must not include any identifying data, such as names of participants, research location, or other related items.

- It should be devoid of bias and stereotypes and follow the guidelines for recording reflective entries.

- It must consist of professional, discrete notations that do not reveal findings prior to the end of the study.

Antonio's Gun & Delfino's Dream:

Perceptions and Views of ELL Immigrants in Schools

Reflective Response Based on Text

Online Discussion Forum Instrument

After reading chapters 1–3, post reflections to the following:

■ What is your position on the current state of immigration?

■ Do you have any suggestions for immigration reform?

After reading chapters 4 and 5, post reflections to the following:

■ We have all mocked and laughed at the "velvet Elvis" or "velvet Jesus" hangings that crop up on corners. In fact, at one time velvet paintings were for sale at the intersection of Memorial Blvd. and Broad Street. After reading the chapters, what are your thoughts regarding this art form and how it relates to economic conditions?

■ Think of the culture tied to the paintings. How would you respond to an ELL who is ridiculed when he or she shares this family tradition within the school environment?

After reading chapters 6 and 7, post reflections to the following questions:

■ The theme running through the chapters is one of betrayal and abandonment. In chapter 6, the high school teacher feels betrayed by his own country because the opera organizers pass him by. The teacher stays in Mexico but feels abandoned.

■ In chapter 7, families striving for a better life move to Chicago but return to their home town to build lavish houses with the intent on returning to Mexico permanently. In time, however, they settle in the U.S. returning to Mexico for brief vacations.

■ Considering the conditions of immigration, which situation cited above is worse? Explain your position.

After reading chapter 8 and the Epilogue, post your reflections to the following:

Chapter 8 illustrates a "dual existence" between immigrant students and U.S. born students. For this forum:

■ Share one instance that you have observed of the "dual existence."

■ If you do not work currently work with ELLs, share an instance that you have observed the "dual existence" between Caucasian students and any other minority (African American students, gender minority, special needs, etc.).

■ How can teachers help to dissolve the "dual existence"?

FIGURE 6.4. *Using Online Forum Postings as a Research Tool*

Some researchers consider a research blog similar to a field journal. However, typically the nature of a blog is not the same because while a field journal is a record of private thoughts, a blog is usually open to the public.

Considering the nature of action research and the practitioner-oriented process, studies focusing on interaction may also include postings to online discussion forums as a source of data. Postings that result from dedicated, focused online discussion are excellent sources that may be considered as a data set in an action research study. For example, a middle school teacher who intends to study student interactions during Socratic seminars may decide to set up an online discussion forum. The forum—structured with specific focus questions—may be the perfect avenue for discussion since the middle school students involved all enjoy working with computers. In addition, the focus questions may be structured in a way that enables open-ended discussion while providing guidance for the middle school student participants. Another example of using postings from an online discussion forum as one data set is illustrated in Figure 6.4. The sample action research study uses a popular book to encourage teachers to explore their views and perceptions of legal and illegal immigration. Information gleaned from the discussions resulting from the focus questions becomes a data set that is later coded and analyzed for themes and categories.

Action researchers who have a laptop or computer available opt to keep an *electronic field journal* instead of a print journal. An electronic field journal is a private record of thoughts, similar to a print field journal. The electronic field journal—although it may be accessed via a computer—is different from a research blog because the research blog is public and may be viewed by many people. In the event that the researcher decides that an electronic field journal bests suits the inquiry, the following points should be considered:

- If the electronic field journal will be kept on a computer that can be accessed by multiple users, consider password-protecting the journal.
- Be sure to use a coding system that deidentifies all participants as well as the research site.
- Remember to use the guidelines for recording descriptive and reflective entries.

SUMMARY

The action researcher typically identifies the research tools needed to complete the study and develop the action plan. Just as data are readily available in the practicing environment, so are the tools needed for conducting action research. In many instances, the data are also the tools that are critical for action research. This is especially true if the action research uses a qualitative approach. The field journal is a research tool. The researcher's field notes, which are recorded in the journal, are also part of the data collected to inform the inquiry. Several research tools that are vital to action research include field journals, artifacts, electronic materials, and—if appropriate—photos.

The researcher's field journal may consist of a notebook, a decorative journal, or a running log entered electronically via a word processing program. The field journal helps the researcher carry out the inquiry through the physical act of recording notations. When working with small groups of participants, a researcher may require each participant to keep a journal to record information regarding views, perceptions, and ideas surrounding the study. Research orientation develops as a result of thinking through a study from beginning to end and combining that thought process with the actual act of implementation. The successful implementation of a project ensures that a researcher is developing research orientation, a kind of literacy. The field journal or research journal is one tool that enables the development of research orientation and research literacy. In addition to the field journal, electronic tools and technology should be considered as tools to facilitate research.

KEY TERMS

Blog
Blogger
Descriptive entries
Electronic field journal
Field journal
Ongoing recording
Participant field journal
Prospect thinking
Reflection-in-action
Reflection-on-action

Reflective entry
Reflective recording
Reflective self
Removed recording
Research imagery
Research orientation
Researcher's field journal
Retrothinking
Theory of symbolic interaction

DISCUSSION QUESTIONS

1. Discuss the researcher's field journal and the importance of the field journal to the action research process.

2. Discuss symbolic interaction and the relationship between symbolic interaction and research.

3. Describe the relationship between literacy and research orientation. Provide several suggestions to help beginning researchers develop research orientation.

4. Define ongoing recording and reflective recording. Compare and contrast the differences between the two types.

5. How does a participant field journal relate to action research? Provide an explanation regarding the uses of a participant field journal.

6. Compare and contrast descriptive and reflective field journal entries. Provide an example of when a descriptive entry would be appropriate and when a reflective entry would be appropriate.

7. Discuss the characteristics of descriptive entries and reflective entries.

8. Explain the difference between retrothinking and prospect thinking. Provide examples.

9. Compare and contrast reflection-in-action and reflection-on-action. Explain when each would be used.

10. Discuss negative imagery and accurate imagery. Provide an example of each.

SUGGESTED TOPICS

1. What negative images, ideas, preconceived notions, or stereotypes might an action researcher hold that would promote negative imagery in each of the following action research studies?

    a. Views and perceptions regarding clothing worn by Hispanic females and how these perceptions affect academic success

    b. A study of the dropout rate among students enrolled in an urban high school

2. Conduct a short observation at a possible action research site (or in your own practicing environment). Practice writing a descriptive field journal entry. Once the session ends, enter a reflective entry in the field journal.

3. Conduct a short Internet search of several newspaper sites as well as online news sites. Locate links for one or two reporters' blogs. View the information critically, looking for negative and accurate imagery.

4. This assignment requires you to analyze field notes in order to determine evidence of researcher bias, descriptive language, and thoroughness. Begin by examining the sample field notes in Exhibit 6.3. Analyze the notes for the following:

    ▪ Researcher bias

    ▪ Appropriate descriptive language

    ▪ Thoroughness—date, time, location, situation, subjects

ONLINE ACTIVITIES

1. Select one or two of the discussion questions provided to set up an online forum. Have students support their ideas with outside sources. Use a rubric for evaluating the postings. (*Note:* This may be completed in small groups or with the entire class.)

EXHIBIT 6.3. Sample Field Notes

Overview of the study: This study seeks to examine the perceptions held among 70- to 75-year-old females with regard to personal social image and the effect on aging.

Date:

Location:

Subjects: BM, VL

Situation: Observation of two females at a church function (age:)

BM: I can't believe that he is looking at me—OK, yes, I can. What do you think of my hair today? I know it makes me look younger than that oldie over there!

(*Notes:* What kind of accent does she have? She is full of herself! The outfit alone makes her look like a complete tart—the color is hideous and makes her skin look yellow . . . no, almost green! The makeup alone makes her look like a cadaver. And . . . what's with the orange hair and the bright red lips? Ahhhhggghhh—how much longer do I have to observe these two old bats?)

VL: I don't think he's looking over here; it looks to me like he's looking for somewhere to throw trash away. And you are kidding, aren't you, about your hair? I think it makes you look like you're stuck in the eighties.

(*Notes:* You go, old girl! Someone has to tell her! I like this one's style—the hair is appropriate for the age, and although her voice is driving me crazy, I think she isn't trying to look younger so she can snag the old guy they keep talking about.)

Other Person: (I didn't get the name): What are you girls doing over here? Why don't you come and help me clean up the church kitchen?

BM: Are you crazy? I can't do that today—I just bought this skirt and I don't want to get anything on it. Maybe you can get one of the older girls to help.

(*Notes:* Can you believe this? The skirt is too tight and too short. It's embarrassing to watch this!)

2. Complete "Suggested Topics" exercise 1. Share your responses with your group members by posting to the forum. After examining all group members' responses, answer the following questions:

Were there any additional negative items that you would add?

What two suggestions can you offer to beginning action researchers to assist with eliminating negative imagery?

Post your responses to the forum.

3. Conduct a short observation at a possible action research site (or in your own practicing environment). Practice writing a descriptive field journal entry. Once the session ends, enter a reflective entry in the field journal. Post your entries on your group's dedicated discussion forum. Be sure to remove all identifying information before posting. Read other group members' postings. Offer suggestions for improving the entries.

4. Conduct a short Internet search of several newspaper sites as well as online news sites. Locate links for one or two reporters' blogs. View the information critically, looking for negative and accurate imagery. Post the following information to the discussion forum:

   Site name and URL

   Name of blog and blogger

   Summary of negative or accurate imagery

CHAPTER

7

ORGANIZING, CODING, AND ANALYZING QUALITATIVE DATA

LEARNING OBJECTIVES

After reading Chapter Seven, you should be able to:

- Identify the steps involved in organizing, coding, and analyzing qualitative data
- Discuss different qualitative analysis approaches
- Explore a variety of coding processes
- Identify typical codes used when analyzing qualitative data

GETTING STARTED

Action research studies that employ a qualitative approach to inquiry require the researcher to collect multiple forms of data in order to ensure triangulation. The triangulation process validates the study and supports the findings, which in turn add to the relevancy and importance of the study. As a study gets under way, the action researcher—working within the framework of qualitative methods—begins to collect data sets. The data sets pile up quickly as the researcher identifies emerging questions and accumulates additional unanticipated data sets. Because data in a qualitative action research study may consist of artifacts, pictures, samples, and other items, the researcher is inundated with information. The amount of data typically collected to inform inquiry in a qualitative action research study is immense, leaving the researcher to deal with issues related to organization, analysis, storage, and available space. In addition, the data must be deidentified, leaving no information that may reveal the participants' identity. Because action research takes place in the practicing environment, researchers find it difficult to store collected data due to space as well as anonymity factors. This is especially trying in situations where the participants are minors in that extra precautions must be taken to protect identity.

Action researchers are all individual learners, practitioners, and researchers. Many have their own style and preferences with regard to organization. The manner in which data are organized is not as important as a researcher's organization style. It is all too easy to collect data sets and then set the information aside to analyze "later." As large amounts of data pile up, procrastination in organizing and analyzing works against the researcher and may even derail the study completely. The key is to collect, organize, analyze, code, reanalyze, and collect—and to do all of this on a continuous, ongoing basis.

Think of the process as a circle, with data examined regularly. This is important because if the action research adopts a qualitative approach, the researcher continually looks for emerging questions, themes, and patterns throughout the study. If the data are left unorganized and unanalyzed until the end of the study, the researcher runs the risk of missing vital questions that emerge during the study itself, overlooking crucial information and inquiry that would have provided insight for improving practice. The data collection and analysis process mirrors the action research process. The researcher begins by identifying problems and collecting information. From there, information is organized into a literature review. Next, the researcher looks for themes and patterns in the existing body of knowledge via literature review. The hypothesis, research questions, or overarching questions are developed and defined. The questions are reexamined and refined as the study begins and progresses. Finally, findings are used to examine further and improve practice.

COLLECTING AND ANALYZING DATA

All too often researchers hold misconceptions regarding qualitative action research, including the following:

- Data consist entirely of notes recorded while observing.
- Analysis does not extend beyond data collection.
- Analysis involves reviewing the notes and reporting what took place.
- Analysis consists largely of the researcher's point of view.
- Findings may or may not be useful due to the lack of rigorous statistical analysis.

In many instances, these misconceptions deter many action researchers from taking a qualitative approach to inquiry. The same holds true for beginning researchers who may be considering a qualitative approach to a dissertation study. However, none of these misconceptions hold true. Qualitative data analysis may consist of reporting—in rich, descriptive language—what took place in a specific research setting. If the study demands this approach, a low level of analysis is needed. However, the raw data collected in the form of field notes must be converted into a transcript that is then triangulated before it can be used in reporting findings.

In reality, qualitative data analysis examines meaning within the context of a specific phenomenon being studied. The qualitative action researcher is immersed in the research setting in order to comprehend the situation fully and provide insight to other practitioners. Understanding and meaning are the direct results of data collection and analysis. The job of the action researcher who employs a qualitative approach does not end with data collection.

There are similarities and differences between analyzing quantitative data and analyzing qualitative data collected as a result of action research. As with quantitative methods, once data have been collected in a qualitative action research study, they must be analyzed to draw conclusions and present findings. Quantitative data may be collected prior to the study and then again at the end of the study. Qualitative data may also be collected prior to the study and again at the end. Analysis tests are usually run following each collection period. However, qualitative data may also be collected throughout the study—which is typically the case for most action research that takes a qualitative approach. Qualitative data may be analyzed throughout the study in order to identify emerging research questions and to determine if additional data sets are needed. Depending on the structure of the study and the focus of the inquiry, qualitative analysis is ongoing, recursive, and blended into the actual inquiry activities. In addition, qualitative analysis may include several steps that are revisited as the analysis progresses. Unlike a statistical analysis test that is conducted in order to gather specific information that is then examined, qualitative analysis is time-consuming and ongoing.

Basically, there are three approaches to qualitative data analysis as related to action research, ranging from a simple, low level of analysis that doesn't require lengthy examination to a more complex, in-depth level of analysis that is lengthy and time-consuming. These approaches are known as *reporting*, *descriptive reality*, and *grounded theory*. The *reporting approach* requires the researcher to report and present findings with little analysis other than transcribing and examining data sources. In action research, this approach is appropriate in a situation where a practitioner is examining one small piece of a larger context in the environment. Two examples are presented in Exhibit 7.1.

The examples illustrate action research studies that are based on a specific problem or focus, a situation in the practicing environment, collecting data, triangulation, and reporting findings. Little analysis was needed due to the structure of the action research. Although triangulation took place, analysis was not lengthy as the main goal of each study was to report findings. Example 1 used the teacher and student experiences during lessons to share and report findings to colleagues. Example 2 used the experiences of the students visiting the recreation center, staff observations, and records to report why students were not using exercise machines.

The *descriptive reality approach* requires the researcher to engage in a more systematic analysis of data sets. The goal of descriptive reality is to use raw data in a manner that ensures triangulation and presents a vivid, descriptive picture of what took place in a specific environment. This is accomplished by following four systematic steps: collecting at least three forms of data, examining the data to interpret what took place, integrating the data in a way that creates a richly detailed description, and reporting interpretive, integrated findings.

Once the data have been collected, the action researcher examines each data set to interpret what actually took place in the practicing environment. Raw data are converted to transcripts. Then the data sets are integrated to develop a narrative that paints a picture of the situation and interactions. The narrative presents a picture of reality as interpreted by the action researcher. Finally, a detailed report is prepared to share findings, provide insight, and improve practice. Exhibit 7.2 provides two examples of action research that takes the descriptive reality approach.

A systematic approach to analysis was needed for the studies discussed in Exhibit 7.2 due to the structure of each study and the nature of the inquiry. Multiple forms of data were used to ensure triangulation. In each, the researcher was able to collect data, analyze the data, and integrate each data set so as to re-create reality with words. The goal in these studies was to provide a picture of reality. This was accomplished by examining the data and developing a descriptive narrative that integrated all aspects of the situation. Example 1 in Exhibit 7.2 used the data to present a vivid picture of the diaspora experience. The findings were used to provide insight to other ELL professionals in an attempt to meet the needs of their students more effectively. Example 2 used the experiences of the mentors and participating teachers to illustrate an integrated picture of reality as seen in the context of a pilot study. The findings

EXHIBIT 7.1. Reporting Approach: Two Examples

Example 1: Teaching Patterns

Ms. Hall, a kindergarten teacher, implements an idea that consists of using colorful candies to teach the concept of patterns. After using the candies for two lessons, the students seem to grasp the concept. In fact, they are using the knowledge to construct simple graphs illustrating the patterns. Ms. Hall decides to videotape a lesson, transcribe the tape, and report findings to the kindergarten teaching team. After sharing her findings, the team makes the decision to integrate candies into lessons focusing on patterns, videotape lessons, and compare findings. The teachers plan an action research study, implement the lessons, and compare their findings, which are presented in a report released during a systemwide kindergarten teacher session.

Focus of the Action Research: Using candy to teach patterns

Data: Transcripts of videotaped lessons recorded by five kindergarten teachers

Triangulation: Transcripts

Report: Presented to colleagues

Example 2: Recreation Center

Dr. Stone, a university instructor, visits the university recreation center and notices that students are using only the track and the climbing wall, leaving all the exercise machines vacant. Discussions with recreation center staff reveal that this is typical throughout the day. Dr. Stone discusses the situation with his colleagues, and the discussions are recorded and transcribed. Next, he examines recreation center records, which show how many students sign in each day and which activities they engage in. The information is recorded and compiled. Dr. Stone then designs a simple open-ended interview instrument consisting of five questions in order to gather information regarding student preferences and use of the university recreation center. He gains permission to interview incoming freshmen attending university orientation sessions. After interviewing one hundred students, Dr. Stone examines the student responses and compiles results into a simple table. Findings show that students prefer the climbing wall, the track, the pool, and the sports courts because these areas are well lighted, well maintained, and temperature-controlled. Findings also indicate that the exercise machines are located in dim, cramped areas that are either very warm or uncomfortably cold. Dr. Stone uses the data collected and findings to design an action plan for improving recreation center space. The plan is shared with recreation center staff, budget heads, and university administrators.

Action Research Focus: Use of recreation center facility

Data: Interviews and recreation center records

Triangulation: Student interviews, recreation center staff interviews, records

Report: Presented to recreation center staff, budget heads, and administrators

EXHIBIT 7.2. Descriptive Reality Approach: Two Examples

Example 1: The Diaspora Experience

Mrs. P. notices that many of her middle school English language learners (ELLs) engage in detailed drawing during classroom downtime. After approximately two weeks of daily observations, Mrs. P. decides to ask students to share their drawings. She quickly notices that although the ELL students represent South American, Asian, and Middle Eastern countries, their drawings consist of images typically seen in *barrios*. After conducting a preliminary literature review, Mrs. P. decides to conduct an action research study on the phenomenon of diaspora. Diaspora is the concept of displacement that is typically experienced by people who leave their native country behind to make a new life in an unfamiliar place. Mrs. P. structures the study in a way that allows for her to collect student drawings and samples of student writing and to engage the students in discussions regarding their displacement experiences. Mrs. P. also keeps a field journal in which she makes both descriptive and reflective entries. Data are collected for twelve weeks. Drawings, samples of writing, and student responses during discussions are organized by participant. Data are examined carefully. Then Mrs. P. begins writing an integrated narrative on each participant, presenting a picture of the journey each traveled from the home country to the classroom. Each narrative is integrated to illustrate a descriptive reality of the ELL classroom. Finally, a detailed report that includes an integrated narrative is prepared and presented at a districtwide meeting of ELL professionals. Findings are then used to design an action plan to assist students who experience diaspora throughout the school system.

Example 2: Art Mentoring

Mr. West is a district technology director. He works regularly with K–12 teachers on effective use of technology in classrooms. After speaking with several high school teachers, Mr. West finds out that art teachers at CHS would like to create mentor teams of high school art students and K–6 students who are enrolled at a local elementary school that does not offer art classes. The teachers feel that the project would benefit the elementary students. In addition, they feel that there would be great benefit for high school students who would serve as mentors with regard to developing skills in painting, drawing, and clay. Mr. West likes the idea; however, he is not sure how effective or feasible it would be due to factors such as location of the schools, equipment needed, and lack of materials. To provide a rationale for funding, Mr. West designs an action research study to examine the effectiveness of high school art mentors. Working with the high school and elementary teachers, Mr. West sets up the study and helps teachers design a set of overarching questions matched with data sets. The teachers agree to collect data for two marking periods. Data sets include samples of high school student artwork prior to the study, high school student responses regarding their views and perceptions of the mentoring experience, elementary student responses regarding the high school mentors, and elementary teachers' responses during open-ended interviews regarding the effectiveness of the program. All participants agree to keep reflective field journals in which entries are recorded after each mentoring session. Data are forwarded to Mr. West on a weekly basis. Mr. West organizes the data and examines each data set to provide an integrative description of reality as seen through the eyes of the mentors and teachers. Finally, a detailed report that includes an integrated narrative is prepared and presented at the fall budget meeting. Findings are then used to design an action plan to implement the art mentoring program at two more high schools and elementary schools.

were used to provide a rationale for funding effective art mentoring programs at other schools.

The last approach, *grounded theory*, requires the action researcher to engage in the highest-level, most in-depth analysis of the three approaches. Glaser and Strauss (1967) developed the grounded theory approach. The notion of grounded theory is that through data collection and systematic analysis, the researcher is able to derive theory from the phenomena that make up the research environment, including the interactions and activities that took place throughout the study. The researcher is required to use the *constant comparative method* when analyzing data. The method involves detailed coding in order to identify categories and attributes. The process is lengthy and time-consuming and is typically part of an in-depth study. The analysis of data results in the development of a theory that is grounded in triangulated data. The grounded theory is then used to provide a detailed explanation of the situational milieu. The approach described aligns with the qualitative approach in that ongoing analysis allows the action researcher to look for emerging categories, themes, and patterns across the data sets, thus enabling findings that are grounded in research contexts. Further discussion of the grounded theory approach and the constant comparative analysis method as related to action research comes later in this chapter.

The level of analysis and approach employed for analyzing qualitative data for an action research study are based on all of the following factors:

- The design of the study
- The set of overarching questions
- The data sets
- The nature of each piece of data collected
- The timeline for completing the action research
- The experience and expertise of the action researcher
- The nature and focus of the inquiry

For newcomers to the action research process, the reporting approach is recommended for conducting a first or second study. After that, researchers should consider the descriptive reality approach. Grounded theory should be employed only after researchers are comfortable with the components of action research as well as their own research skills and experiences. However, there are some researchers who will innately adopt grounded theory as an analysis approach and method. If this is the case, the approach should be selected as it is intricate, interesting, and valid when conducting qualitative action research.

ORGANIZING DATA

Action researchers who adopt a qualitative approach find that data accumulate quickly. As the study progresses, the amount of data grows and grows to the point where it can get unmanageable very rapidly. Therefore, organization is critical and must be addressed before the first data are collected. In addition to organization, once data are collected, the researcher is faced with the task of making sense of the data as well as the relationships within each data set. Several organizational tips may help both the beginning researcher and anyone new to qualitative action research prepare for analysis. Because many data collected for qualitative action research consists of artifacts, notes, and recordings, the data must be transferred or converted to an analyzable form. The data should be converted to a format that is easy to read, easy to manipulate, and easy to organize and store. The following tips involve converting raw data into analyzable data.

■ *Transcribing*. Field notes, audiotapes, and videotapes should be transcribed into print format. Some researchers find that once transcribed, the data can then be easily organized and stored in notebooks. Others prefer transcribing and printing the data so that later, when coding, the information can be segmented and pasted on note cards for analysis. The note cards can then be stored in small boxes and rearranged during analysis.

■ *Simple coding*. Use a simple coding system prior to organizing or copying any transcribed data. For example, an interview transcript may be coded "T/I" (for *transcript* and *interview*). Going a step further, the researcher could add a code for a participant respondent: "T/I/P#1" (for *transcript, interview, participant 1*). A field journal transcript might be coded "T/RFN" (*transcript, researcher's field notes*). Open coding—a process that is conducted in the initial stages of data analysis—is discussed later in the chapter.

■ *Dating*. Before making photocopies of any data, the data should be dated at the top or bottom of each transcribed page. The dates on the data can be useful when reporting findings.

■ *Copying*. Once transcripts have been prepared, it is strongly suggested that the researcher make photocopies of all transcripts. The copies can be used for coding and analysis while the originals remain safely stored away. When working with field notes, the notes—if legibly printed—may be photocopied without transcribing and used for coding, leaving the original journal intact for future reference.

■ *Artifacts*. When using artifacts such as student samples, photos, diagrams, and drawings, accompany the data with a brief description of the data and the date collected. If the artifact consists of a student sample, diagram, or project, record the collection date, a brief description of the data, and the participant code. Date photos, and record the nature of the picture. The simple coding and brief descriptions will help during analysis. Make photocopies whenever necessary or appropriate.

■ *Memos*. If the researcher records any memos or notes outside the field journal, these should be dated, coded, and copied. Coding on a memo may consist of a brief description of what prompted the memo or note. For example, the memo may have been prompted by a participant question, a research event, or a related activity.

REVISITING THE TRIANGULATION MATRIX

After the initial organizational activities—transcribing, simple coding, dating, and copying—are complete, it's time to revisit the triangulation matrix. By doing so, the action researcher is better able to decide how to organize the data before beginning the analysis process. The triangulation matrix provides an organizational framework in that the data may be arranged and aligned with each overarching question. An action research study that requires data collection of student writing samples, field notes, survey responses, interviews, and artifacts may be organized in files based on the corresponding overarching question. This organization technique helps during analysis as well as later in the process when writing the final report.

In addition, since one data set may be used to inform more than one question, the researcher has an opportunity to make duplicate copies. For example, a study may require that the researcher collect the following data:

Overarching Question	Data Sets Needed
1	field journal notes, *student writing samples*, open-ended interview responses
2	survey responses, *online forum responses*, *student writing samples*
3	student projects, *online forum responses*, participant field journals

As you can see, student writing samples are aligned with overarching questions 1 and 2, and online forum responses for questions 2 and 3. The researcher would make duplicate copies of the student writing samples and the online forum responses when preparing and organizing data for analysis. The duplicate copies may be aligned with the overarching question and would allow for manipulation during analysis. Organizing data according to the corresponding overarching question makes triangulation of the data easier.

EXAMINING THE PIECES

Once organization is complete, the action researcher can begin the task of examining the data separately and integratively. Before starting the analysis process, however, the researcher must reflect on the concept of researcher-as-instrument. Due to the naturalistic process of qualitative action research, it is much too easy for a researcher to rely on preferences, biases, and views when analyzing data. Action research that takes a qualitative approach requires the researcher to engage in inquiry as a participant observer, which allows the researcher to acquire a unique sense of the research environment and participants. The researcher's perspective is crucial because it can either slant the analysis or guide it accurately. So the researcher must take a moment to examine perspectives regarding the inquiry before engaging in analysis.

Patton (1990) suggests that when working with qualitative methods, researchers must engage in *epoche* (pronounced "EP-uh-kee"). *Epoche*—Greek for "suspension of judgment"—is a process that requires the action researcher to reflect on and remove any biases, perceptions, preconceptions, and assumptions regarding the research environment, interactions, and related activities prior to engaging in the analysis process. Epoche helps the researcher examine the data from a fresh viewpoint. By consciously setting aside imposing factors, the researcher is able to analyze the data objectively, thereby encouraging valid, informative findings and conclusions.

With epoche out of the way, the analysis may begin. Typically, data analysis in a qualitative action research study is inductive as opposed to deductive. Deductive analysis—typically used in quantitative analysis—mirrors the research process in that a hypothesis is designed, data are collected and statistically analyzed, and the hypothesis is revisited to prove or disprove. Inductive analysis involves collecting data to inform inquiry. There are no predetermined ideas regarding the action research. The data are collected and examined in order to identify emerging categories, themes, or patterns. The basis for analysis comes from the themes and patterns that emerge as the study progresses. Although systematic and time-consuming, the analysis process takes place in a similar manner as the actual research. For example, the qualitative action research study begins with a set of overarching questions. Data sets are aligned with each overarching question. Data sets are collected and examined. The researcher adds overarching questions based on early examination, research activities, and emerging patterns. The data analysis is conducted similarly with the researcher examining the data sets, conducting analysis, and identifying themes, patterns, and categories.

Once raw data have been transcribed, simple coded, dated, and copied, the researcher formally begins the process of analysis (Maykut & Morehouse, 1994). The first step in the analysis process is to identify *chunks of meaning* in each data set. The chunks of meaning are derived from the emerging patterns and themes, which are then organized into categories with distinct attributes. This is accomplished by *subsetting* the data. Subsetting takes place when the researcher examines the data sets—organized around the overarching questions—and identifies subsets of related data within each data set. The smaller subsets provide information that enables the researcher to develop meaning regarding the inquiry. The subsets assist the researcher in identifying and defining the larger categories that emerge as a result of data analysis. However, each subset of data must be understandable and must consist of themes or patterns related to the focus of the action research inquiry. When identifying subsets, the researcher should be sure to include all relevant data in order to create meaning and promote understanding. For example, if data collected as a result of an open-ended interview are used to inform an action research study, the researcher must include both question and response as part of a subset of data. Subsets of data may consist of several related sentences, short paragraphs, or even page-long excerpts. Examples of data subsets are illustrated in Figure 7.1 and Figure 7.2.

Working with photocopies of each data set, the subsets of data were gleaned from larger data sets. As the researcher examined each data set, a theme emerged. The phrase "computers in the classroom" was assigned to the subsets of data in Figure 7.1. The phrase "student design preferences versus assignment guidelines" was assigned to the subsets of data in Figure 7.2. Specific subsets related to the theme are identified and then removed from the larger data set. This may be accomplished by cutting apart and manipulating the photocopies, leaving the original transcripts and field notes intact. The subsets are then arranged in either a notebook or taped on 5-by-8-inch index cards. If using a notebook, the subsets may be cut from the entire transcript or copies of field journal notes and taped together. A similar process is followed if index cards are preferred with subsets taped to individual cards. Index cards are a little easier to manipulate. In addition, clarifying notes and information may be recorded on the back of each card in order to facilitate the analysis process. The subsets are revisited and coded for further clarification and meaning during analysis.

EXAMINING INDIVIDUAL DATA SETS AND SUBSETS

Defining and identifying the subsets is the first step toward analysis. The researcher must revisit each data set a few times to be sure that all subsets are addressed. During this process, the subsets have a dynamic relationship in that on first examination, a minimal degree of relationships and themes emerge. However, as the data sets are revisited, additional relationships and themes may be revealed. The action researcher must reexamine the data sets with an open mind until the subsets are exhausted and no new themes or patterns emerge. It is also a good idea to record any thoughts, recurring questions, or ideas during subsetting. These can be recorded in the field journal so that the researcher can engage in continuous reflection during the analysis process. The notations also help in coding and defining categories later in the analysis. The act of recording while subsetting is sometimes referred to as *discovery* (Taylor & Bogdan, 1984). During discovery, the action researcher identifies a wide range of recurring ideas, concepts, themes, and patterns across data sets and subsets. Discovery is ongoing and continues throughout the analysis process, from the initial stages until the analysis concludes. It is during discovery and subsetting that the action researcher begins to see patterns of meaning develop. The meanings are further defined as the analysis process continues. Through careful examination and reexamination, the action researcher asks the following questions:

- What words or phrases recur throughout the data sets and subsets?
- Which pattern concepts are present in several data sets and subsets?

Overarching Question:

What are teachers' views of integrating technology into writing lessons, and how do these views relate to *current practice?*

Data Subset:

Individual open-ended interviews

Theme: Computers in the classroom

Individual Open-Ended Interview Transcript
October 16, 2009

Q#1: What are your thoughts regarding current practice with regard to integrating technology into writing lessons in middle school?

1 R/I/JC: At my school, there aren't enough computers to go around. If
2 a teacher wants to use computers there just are not enough for even
3 one classroom. For example, if I wanted to use computers during a
4 brainstorming session, it would be great for students to construct
5 webs of their ideas. This can be done with one computer per two
6 students. But with only two computers in the classroom and twenty-six
7 students, it is not possible.
8 R/I/AC: I agree—I read this article on how to use computers with
9 writing instruction, but basically the computer (one) was being
10 used by the teacher, not the students.
11 R/I/BB: I find that true. "Integrating technology" is code for "the
12 teacher uses the machine, and the students watch." I don't think that
13 integrating technology in classrooms was meant to be for teachers
14 only, but due to lack of funding, that's what it means now.

FIGURE 7.1. *Data Subsets: Example 1*

Overarching Question:	Data Subset:	Informal Inventory of Classroom Technology October 1, 2009

What are teachers' views of integrating technology into writing lessons, and how do these views relate to *current practice?*	Informal inventory of classroom technology
	
	Theme: Computers in the classroom
		Classroom 1: - one working computer located on the teacher's desk
		Classroom 2: - one working computer on a table in the front of the room
		    - two working computers toward the back of the room
		Classroom 3: - no working computers
		Classroom 4: - three working computers on a worktable to the right of the room
		Classroom 5: - one working computer on the teacher's desk
		    - one working computer on a student desk at the back of the room

FIGURE 7.1. *(continued)*

Overarching Question:	Data Subset:	Field Notes / Classroom Visits October 7, 2009
What are teachers' views of integrating technology into writing lessons, and how do these views relate to *current practice?*	Field notes of classroom visits Theme: Computers in the classroom	Classroom visit/JC/ 26 students present, sitting in teams of two 1 I entered the classroom while the students were beginning a team 2 writing assignment. JC directed students to examine the topic for 3 the day. Students were then asked to brainstorm ideas for a 4 writing piece. JC reminded students to record 5 the team ideas in the writing journals. Students worked quietly 6 and recorded ideas. JC moved to the computer at the front of the 7 room and turned on the projector to display the computer monitor 8 on the screen. Students were asked to share ideas. As they 9 shared, JC typed the ideas so that students could view. All team 10 responses were recorded. A discussion of ideas followed. Note: One computer in use by teacher (JC). Student computers were on but not in use for the lesson.

Note: Data selected from *Action Research Study: Integrating Technology into Classroom Lessons at the Middle School.*

FIGURE 7.1. *(continued)*

Transcript / Videotaped Observation
March 1, 2009

Overarching Question:	Data Subset:	Observation: Classroom session of students working in a computer lab. Students using computers to design their own Web sites. Assignment distributed prior to my arrival (copy attached). Observation focuses on two students working together.
What personal design *preferences do students have* with regard to Web site design, and do these *preferences affect the actual design?*	Observation transcript Theme: Design preferences versus assignment guidelines	1 S#1: Are you using FrontPage or Dreamweaver? 2 S#2: I like FrontPage but decided to go with Dreamweaver. 3 S#1: Why? What's the difference? Hey, look at this background—do you 4 think it's too distracting? 5 S#2: I have a Mac at home, and we have Dreamweaver on it. If I use 6 Dreamweaver, I can work more at home. I like the design part and need 7 more time to do the logo at the top. Let me see the background again. 8 What site did you find that on? 9 S#1: Here's the site address. It has all kinds of backgrounds. 10 S#2: Take a look at what I did—what do you think? 11 S#1: I like it, but I don't see the links right away. Maybe you should 12 put a menu across the top. What else do we need to add to these? 13 S#2: Let's look at the rubric—I think there's a list of stuff attached.

FIGURE 7.2. *Data Subsets: Example 2*

Artifacts / Student Web Sites "Snagged" and Saved as PDF Files
Preliminary Designs
Collected March 15, 2009

Overarching Question:	Data Subset:	Student Participant Site	Criterion 1 Use of Color	Criterion 2 Menu Design	Criterion 3 Integration of Graphics	Criterion 4 Attention to Details	Criterion 5 Overall Design and Components (scale: 1–5)
What personal design *preferences do students have* with regard to Web site design, and do these *preferences affect the actual design?*	Informal evaluation of preliminary design of student Web sites Note: Evaluation based on rubric provided by teacher Theme: Student design preferences versus assignment guidelines	S#1 site	Blue background with pink text	Top menu bar, easy-to-find links	No graphics	Spelling errors	Preliminary design: 3
		S#2 site	Black background with inserted tables (white background) with black text	Top menu bar with side bar that repeats links	Student-designed logo at top of opening page (name, e-mail, graphic)	No spelling or mechanical errors present	Preliminary design: 4

FIGURE 7.2. *(continued)*

Participant Field Journal / Entries Recorded After Two Design Sessions

March 5, 2009

Overarching Question:	Data Subset:	Participant Field Journal / S#1 March 5, 2009
What personal design *preferences do students have* with regard to Web site design, and do these *preferences affect the actual design?*	Field notes gleaned from student participant field journals Theme: Student design preferences versus assignment guidelines	First Entry 1 I'm having trouble with the design aspects. I feel like I want to 2 design the site like I did my MySpace page. I can't do that 3 because we have all these criteria that the teacher gave us. We 4 have different components that need to be included, and it's making 5 me have trouble. I know that we're not supposed to use bright 6 colors, but I think the site looks better when color is used. I 7 decided to go with what I want. 8 Now I'm looking for some music that I can load somehow. The 9 design is different than MySpace because we have to use a 10 program. We do have a choice, and I took FrontPage. 11 Overall, it's going OK.

FIGURE 7.2. *(continued)*

179

Participant Field Journal / S#2
March 5, 2009

First Entry

1 I planned out my site before I did anything on the computer. I

2 sketched the design and then realized that I wanted some graphics

3 that would be mine alone. I used Paint to make a logo. It's

4 simple but understated and really personalizes the site.

5 I looked at the assignment and the components. I decided to use

6 Dreamweaver because I have it at home and can work more later.

7 I read somewhere that Web pages look really good with dark

8 backgrounds. I tried black with white writing but didn't like it.

9 I got the idea to insert a white table on the black page. This looked

10 really sharp. I decided to use black text and that looks really

11 good.

12 The only trouble I had was the menu bar. I first had it on the side.

13 Then I moved it to the top but thought that it would be good to

14 see it in two places—you know, because people like things in

15 different places. So I put it at the top and then on the side.

Note: Data selected from *Action Research Study: Examination of Student Web Design.*

FIGURE 7.2. *(continued)*

- Are there any recurring terms used by participants that appear in multiple data sets and subsets?

- What themes emerge throughout the data sets and subsets?

- Are there any overall, recurring ideas integrated in data sets or subsets?

Responses to each question are recorded in the field journal. Many action researchers prefer transferring the responses to chart paper so that the initial themes and patterns may be reviewed throughout the analysis process. Once initial themes have been identified, notations may be added to the chart as data sets and subsets are reexamined. Charting the themes from beginning to end also helps when defining categories and attributes during coding.

Looking for Relationships

Discovery and subsetting charts are intricate tools that enable the researcher to identify relationships among data sets and subsets. A discovery and subsetting chart clearly illustrates each theme. Once the chart is complete, it is compared to the original triangulation matrix as some data sets are used to inform one or more questions. Because the data sets may overlap between overarching questions, the discovery and subsetting charts provide a visual description of the overlap in relationships among data. The relationships are critical because they also ensure triangulation of data, thus providing validity to the action research. However, owing to the recursive nature of the action research process, the researcher must return to the discovery and subsetting chart to add, revise, and reconsider relationships among data sets and subsets. The continual reexamination encourages ongoing analysis and enables the researcher to address all emerging patterns.

Patterns and Themes

Patterns and themes identified during subsetting should be noted and revisited throughout the recursive process. Once all data have been examined and all subsets have been identified, the researcher returns to the data to confirm emerging themes and patterns. Additional notations are made for clarification and to prepare for in-depth coding, which comes next in the analysis process. Using the data sets illustrated in Figures 7.1 and 7.2, the notations in Figures 7.3 and 7.4 show the patterns and themes as confirmed by the researcher. Keep in mind that the confirmed patterns and themes are recurring and appear and reappear throughout the data subsets.

As the researcher enters additional notations, the patterns are clarified. Use of underlining or highlighting helps the researcher define the patterns and confirm the information gleaned from the data subsets. This information is again revisited during the coding stage of analysis.

Individual Open-Ended Interview Transcript
October 16, 2009

Overarching Question:

What are teachers' views of integrating technology into writing lessons, and how do these views relate to *current practice?*

Data Subset: Individual open-ended interviews

Theme: Computers in the classroom

Pattern: Inadequate resources hinder student use

Q#1: What are your thoughts regarding current practice with regard to integrating technology into writing lessons in middle school?

1 R/I/JC: At my school, there *aren't enough computers* to go around. If

2 a teacher wants to use computers, there just *are not enough for even*

3 *one classroom.* For example, if I wanted to use computers during a

4 brainstorming session, it would be great for students to construct

5 webs of their ideas. This can be done with only one computer per two

6 students. But *with only two computers in the classroom and twenty-six*

7 *students, it is not possible.*

8 R/I/AC: I agree—I read this article on how to use computers with

9 writing instruction, but basically the computer (one) was being

10 used by the teacher, not the students.

11 R/I/BB: I find that true—"integrating technology" is *code for "the*

12 *teacher uses the machine, and the students watch."* I don't think that

13 integrating technology in classrooms was meant to be for teachers

14 only, but *due to lack of funding,* that's what it means now.

FIGURE 7.3. *Confirming Patterns: Example 1*

Informal Inventory of Classroom Technology
October 1, 2009

Overarching Question:

What are teachers' views of integrating technology into writing lessons, and how do these views relate to *current practice?*

Data Subset:

Informal inventory of classroom technology

Theme: Computers in the classroom

Pattern: *Inadequate resources hinder student use*

Classroom 1: - *one working computer* located *on the teacher's desk*
Note: 26 students enrolled

Classroom 2: - *one* working computer on a table in the front of the room
- *two* working computers toward the back of the room
Note: 27 students enrolled

Classroom 3: - *no working computers*
Note: 27 students enrolled

Classroom 4: - *three* working computers on a worktable to the right of the room
Note: 28 students enrolled

Classroom 5: - *one* working computer on the *teacher's desk*
- *one* working computer on a student desk at the back of the room
Note: 27 students enrolled

FIGURE 7.3. *(continued)*

Field Notes / Classroom Visits

October 7, 2009

Overarching Question:	Data Subset:	Classroom visit/JC/
What are teachers' views of integrating technology into writing lessons, and how do these views relate to *current practice?*	Field notes of classroom visits Theme: Computers in the classroom *Pattern: Inadequate resources hinder student use*	26 students present sitting in teams of two 1 I entered the classroom while the students were beginning a team 2 writing assignment. JC directed students to examine the topic for 3 the day. Students were then asked to brainstorm ideas for a 4 writing piece. JC reminded students to record 5 the team ideas in the *writing journals.* Students worked quietly 6 and recorded ideas. *JC moved to the computer at the front of the* 7 *room and turned on the projector to display the computer monitor* 8 on the screen. Students were asked to share ideas. As they 9 shared, *JC typed the ideas so that students could view.* All team 10 responses were recorded. A discussion of ideas followed. Note: One computer in use by teacher (JC). Student computers were on but not in use for the lesson.

Note: Data selected from *Action Research Study: Integrating Technology into Classroom Lessons at the Middle School.*

FIGURE 7.3. *(continued)*

Transcript / Videotaped Observation
March 1, 2009

		Observation: Classroom session of students working in a computer lab. Students using computers to design their own Web sites. Assignment distributed prior to my arrival (copy attached). Observation focuses on two students working together.
Overarching Question:	Data Subset:	
What personal design *preferences do students have* with regard to Web site design, and do these *preferences affect the actual design?*	Observation transcript	1 S#1: Are you using FrontPage or Dreamweaver?
	Theme:	2 S#2: *I like FrontPage but decided to go with Dreamweaver.*
	Design preferences versus assignment guidelines	3 S#1: Why? What's the difference? Hey, look at this background—do you
		4 think it's too distracting?
	Pattern:	5 S#2: *I have a Mac at home and we have Dreamweaver on it. I'll use*
	Preferences over guidelines	6 *Dreamweaver I can work more at home.* I like the design part and need
		7 more time to do the logo at the top. Let me see the background again.
		8 What site did you find that on?
		9 S#1: Here's the site address. It has all kinds of backgrounds.
		10 S#2: Take a look at what I did—what do you think?
		11 S#1: *I like it, but I don't see the links right away.* Maybe you should
		12 put a menu across the top. What else do we need to add to these?
		13 S#2: *Let's look at the rubric*—I think there's a list of stuff attached.

FIGURE 7.4. *Confirming Patterns: Example 2*

185

Overarching Question:	Data Subset:	Student Participant Site	Artifacts / Student Web Sites "Snagged" and Saved as PDF Files Preliminary Designs Collected March 15, 2009				
			Criterion 1 Use of Color	Criterion 2 Menu Design	Criterion 3 Integration of Graphics	Criterion 4 Attention to Details	Criterion 5 Overall Design and Components (scale: 1–5)
What personal design *preferences do students have* with regard to Web site design, and do these *preferences affect the actual design?*	Informal evaluation of preliminary design of student Web sites Note: Evaluation based on rubric provided by teacher Theme: Student design preferences versus assignment guidelines *Pattern:* *Preferences over guidelines*	S#1 site	Blue background with pink text	Top menu bar, easy-to-find links	No graphics	Spelling errors	Preliminary design: 3
		S#2 site	Black background with inserted tables (white background) with black text	*Top menu bar with side bar that repeats links*	*Student-designed logo* at top of opening page (name, e-mail, graphic)	No spelling or mechanical errors present	Preliminary design: 4

FIGURE 7.4. *(continued)*

Participant Field Journal / Entries Recorded After Two Design Sessions

March 5, 2009

Overarching Question:	Data Subset:	Participant Field Journal / S#1
What personal design *preferences do students have* with regard to Web site design, and do these *preferences affect the actual design?*	Field notes gleaned from student participant field journals Theme: Student design preferences versus assignment guidelines *Pattern: Preferences over guidelines*	March 5, 2009 First Entry 1　I'm having trouble with the design aspects. I feel like *I want to* 2　*design the site like I did with my MySpace page.* I can't do that 3　because *we have all these criteria that the teacher gave us.* We 4　have different components that need to be included and *it's making* 5　*me have trouble.* I know that *we're not supposed to use bright* 6　*colors, but I think the site looks better when color is used. I* 7　*decided to go with what I want.* 8　Now I'm looking for some music that I can load somehow. The 9　design is different than MySpace because we have to use a 10　program. We do have a choice and *I took FrontPage.* 11　Overall, it's going OK.

FIGURE 7.4. *(continued)*

187

Participant Field Journal / S#2
March 5, 2009

First Entry

1 *I planned out my site before I did anything on the computer.* I
2 sketched the design and then realized that *I wanted some graphics*
3 *that would be mine alone.* I used Paint to make a logo. It's
4 simple but understated and *really personalizes the site.*
5 I looked at the assignment and the components. *I decided to use*
6 *Dreamweaver because I have it at home and can work more later.*
7 I read somewhere that Web pages look really good with dark
8 backgrounds. *I tried black with white writing but didn't like it.*
9 I got the idea to insert a white table on the black page. This looked
10 really sharp. *I decided* to use black text and that looks
11 really good.
12 The only trouble I had was the menu bar. I first had it on the side.
13 Then I moved it to the top but thought that *it would be good to*
14 *see it in two places—you know because people like things in*
15 *different places.* So I put it at the top and then on the side.

Note: Data selected from *Action Research Study: Examination of Student Web Design.*

FIGURE 7.4. *(continued)*

CODING AND ANALYZING

Coding is the most interesting stage of data analysis. Coding involves further examination of the data sets and subsets and further organizing, manipulating, dissecting, and reconnecting the information to create an intricately woven picture of the research phenomenon. Unlike quantitative analysis, which involves a statistical test that assigns a numerical value, the coding process in qualitative analysis allows the researcher to use creativity as a researcher and an expert in creating categories, defining attributes, and explaining what took place in the research environment through *descriptive storying*. Descriptive storying takes place as the researcher re-creates the research environment and interactions through descriptive language. However, it is the coding that truly creates the picture of events. At this point, the data sets and subsets have preliminary codes attached. Now it's time to expound and expand the preliminary codes and compare the information, a process consisting of reexamination of the data sets and subsets; analysis through manipulating the information; noting overlapping themes, patterns, and concepts that appear in multiple data sets and subsets; and putting the pieces back together to create a continuum of research and a clearly defined picture. As noted earlier in this chapter, the *constant comparative method* of analysis involves combining inductive codes and categories assigned to data sets and subsets and comparing all data in order to reorganize the information into similar groups with similar meanings (Glaser & Strauss, 1967). This is why using index cards is efficient and effective because the cards may be easily manipulated during comparison. The purpose of the constant comparative method is to make certain that all of the following occur:

- Triangulation occurs across data sets.
- Categories of related and interconnected information are defined.
- Reconstruction of the data is complete.
- Attributes are identified that substantiate each category.
- Meaning is derived from the process.

Figure 7.5 illustrates the constant comparative method of data analysis. It should be noted that when using the method as part of analysis in action research, the researcher must once again rely on expertise, experience, and researcher-as-instrument in analysis.

Coding Processes and Types of Coding

As the analysis continues, the action researcher engages in coding. Typically, when employing the constant comparative method of analysis, several types of codes may be used to help define themes, patterns, and categories. Basic coding involves three processes: *open coding*, *selective coding*, and *axial coding* (Corbin & Strauss, 2007). The researcher begins with *open coding*, which involves breaking down the data, examining, comparing, and categorizing. For example, an entry of an observational

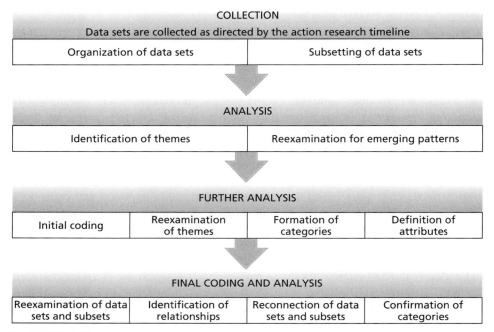

FIGURE 7.5. *Overview of the Constant Comparative Method of Data Analysis*

field note may be broken apart into a word, a sentence, or a paragraph. The researcher is then able to give each incident a name or assign a label. Next, the action researcher engages in *selective coding*. Selective coding requires the researcher to identify a core category, systematically relating the core to other categories and validating the relationship among data sets and subsets by comparing the information for refinement and development. Last, the researcher conducts *axial coding*. Axial coding is a process that enables the action researcher to put the data back together by making meaningful connections between categories. This is accomplished by re-examining the categories in order to identify any commonalities or relationships.

In addition to coding processes, there are several types of codes that may be used to analyze qualitative data collected during an action research study. The action researcher determines which codes are appropriate for a particular study. The researcher—relying on expertise as a practitioner—uses an individually preferred system, such as underlining, highlighting with colored markers, or the like. Bogdan and Biklen (1998) suggest the following coding categories:

■ *Setting or context codes*. *Setting codes* or *context codes* provide information regarding the setting, location, and action research environment. These codes help the researcher in analyzing specific information in the context of the research setting.

■ *Situation codes*. *Situation codes* highlight information that provides insight regarding how the participants interact in specific situations related to the action research. Situation codes may also draw attention to participant perceptions, views, beliefs, and preferences. The codes provide information regarding how participants construct meaning in the practitioner-based setting. The situation code helps the researcher view the research environment from the participant's perspective.

■ *Process codes*. *Process codes* consist of words, phrases, or terms that help the researcher categorize research events, sequences of activities, or any changes in the environment that take place during the research period. Process codes reveal passages and transitions as well as steps in a process, chronologies, or periods of time. Process coding enables the researcher to reconstruct the events and activities that played out during the action research study.

■ *Activity codes*. *Activity codes* illustrate specific behaviors and interactions. Activity codes tend to be particularly interesting because they relate directly to the participants and how they interact and communicate.

■ *Event codes*. *Event codes* note personal activities and events that take place in the daily routine and lives of the participants. Event codes are typically used when analyzing interview responses, as the participants often offer unsolicited information regarding individual, personal activities.

■ *Strategy and methods codes*. *Strategy codes* point to specific strategies, techniques, and processes participants use when acting and interacting in the practitioner environment. Strategy codes may provide information regarding student participants as well as teacher or practitioners working in the action research setting. *Methods codes* separate specific research processes that may emerge as the action research study progresses. Methods coding is typically used when analyzing researcher reflective field notes or participant reflective field notes.

■ *Relationship codes*. *Relationship codes* are used to note any specific relationships among participants, activities, data sets, or subsets. Personal relationship codes are typically noted when analyzing interactions between participants. Overall relationship codes are used when analyzing data sets and subsets, emerging patterns, categories, and themes.

With experience, action researchers who employ a qualitative approach to inquiry may develop their own meaningful codes to suit their particular study, relying on their expertise and experience as practitioners. Table 7.1 provides examples of specific codes.

IDENTIFYING CATEGORIES AND DEFINING ATTRIBUTES

Once the coding process is complete and specific codes have been assigned, it's time for the researcher to identify and label the emerging categories. Any data or subsets assigned to a specific category become part of a group of information. These data or subsets remain in the categorical group based on the attributes that define the

TABLE 7.1. **Sample Codes for Use in Data Analysis**

Type of Code	Sample Data Set or Subset
Setting or context code: Available technology	*Informal Inventory of Available Computers* Classroom 1: <u>one working computer</u> located <u>on the teacher's desk</u> *Note: 26 students enrolled* Classroom 2: <u>one</u> working computer on a table in the front of the room <u>two</u> working computers toward the back of the room *Note: 27 students enrolled*
Situation code: Student interaction in a classroom situation	*Researcher's Field Notes / Observation of Group Projects* Prior to my arrival, Mr. Z. distributed the assignment guidelines. Students are working in teams of two on the project, which involves online research and designing a presentation. S#1: Here are my notes, but I am not comfortable with writing. S#2: You don't think you write well enough to do the paper? Why? S#1: It's not that; I just don't feel comfortable sitting here writing—I don't like the computers we have, and I absolutely hate knowing that Mr. Z. may appear at any time and look over my shoulder. I like to work alone, not in the middle of everything.
Process code: Transition of preparation	*Transcript / Informal, Unstructured Group Interview* Question: What are your thoughts about going to college in the fall, and do you feel prepared? 1. P#1: I don't feel fully prepared. I mean, I know I'm only seventeen, but I 2. think there's much more in preparing for college than just getting ready 3. and practicing for exit exams. It seems so useless. 4. P#2: I think that we should cover things like how to manage our 5. scholarship funds and how to prioritize things such as classes and 6. schedules. I know we have to finish here, but we still have time for the 7. counselors to help us with the other stuff.
Activity code: Web designer team interactions	*Observation / Classroom Session of Students Working in a Computer Lab* Students are using computers to design their own Web sites. Assignment was distributed prior to my arrival. Observation focuses on two students working together. S#1: Are you using FrontPage or Dreamweaver? S#2: I like FrontPage but decided to go with Dreamweaver. S#1: Why? What's the difference? Hey, look at this background—do you think it's too distracting?

(Table 7.1 continued)

	S#2: I have a Mac at home, and we have Dreamweaver on it. If I use Dreamweaver, I can work more at home. I like the design part and need more time to do the logo at the top. Let me see the background again. What site did you find that on?
	S#1: Here's the site address. It has all kinds of backgrounds.
	S#2: Take a look at what I did—what do you think?
	S#1: I like it, but I don't see the links right away. Maybe you should put a menu across the top. What else do we need to add to these?
	S#2: <u>Let's look at the rubric</u>—I think there's a list of stuff attached.
Event code: Personal-home connection	*Transcript / Structured Individual Interview with a Teacher Participant* Question: If the sky's the limit, what ideas do you have for integrating technology into your daily lessons? 1. JC: I think that since money would not be a problem, I would like to 2. have at least one computer per student—preferably laptops—which 3. would be used in class and then checked out. I know this sounds lofty 4. because you may think I would never see the computers again—possibly 5. they might be sold on the street—but there is so much that could be 6. done if there were computers for each student. For example, I would 7. structure writing lessons so that the students brainstormed, drafted, 8. and so on, with the assistance of a word processor.
Strategy code: Mastering APA documentation style	*Transcript / Audiotaped Conversation Between Two Participants (Graduate Students) Working on Position Papers* 1. P#1: I can't seem to master APA formatting. Just when I think I have it, I 2. find that the format is incorrect. This throws me off, and I get bogged 3. down trying to find the correct format for citing specific sources. . . . 4. Have any suggestions? 5. P#2: Whenever that happens to me, I think hard about including the 6. source. If it's too difficult to cite, is it worth using it? If I think that I 7. have to use the source, I first go to the university research Web site. It's 8. pretty comprehensive and has great examples. If I can't find it there, I 9. use this little pocket guide that I found online. It's a little better than 10. poring over the entire manual. But I suggest that you begin with 11. looking at the research link from the main site. That should help.

Continued

(Table 7.1 continued)

Type of Code	Sample Data Set or Subset
Overall relationship code: Patterns and preferences held by male students and female students	*Researcher's Reflective Field Notes* (Recorded after conducting open coding) There seems to be a pattern and relationship developing between student choice of group members and project design. *Transcripts:* Female students selected other females to work with as group members. *Transcripts:* Female students chose to work in groups of three or four. *Transcripts:* Male students selected only one other male to work with on the project. *Interviews:* Female students preferred working with other females and liked to work with more than one other (three or four). *Interviews:* Male students just wanted to work with one "buddy" and didn't need more than one other student per group. *Artifacts:* Female group projects were neat, organized, and colorful and consisted of several components (booklet, presentation, video, and so on). *Artifacts:* Male projects were not as colorful as female group projects. Artwork was included but in the form of black-and-white diagrams and charts. Male projects consisted of one component (presentation, booklet, or diagram).

group. During this process, the action research is encouraged to use creativity and rich description when labeling the categories. A label should create an interesting picture that implies the attributes. Each category must be assigned specific attributes that provide clarification for the organization. Using the final example provided in Table 7.1, the researcher, after assigning the data subsets an "overall relationship" code, may label the category and define the attributes as in Table 7.2.

The example in Table 7.2—which reflects data collected from an action research study examining student preferences when working in groups—illustrates that a specific pattern emerged through data analysis. After examining transcripts of observations, transcripts of individual, structured interview responses, and artifacts, the researcher recorded reflective field notes. The field notes describe the pattern that emerged as a result of the analysis. After examining all data sets and subsets, the researcher is comfortable defining specific phenomena present in the research environment that reflect student preferences and patterns. The researcher then names the category using a descriptive, interesting label. Last, the category is defined using descriptive attributes. All data that reveal any of the attributes are included in the category. Triangulation occurs because at least three forms of data reveal a similar pattern.

TABLE 7.2. Categories and Attributes: An Example

Type of Code	Category and Attributes	Sample Data Set or Subset
Overall relationship code: Patterns and preferences held by male students and female students	Category: *It's a Man's World . . . but . . . All Chicks All the Time* Attributes: Data and data sets that show the following: - Male students select only one other male to work with - Males prefer a "buddy system" - Females students select only other females - Female groups are "chick cliques" - Female projects use pastels in design - Female projects are multidimensional - Male projects are black-and-white - Male projects are unidimensional	*Researcher's Reflective Field Notes* There seems to be a pattern and relationship developing between student choice of group members and project design. *Transcripts:* Female students selected other females to work with as group members. *Transcripts:* Female students chose to work in groups of three or four. *Transcripts:* Male students selected only one other male to work with on the project. *Interviews:* Female students preferred working with other females and liked to work with more than one other (three or four). *Interviews:* Male students just wanted to work with a "buddy" and didn't need more than one other student per group. *Artifacts:* Female group projects were neat, organized, and colorful and consisted of several components (booklet, presentation, video, and so on). *Artifacts:* Male projects were not as colorful as female group projects. Artwork was included but in the form of black-and-white diagrams and charts. Male projects consisted of one component (presentation, booklet, or diagram).

THE BIG PICTURE

The process of labeling categories and defining attributes continues until all data sets and subsets have been thoroughly examined and reexamined. The recursive process ends when the researcher determines that all patterns have been identified. Depending on the overarching questions and data sets, the researcher may arrive at this point quickly. However, if new questions and data sets were added to the original set of overarching questions as a result of the inquiry, the process may continue for a while before the researcher determines that the emergence of patterns has ended. When is the analysis process complete?

- When all categories have been creatively labeled with interesting and descriptive identifiers

- When descriptive, clarifying attributes have been assigned to all labeled categories

- When relationships between categories have been defined

- When connections have been established

- And when the researcher is able to establish meaning through the analysis

The Last Step in Analysis

With categories established, it sometimes helps to see an actual visual in the form of a table or chart that outlines each category along with its attributes. The visual may be simple or elaborate and may later be used when designing the action plan and writing the final action research report. By constructing a table or chart showing the hierarchy of categories matched with the relationships or connections, the researcher creates a picture of how all data are interconnected. Having a visual on hand also assists in creating meaning and describing the various phenomena. Many researchers prefer using a word processing program that has the capability to design flowcharts or relationship charts. The categorical information may be entered along with the set of attributes and the data sets and subsets that reflect the patterns that make up each category.

Another means for illustrating the connection between the categories is to use a simple table. Categories, labels, and attributes can easily be aligned with the data sets matched with overarching questions showing the triangulation that took place as a result of analysis. The table also helps the researcher to take one last look at each category to reconfirm the label, attributes, and aligned data sets. Finally, any type of visual constructed to show categories and related information provides an opportunity for the researcher to compare the results of analysis with the original triangulation matrix—confirming all of the following:

- Each overarching question was addressed and pursued fully through inquiry.

- All data sets were collected, organized, and analyzed.

- All patterns were identified until exhausted.

- Triangulation was established.

SUMMARY

Action research studies that employ a qualitative approach to inquiry require the researcher to collect multiple forms of data in order to ensure triangulation. The triangulation process validates the study and supports the findings, which in turn add to the relevancy and importance of the study. As a study gets under way, the action researcher begins to collect data sets. As data sets pile up, the researcher must deal with organization, analysis, storage, and available space. Qualitative data may be analyzed throughout the study to identify emerging research questions and to determine if additional data sets are needed. Depending on the structure of the study and the focus of the inquiry, qualitative analysis is ongoing, recursive, and blended into the actual inquiry activities. To facilitate the analysis process in a timely manner, the action researcher relies on expertise and the concept of researcher-as-instrument in conducting the analysis.

Using several coding processes and multiple types of codes, the researcher systematically analyzes, examines, and reexamines the data sets and subsets. Beginning with open coding, the data sets and subsets are manipulated, taken apart, and reassembled. The researcher then defines specific categories, labels the categories, and assigns descriptive attributes. Last, the categories are examined to ensure that all overarching questions were addressed, all data sets were collected and analyzed, and triangulation has occurred.

KEY TERMS

Activity codes	Methods codes
Axial coding	Open coding
Chunks of meaning	Process codes
Constant comparative method	Relationship codes
Context codes	Reporting approach
Descriptive reality approach	Selective coding
Descriptive storying	Setting codes
Discovery	Situation codes
Epoche	Strategy codes
Event codes	Subsetting
Grounded theory	

DISCUSSION QUESTIONS

1. Compare and contrast the reporting approach to data analysis and the descriptive reality approach. What are the differences? What are the similarities?

2. Provide an explanation of grounded theory. In what ways is it relevant to action research studies?

3. Describe the constant comparative method of analysis. What is the relationship between the method and data analysis?

4. Define *epoche* and provide an example.

5. Discuss the concepts of chunks of meaning and subsetting. Explain how these concepts aid the analysis process.

6. Compare and contrast open, selective, and axial coding. Describe when each type of coding is typically used.

7. Define each of the types of codes assigned in qualitative data analysis—setting, situation, process, activity, event, strategy, and relationship.

SUGGESTED TOPICS

1. Examine the data in Exhibit 7.3. Assign appropriate codes. Be prepared to discuss the assigned codes in small groups.

2. Using the information in Exhibit 7.4, label each category with a descriptive title.

ONLINE ACTIVITIES

1. Select one or two of the discussion questions provided to set up an online forum. Have students support their ideas with outside sources. Use a rubric for evaluating the postings. (*Note:* This may be completed in small groups or with the entire class.)

EXHIBIT 7.3. Examples of Transcript Data

Transcript/Individual Interview

1. During the pre-seminar interview session, SE stated that, "Computers were fun and had
2. a lot of information to give out."

Transcript/Observation

1. Female students selected markers over colored pencils for project design. They asked
2. Ms. J for: felt or construction paper, glitter, and fabric.

Transcript/Participant Field Journal/Reflective Notes / P#6

1. I found a lot of information on *American Idol* on the home page. I'm surprised that there
2. was no mention of my favorite Idol from last year. I plan to look again tomorrow,
3. but—I have to be sure that I find something to use for the group project.

EXHIBIT 7.4. **Examples of Categories**

Category #1:

Attributes:

Thoughts about computers

Levels of fluency and comfort using computers

Having fun with computers

Surfing easily

Accessing, navigating, and operating

Manipulating information

Selecting relevant information

Category #2:

Attributes:

Using organizers

Planning before designing

Group members and makeup

Interactions

Project design and components

Work patterns

---

2. Discuss the analysis process used for qualitative action research. Post at least two questions regarding the process. Select two other postings. Respond to the questions posted with suggestions for effectively analyzing qualitative data.

3. Use the example provided in "Suggested Topics" exercise 1 to assign codes. Post your results to the dedicated forum. In small groups, compare results. Did others assign similar codes? If not, what explains the differences?

4. Use the examples provided in "Suggested Topics" exercise 2 to label the categories. Share your labels in the dedicated forum. Post initially and respond to at least two others.

CHAPTER

THE ACTION RESEARCH REPORT

LEARNING OBJECTIVES

After reading Chapter Eight you should be able to:

- Discuss the rationale for writing the action research report
- Identify the components typically included in an action research report
- Examine different styles of effective writing
- Explore the importance of audience and voice
- Discuss appropriate ways to present findings

WRITING THE ACTION RESEARCH REPORT

For any research to become applicable and relevant, findings gleaned from the inquiry must be disseminated and shared. In the case of action research, presenting findings is crucial to the action plan and consequently to improving practice. It is very important to share findings because it is through dissemination of information that practitioners gain expertise, examine practice, and apply new information. In addition, the action research report enables the researcher to describe relevant research activities, offer suggestions, and discuss events that lead to meaning and understanding of a particular situation or phenomenon. The *action research report* allows the researcher to compile information regarding focus of the study, background, subjects, methods, and conclusions. The report consists of several components and is often paired with some type of formal presentation. The presentation allows the researcher to make a formal case for the action plan and offer a rationale regarding the importance of the inquiry as it relates to improving practice.

Although conducting the action research is challenging enough, practitioners often struggle with writing the action research report, for several reasons. Working in a practitioner-based setting, the researcher may not feel comfortable writing a formal report. Reporting the events and results of an action research study is not the same as writing a paper. The action researcher may not have any experience or training doing formal research, which means that the process may be unfamiliar and uncertain. Interacting informally with colleagues does not require polished presentations. The idea of writing a report that will later be available for others to examine evokes hesitation and apprehension. And the thought of sharing the action report with administrators and others in decision-making positions in one's own environment leaves the novice action researcher feeling at risk. Action researchers who are also full-time graduate students, who generally lack experience in making formal presentations, have similar apprehensions. First-time action researchers ponder questions such as these:

- How will I know what to report?

- What information must be included?

- What information should be omitted?

- How will I determine which information is most important?

- How much background information is needed to convey meaning and promote understanding?

- How can I present information without revealing confidential details regarding participants or location?

- What format is best for presenting findings?

- How long should the action research report be?

- What should be included in the report?

- What can be done to incorporate theory as well as relevant information understandable to a wide audience?

- Should I include examples of data and artifacts?

- What related materials should I have on hand when making my presentation?

RATIONALE FOR WRITING THE REPORT

Despite the uncertainty and apprehension that come with the prospect of writing an action research report, the practitioner researcher is obligated to prepare a well-written, well-organized paper that presents findings in a systematic manner. The action research report serves as the basis for the action plan. The report outlines what took place during the inquiry. The chronology of the events and activities enable the researcher to re-create the study with words, tables, and figures. Findings—based on data collection and analysis—are used to put together the action plan, which is then implemented to improve practice.

The action research report also serves to support the need for examining a specific problem, issue, or concern in the practicing environment. The report assists when presenting the findings and substantiating the research through informed conclusions. The informed conclusions lead to informed decisions for improving practice. Thus the report provides the information needed to make changes, implement new techniques and methods, request funds for additional programs or resources, generate solutions to problems, and support theories.

The formal presentation matched with the action research report should paint a professional portrait of expertise, knowledge, and true understanding of the specific practitioner-based environment. The importance attached to both the report and the presentation enables the researcher to engage in professional discourse with colleagues, administrators, and others in decision-making positions. It is the professional discourse that promotes further examination, which leads to improved practice.

COMPONENTS

Although there is no standard format for action research reports, the following components are vital for describing the inquiry and explaining the findings.

- *Introduction to the focus of the study.* This section introduces the focus of the inquiry and provides information regarding the nature of the inquiry.

- *Overarching questions, hypothesis, research questions, and research statement.* This section outlines the overarching questions in a qualitative action research study or provides the hypothesis and research question in a quantitative action research study. The research statement is presented here as well.

- *Literature review.* The literature review presents information regarding the already established body of knowledge related to the action research focus. The literature review provides an integrated, thematic account of previously conducted research as related to the action research.

■ *Research location and subjects or participants.* Information regarding the research site is described in this section, and a description of the participants is provided. However, all information must be deidentified to protect participant identity.

■ *Methodology.* The methodology section offers information as to why the selected method best meets the needs of the inquiry. The methodological approach is outlined, along with a rationale for its selection. If a statistical analysis test was used, this section will describe the type of data and what the selected test will measure. It briefly describes the analysis procedures for qualitative data, if applicable. An action research timeline should be included in the methodology section as it provides a chronology of the research activities and tasks.

■ *Data sources and data collection schedule.* The researcher must provide a brief explanation of each form of data aligned with the overarching questions for a qualitative action research study or an explanation of the data aligned with the hypothesis for a quantitative study. The triangulation matrix—aligning the questions and data sets—should be included. A well-organized, chronological data collection schedule inserted in this section helps illustrate what took place throughout the action research study.

■ *Data analysis.* The analysis procedures are described in full. If a statistical analysis test is required, offer an explanation regarding the type of data collected—parametric or nonparametric. Be sure to describe the testing procedures and measurement. Fully describe the analysis procedures for qualitative data. Include information regarding coding, categorizing, and attributes.

■ *Findings or conclusions.* This section includes an explanation and presentation of findings in chronological order. The triangulation matrix is revisited, with suggestions offered to improve practice. The section also includes the action plan for implementing the findings in order to effect change.

■ *References.* Be sure to include a reference list of all sources consulted in preparing the study and the report.

A typical action research report is twenty to twenty-five pages long. Action researchers are encouraged to include appendixes in order to provide examples of artifacts, field journal notes, copies of surveys or interview instruments, and information regarding the statistical test, if applicable.

TIPS FOR WRITING

Many newcomers to the action research process fall into undesirable patterns when writing the action research report, due in part to inexperience, writing style, and writing preferences. Inexperience causes the action researcher to write the action report in a manner that does not display a sound research orientation. Though tempting, the use of the first person ("I," "we") and a subjective tone and "personal" voice makes the report seem more an informal discussion than a formal presentation of research findings. As researchers engage in ongoing action research, they begin to build the skills needed to write effectively and report findings in an objective, professional, and scholarly manner. The research literacy that comes with experience allows the action researcher to glean the most important information gained from the study and report findings in a well-written, highly organized report (Craig & Patten, 2006).

The researcher's writing style may also influence the effectiveness of the report. When the writing style is informal, it makes the report sound amateurish and unprofessional. A scholarly writing style is preferred when reporting research findings, as the style demands attention and conveys expertise. General elements of scholarly writing include the following:

- Reporting from the stance of researcher-as-instrument, which requires writing in the third person ("they," "the research team")

- Integrating professional references when appropriate and as needed

- Presenting the information in a highly organized and chronological manner

- Using descriptive language in a formal manner

- Writing in a way that describes, explains, and clarifies

A scholarly writing style presents information in an objective and professional manner that provides support for the research and solidifies the importance of the study (see Exhibit 8.1). As you can see from the examples, the amateurish style of writing is fine for an informal narrative; however, the scholarly style commands attention and presents a strong, knowledgeable voice in reporting. By using a scholarly style of writing, the researcher displays confidence and expertise.

The following tips will help action researchers develop a more scholarly voice when writing research reports:

- Be sure to "remove yourself" from the researcher. This is accomplished by returning to the concept of researcher-as-instrument. In writing, this means omitting any first-person references. Replace "I" with "the researcher" to illustrate a professional voice and point of view.

- All verbs describing research actions must be in the past tense. The action research report presents findings related to a study that has already been completed; therefore, the past tense is appropriate.

- Use references as needed to support the inquiry, methodology, and findings.

- If using overarching questions, be sure that they are open-ended and well designed.

- Never identify participants or locations by name. Instead, use contextual factors to describe participants and research locations. This allows the research to provide detail without identifying people and places involved in the study.

EXHIBIT 8.1. Examples of Writing Styles

Amateurish Writing Style

In this study, I examined the process of students conducting semester projects. All of the student participants were enrolled in my online classes. I used a set of overarching questions as I conducted the research. The questions were as follows:

— Would the online learning environment help students conduct action research?

— Would students be able to reflect on their research?

— Would students be able to develop research skills without interacting face to face with the professor?

— What patterns would emerge, and could these patterns be used to help other university professors?

Before the semester started, I looked carefully at my course content and decided to add a research assignment. The courses were revised. . . .

Scholarly Writing Style

This study examined the process, discourse, and patterns that emerged as students conducted one-semester projects. Student participants included graduate students enrolled in several master's programs. The following set of overarching questions framed the study:

— Would the online learning environment facilitate the action research process in providing an avenue for discourse, dialogue, and reflection in order to improve practice?

— Considering the online environment and the absence of face-to-face interaction, could students truly develop the skills needed to design and implement projects that would improve learning and effect change?

— What patterns and preferences with regard to the inquiry process would emerge as the projects progressed, and would these findings inform practice at the university level?

Prior to the semester, course content was carefully examined and redesigned to include a research component. Following guidelines outlined by Palloff and Pratt (1999), course instructors and researchers designed the courses to include . . .

REPORTING AND PRESENTING FINDINGS

Writing the action research report provides an opportunity for the researcher to reexamine the study in chronological order one last time before formally presenting findings and designing the action plan. The writing process helps the researcher determine what information should be highlighted when presenting findings. As the writing progresses, the researcher has a chance to reflect on the following aspects:

- *Audience:* Which members of the professional community will be included in the audience?

- *Voice:* Whose voice needs to be strongest—the researcher, participants, or advocates for the research environment?

- *Reporting:* What mode of reporting is most appropriate for this particular audience?

- *Action plan:* What is the best method to present the action plan and related information?

In general, the four key issues—audience, voice, reporting, and action plan—must be fully addressed prior to the presentation of findings. If any one is ignored, the information resulting from the study will not be fully conveyed. This may lead inadvertently to a halt in progress or even a stalemate with regard to improving practice.

Audience and Voice

Audience and voice must be addressed first. By considering the audience, the action researcher is better able to determine which information should be selected from the action research report and converted into a formal presentation. Although the report itself remains the same, the presentation of findings may be altered to suit a specific audience. For example, if findings are to be presented to colleagues, information and terminology common to all practitioners can be included. In addition, specific information regarding environmental strategies, programs, or resources may be presented in an abbreviated manner if the researcher determines that these things are common knowledge among audience members.

However, if findings must be presented to board members, policymakers, or individuals removed from the practicing environment, the researcher must determine all of the following:

- What degree of background information must be presented to ensure understanding?

- What terms and strategies require definition or explanation to inform an audience that is removed from the practicing environment?

- What types of materials and resources are needed to overcome the lack of common knowledge among the audience?

Knowing the audience makes the job of designing an informative, relevant presentation much easier and also helps the action researcher tailor the presentation to that audience.

Voice in presentation must be considered to the same degree as audience. Depending on the inquiry, the researcher must determine the voice that will be included in the presentation of findings. Of course, the researcher—who will also be taking on the role of presenter—will use the voice of the practitioner researcher; however, there may be several other entities whose voice must be integrated into the presentation. For example, if the action research focused on student participants' views and perceptions, the voice of the participants must be strong within the context of the presentation. In addition, the student participants' voice should be integrated into findings, as the views and perceptions held by participants usually help inform practice. A different voice may be that of advocates for the practicing environment. For example, a study focusing on lack of technology or resources would include the voice of advocates of improving the practicing environment.

Awareness of voice helps the action researcher describe the most important elements of a specific research situation and the phenomena that occurred in the environment that was studied. Voice also helps provide a strong rationale for the action plan and support for the inquiry. One means of achieving a strong voice is to integrate artifacts and data sources into the presentation. By selecting key data sets and subsets, the action researcher is able to support the study and explain what took place. Using examples of student projects, writing samples, interview responses, and participant field notes highlights the voice of both participants and researcher.

Appropriate Reporting

Typically, once the action research report is complete, the researcher begins planning and designing the presentation of findings. As noted, equipped with information regarding audience, the researcher then identifies the voice that will be most effective to convey meaning while presenting findings. The next step is to plan how the information will be presented and design the presentation itself. At this stage, several reflective questions may be considered:

- What method of presentation will be used?
- What is the time frame allotted for the presentation?
- How many people will be in the audience?
- What equipment, if any, will be needed?
- What other resources should be distributed?
- Would a question-and-answer session be appropriate afterward?
- How can feedback be integrated?

Regarding the presentation method, the action researcher has several options. The option selected will depend on the audience and time allocated for the presentation. General methods of presenting findings include presentation aided by a computer-generated slide show, presentation aided by short video clips of key events that took place during the action research, presentation of an informative video or

DVD followed by a question-and-answer session, a poster-session-style presentation that allows the researcher to use and display pictures and related data while answering specific questions, a panel-style presentation that requires the researcher to present findings as part of a series of short reports followed by questions from the audience, or a brief, unassisted presentation consisting of a short verbal report of key findings (see Table 8.1).

The best method for presenting findings is to opt for a presentation that includes an informative video or DVD compiled by researchers and participants. The collaborative voice of researcher practitioner and participants establishes interest, importance, understanding, and meaning. (Of course, this will work only if the appropriate technology is available.) Another excellent method for presenting findings is to design a poster-style session, which displays key information blended with samples of artifacts and data. The poster-style presentation enables the researcher to answer key questions from the audience. It also presents information in a manner that is appealing to a wide range of audiences in that the audience members are able to view and examine the action research information and then formulate questions that are of importance to them.

Perhaps the most popular of the presentation methods is to design an informative slide show, which presents findings in a clear, succinct manner that is interesting to a particular audience. The slide show presentation is typically integrated with audience questions so that meaning and understanding may be established. In addition, the slide show presentation works well when time is limited because a well-designed slide show presents key points and information quickly, making more room for audience questions. Again, this presentation method will not work if the necessary technology is not available. It is also not effective if the slide show is poorly designed and boring. The researcher must determine which presentation method best meets the needs of the action research inquiry, the audience, and the presentation location.

Sharing Meaningful Findings

Whatever the presentation method, the action researcher must take precautions that the presentation itself is designed in a manner that promotes audience understanding of the action research study. This is accomplished by doing the following:

- Selecting key information to build background
- Organizing the information to be presented in a logical manner that is understandable to a wide range of audiences
- Establishing meaning through style, description, explanation, and relevancy

The information selected for the presentation must be meaningful to the researcher, participants, setting, and audience. If the members of the audience have no interest in the focus of the study, it is likely that they will not derive meaning regarding the inquiry, events, or phenomena. Knowing the audience beforehand

TABLE 8.1. Overview of Presentation Methods

Presentation Method	Components and Materials
Presentation of findings aided by a computer-generated slide show	Computer-generated slide show Resources such as handouts or brochures Audience questions Media such as video, audio, or online resources Copies of action research report Chronological information
Presentation aided by short video clips of key events that took place during the action research	One or more short video clips Handouts, resources, or brochures outlining the study Questions and answers Copies of action research report Narration of project
Presentation of an informative video or DVD followed by a question-and-answer session	Longer-length informative video or researcher-generated (or participant-generated) DVD Handouts or brochures Participant-generated materials Pre-narration question-and-answer session Narration of project Post-narration questions Copies of action research report
Poster-session-style presentation that allows the researcher to use and display pictures and related data while answering specific questions	"Poster" display or trifold presentation board Chronology of the study Audience-generated questions Handouts or copies of the action research report
Panel-style presentation that requires the researcher to present findings as part of a series of short reports followed by questions from the audience	Panel of researchers or presenters One-page handout Question-and-answer session
Brief, unassisted presentation consisting of a short verbal report of key findings	Narration Discussion Handout or brochure Action research report

helps avoid a situation such as this. Another technique is to use a large number of relevant examples blended with light, general humor. It also helps if the researcher's presentation style is natural and approachable. Sometimes, a quick run-through before the actual presentation provides a means of rehearsal. The practice assists the researcher in presenting the information in a knowledgeable but comfortable and natural manner. This puts the audience at ease, thereby allowing people to focus their attention on the findings being presented.

Since the slide show presentation method is most popular, a few issues regarding design must be considered. Overall, the general design must hold the attention of the audience. Including too little or too many graphics may be distracting. Including too much text or text typed in a small font leaves the audience frustrated and bored. When designing a slide show with the purpose of presenting research findings, the following tactics are helpful:

- Use colorful but professional templates for the overall design.
- Use a variety of fonts, making sure that the size is appropriate for the presentation area and audience viewing.
- Select relevant graphics, and consider using digital photos taken during the action research study.
- Use digital pictures of artifacts, field notes, and participant journals as appropriate.
- Limit intricate transitions and flash techniques, as they can be distracting when trying to focus an audience on key information.
- If appropriate, opt for short video clips or links for the video integrated into the slide show at relevant and appropriate points.
- Limit text to key points, and use the key points to present information naturally.
- Avoid reading the information on each slide verbatim.
- Consider using tables and charts to present information in an organized, interesting manner.
- If ambitious, use music at appropriate points.
- Limit the number of slides overall; seven or eight usually suffice.
- A final slide may invite questions from the audience if the presentation time frame allows.

Some researchers find it helpful to use a checklist when preparing a slide show presentation for the purpose of sharing findings. The checklist helps ensure that all relevant information is included and that the slide show is professionally designed. Exhibit 8.2 provides an example of such a checklist.

Although the checklist is an excellent tool when preparing for a slide show presentation, it may be adapted to any other method of presenting. The researcher may use the tool to make sure that all critical information is included, materials and

EXHIBIT 8.2. Checklist for Sharing Findings

❏ Title slide includes action research study title, researcher's name, and contact information, including e-mail.

❏ Overview of the study includes background (brief) and overarching questions or hypothesis.

❏ Participant information slide includes the number of subjects or participants, with general information deidentified.

❏ Description of research site, contains general information deidentified.

❏ Overview of selected methodology and quantitative or qualitative approach, with an explanation of those choices is included.

❏ Data slide consists of a clear description of the data and data sets and overview of the analysis performed (may use the triangulation matrix).

❏ Findings are organized in table format.

❏ Conclusions and suggestions are offered.

❏ Brief introduction to the action plan, with rationale included.

❏ Final slide (optional) offers an invitation for questions or provides a list of references and additional contact information.

❏ Handouts, are limited to one page (back and front).

❏ Brochure, if applicable, is organized and informative.

❏ Copies of action research report, if applicable, or one or two examination copies are available.

❏ Approximate number of copies needed: _____

❏ Equipment check complete.

❏ Run-through complete.

❏ Last spelling and grammar check complete.

❏ All materials assembled and ready to go.

resources needed are adequate, and the presentation has been rehearsed and is ready for an audience.

Suggestions for Improvement and Introduction to the Action Plan

It is critically important that the researcher include several suggestions for improving practice that were identified as a result of the action research process. Doing so sets the stage for introducing the action plan. The suggestions are based on informed decision making that came out of the inquiry. The expertise gained from conducting the research enables the researcher to offer insights leading to suggestions. The suggestions are offered as a means for helping others as well as to improve one's own practice. Any suggestions compiled as a result of the action research are later evaluated and addressed, if necessary, when designing the action plan.

One of the last tasks in the formal presentation is to introduce the action plan. The action plan is the result of the inquiry. The plan outlines what steps will be taken and implemented to improve practice and effect change. The action research inquiry and findings inform the design of the action plan. As the recursive process of action research continues, the researcher evaluates both self and situation, compiles suggestions based on the inquiry, and uses the suggestions to design the action plan to improve practice; the action plan is then implemented and evaluated, and the process starts again.

The design and implementation of the plan enable the action researcher to continue the recursive process of self-improvement, situation improvement, and practice improvement. In addition, by using the findings resulting from the actual research, the action researcher continues to use experience and expertise in generating plans for solving problems, which inevitably result in improved practice.

THE ACTION RESEARCH REPORT ASSIGNMENT

Beginning action researchers and graduate students who are embarking on the action research journey may be interested in examining an action research assignment that helps begin the process. A typical graduate-level action research assignment begins with an overview of the assignment followed by guidelines and directions. Graduate students are then encouraged to engage in preproject brainstorming to identify a focus, the research environment, and subjects. Next, a review of literature is required. Research questions are developed and data sets identified. An institutional review board proposal is prepared and submitted for approval. Upon approval, the project is conducted. The culmination is a formal presentation. An electronic copy of a sample action research graduate assignment is located with the online resources for this chapter.

Although the format is used with graduate students who are just beginning to interact with action research, it may be helpful to any practitioner who is also a beginning action researcher. In addition, it is always helpful to have an evaluation rubric on hand prior to completing a study. The rubric provides a framework for the writing the report (see Table 8.2).

Beginning researchers also find it helpful to have an evaluation rubric available for examination when writing any type of report or designing materials for presenting findings. Table 8.3 illustrates an example of an evaluation rubric for a computer-generated slide show.

TABLE 8.2. Action Research Report Grading Rubric

Target	Acceptable	Unacceptable
Evidence of Research Orientation		

Target	Acceptable	Unacceptable
Inquiry clearly defined	Inquiry somewhat defined	Inquiry unclear
Focus of study refined, concise, and targeted	Focus of study somewhat clear and targeted	Focus of study not present
High degree of inquiry and research present	Adequate degree of inquiry and research present	Little degree of inquiry
Overarching questions clearly stated	Overarching questions included *or* hypothesis and research questions included	Inappropriate questions unrelated to the actual study *or* hypothesis poorly formed
Three forms of data defined and appropriate *or* hypothesis well designed and aligned with research statement	Three forms of data included	Fewer than three forms of data
Analysis in place and in-depth	Analysis in place	Little evidence of analysis
Process followed and study carried out	Process followed and study carried out	Process somewhat followed
Literature fully explored and presented	Literature explored and presented	Inadequate literature review

Mechanics

Target	Acceptable	Unacceptable
Paper well written following APA format	Paper well written	Amateur style of writing
Scholarly writing style	APA format followed in some instances	APA format not followed
All components included following guidelines	Somewhat scholarly style	Components missing
Few or no mechanical errors	Most components included	Mechanical errors
	Few mechanical errors	

Notes: 10 points will be added automatically for submitting the draft by the designated date and time; 10 points will be taken off for consistent mechanical errors throughout the paper; 5 points will be taken off for consistently not following APA format.

TABLE 8.3. Electronic Presentation Rubric

Performance Criterion	A+ Exceeds Expectations	A 100–90	B 89–80	C 79–70*
Organization	All criteria were present, and the quality of the overall design exceeded assignment expectations.	Information was presented in a logical, interesting sequence that was easy to follow.	Information was somewhat difficult to follow because student tended to "jump around" from topic to topic.	There did not appear to be any sequence or order to the information presented.
Design	Every slide contained at least one graphic.	All but one slide contained a graphic.	Two slides did not contain graphics.	Three or more slides did not contain a graphic.
	Appropriate slide animations were used.	Some slide animations were used, as needed.	Animations were overused to the point that they were distracting.	No slide animations were used during the presentation.
Mechanics	All criteria were present, and the quality of the overall design exceeded assignment expectations.	Presentation had no misspellings or grammatical errors.	Presentation contained one or two spelling or grammatical errors.	Presentation contained three or more spelling or grammatical errors.
	Presentation contained an introduction, body, and conclusion.	Presentation lacked either introduction or body, or conclusion.	Presentation contained only introduction, body, or conclusion.	Presentation was organized into no discernible sections.
Content	All criteria were present, and the quality of the overall design exceeded assignment expectations. For example, scanned graphic files of student work or other artifacts were included.	Slide show conveyed the action research findings in a detailed, interesting manner. All components were included, and slide limit was not exceeded.	Slide show conveyed the action research findings in a detailed manner. All components were included; however, too many slides were used.	Slide show conveyed information in a boring, dull manner. Components were missing, and slide limit was ignored.

*Below this level, student earns an F; student did not meet the challenges of the task.

SUMMARY

To complete the action research process, findings gleaned from the inquiry must be disseminated and shared. Presenting findings is crucial to the action plan and improving practice. It is important to share findings because it is through dissemination of information that practitioners gain expertise, examine practice, and apply new information. In addition, the action research report enables the researcher to describe relevant research activities, offer suggestions, and discuss events that lead to meaning and understanding of a particular situation or phenomenon. The action research report allows the researcher to compile information regarding focus of the study, background, subjects, methods, and conclusions. The report consists of several components and is often paired with some type of formal presentation. Components include introduction, overarching questions or hypothesis and related discussion, literature review, discussion of subjects or participants and research location or site, overview of selected methodology, discussion of data sets and collection schedule, analysis procedures, findings and conclusions, and references.

The style of writing may influence understanding. Using a scholarly rather than an amateurish style helps the researcher offer expertise through the experience of action research. Critical issues to consider when preparing for presenting findings include audience, voice, reporting, and the action plan. A formal presentation of findings enables the researcher to share the results of the inquiry. Presentation methods may vary and are selected based on the inquiry, audience, and time frame. Newcomers to the action research process find it helpful to examine an action research assignment and guidelines. Rubrics are also used to assist researchers in writing the action research report and designing effective presentations to share findings.

KEY TERM

Action research report

DISCUSSION QUESTIONS

1. Discuss the value in formally presenting findings resulting from an action research study.

2. Discuss components of the action research report. Which is the most critical when presenting findings?

3. Examine the questions that beginning action researchers may have when preparing for a formal presentation of findings. Prioritize the suggested questions, and add at least three more that are equally important.

4. Discuss the different types of presentations. Which do you feel is most effective? Which do you feel is not appropriate?

5. Compare and contrast the amateurish style of writing and the scholarly style. In small groups, compile suggestions to help people develop a more scholarly style.

6. Discuss the importance of audience, voice, reporting, and the action plan. Which do you feel is most critical with regard to presenting findings? Explain and provide support.

SUGGESTED TOPICS

1. Working in teams of two, discuss the action research report. Examine components. Which do you feel are most important when designing the presentation of findings? Be prepared to offer an explanation to support your thoughts.

2. Why is knowledge of audience critical to presenting findings? In small groups, generate a list of ideas to support the concept. Be prepared to share your list with other groups.

3. Examine the following example of amateur writing style. Use the example to note the items that need revision. Rewrite the excerpt in a more scholarly manner. Be prepared to share your work with other group members.

    I followed the action research process for my study. First, I gave a survey to eighteen students at my school. Next, I asked students to write responses to a set of questions. I did this as part of data collection. It helped me triangulate data later. Last, I conducted several open-ended interviews with some of my colleagues, the school principals, and a few special area teachers. I also included the school resource officer to get his views.

ONLINE ACTIVITIES

1. Select one or two of the discussion questions provided to set up an online forum. Have students support their ideas with outside sources. Use a rubric for evaluating the postings. (*Note:* This may be completed in small groups or with the entire class.)

2. Reflect on the specifics of the audience to whom you will be reporting findings related to your action research study. Generate a list of questions regarding how you may design the presentation of findings tailored to the specific audience. Post your overview of the audience and your questions and concerns to the dedicated forum. Then respond to at least two other similar postings.

3. Conduct a brief Internet search to locate two examples of writing style, one amateurish and one scholarly. Critique each, and make a list of suggestions

for improvement. Post URLs for the sites where the examples were found, your comparison of the two styles, and your suggestions for improving the amateurish writing. Respond to at least two other similar postings.

4. Now post your revised version of scholarly writing. Examine other similar postings. Critique and offer suggestions to at least two.

CHAPTER

DESIGNING AND IMPLEMENTING THE ACTION PLAN

LEARNING OBJECTIVES

After reading Chapter Nine, you should be able to:

- Discuss the importance of the action plan
- Examine the phases of the action plan
- Explore the types of decision making involved in action planning
- Identify the components of an effective action plan
- Design an appropriate action plan

THE ACTION PLAN

Many experts in the field of action research consider the action research study and the action research report synonymous with the *action plan*. There is a distinction, however, because the action plan is a direct result of the inquiry. The action research study begins with identification of a focus, problem, issue, or concern present or related to the practicing environment. A hypothesis is formed or overarching questions are designed. Participants are identified. Data sets are identified, collected, and analyzed. Ultimately, the researcher draws conclusion and reports findings. The findings—which result from the inquiry—are used to design an action plan. The action plan is informed by the research conducted in the practitioner-based environment. The plan is designed and implemented, based on findings, generated collections of possible solutions, strategies and interventions identified to improve practice, and continuous evaluation of practice and practitioners.

The action plan follows the inquiry because information gained from conducting the action research is needed to design a "plan of action" to improve practice. The data analysis that takes place during the action research process is used to identify recurring problems and inform decisions regarding improvements in the practitioner-based setting. In addition, the action plan serves as a tool for the researcher's evaluating himself or herself as a practicing professional. The action plan may be likened to a professional development plan or school improvement plan. The difference, however, is that the action plan is informed by inquiry and research conducted by individuals who work in the practicing environment. The closeness of the practitioner to the actual research creates a unique relationship, which draws on experience and professionalism, making the action plan particularly relevant. It is the relevancy of the action plan that encourages "ownership" on the part of the practitioner researcher. When ownership is established, the degree of importance of both the inquiry and implementation of the action plan rises. And the entire recursive process prompts the practitioner researcher to engage in reflection, implementation, review, and self-examination. Each phase requires the researcher to generate questions in these areas that guide the design and implementation of the action plan:

Reflection

■ How can the findings be applied to the design of the action plan in a way that promotes further examination?

■ What possible solutions may be generated?

■ What do the action research findings convey regarding improving practice?

■ What strategies may be integrated into the action plan?

■ Based on the findings, what are the goals of the action plan?

Implementation

■ What materials and resources are needed for implementation?

■ How long will it take to implement the plan?

- Who will be involved?
- Are there any costs involved?

Review

- Were the strategies effective?
- Were the interventions appropriate?
- What changes occurred, and were the changes positive?

Self-Examination

- What additional training do I need to assist the change process?
- What effect do I as a practitioner have on the environment?
- What things can I do differently to improve my own practice?
- What additional interactions do I need to engage to effect positive change?

RATIONALE

The action plan enables the researcher to do all of the following:

- Use the findings gleaned from the action research study to identify needs and problems
- Generate possible solutions
- Identify strategies and interventions that may provide insight and improve practice
- Promote informed decision making through examination, reflection, and evaluation

The action plan may be thought of as an outcome of the action research study. The outcome leads to goals, which are integrated into the action plan. Once the plan is implemented, progress is charted to determine if goals are met and if progress has been made toward improvement.

The action plan serves as a means of attacking a problem and trying to solve it. Design and implementation of the action plan are vital components in the change process. More important, the design of the plan is grounded in informed, systematic inquiry and may be considered as a research-based strategy to improve the working environment.

PURPOSE

The purpose of the action plan is to target specific information gleaned from the action research study findings in order to set goals and establish a plan for meeting the goals. The action plan also serves the purpose of continuing the inquiry, which began with the action research study. The continuation allows the researcher to prioritize information reported in findings and select the most critical problems or situations, which become part of the action plan. Strategies for improving selected problems or situations are integrated into the plan of action, thereby establishing purpose and importance for implementation.

The purpose of any given action plan is based on the individual inquiry. This makes each action plan unique to its specific situation. Formats and components will vary with the situation and the action plan's goals. For example, an action plan designed to improve scheduling at the high school level would have different goals, materials, and strategies than an action plan designed to improve the degree of computer use in elementary school classrooms. The one similarity among action plans is that the core of every plan is driven by the desire to improve practice through action, reflection, and self-evaluation.

WHEN IS AN ACTION PLAN APPROPRIATE?

Once the action research study is complete and findings have been shared with colleagues and other relevant parties, it is usually appropriate to design and implement the action plan. However, an action plan is more appropriate in some situations than in others. As stated previously, some experts in the field consider the action research study the same as the action plan. However, given the nature of action research, the action plan is a distinct component of the entire inquiry process. Therefore, in most cases, designing and implementing an action plan is appropriate. For example, an action research study reveals that students prefer to select members for small group activities themselves. The action researcher shares this information with four colleagues. The colleagues—working at the same school—decide to try student self-selection. Together they put together an action plan, which is implemented in four classrooms. Goals are set and strategies are selected. The action plan is monitored. Teachers engage in reflection and self-evaluation. Progress is charted and changes are noted. In this case, design and implementation of the action plan are relevant and appropriate.

There are situations, however, when an action plan is not appropriate. For example, graduate students who are required to conduct an action research study as part of course requirements may complete the study and design an action plan based on findings. The semester ends, and the plan cannot be implemented due to time factors. In this case, implementation of the plan is not appropriate. Another example is in situations where administrators work with practitioners in conducting action research studies. Once the inquiry is complete, the administrators may not have time to continue collaborating with practitioners. After action research findings are shared, the administrators leave the tasks of designing and implementing the action plan to the practitioners. Although the inquiry continues with the action plan implementation, the administrators are not part of it; therefore, for them personally, the action plan is not appropriate. At the university level, this occurs often when deans and department chairs begin the action research process but due to time constraints leave the design and implementation of an action plan based on findings to faculty members.

INFORMED DECISION MAKING

Informed decision making is a direct result of understanding conditions, situations, and phenomena. The process of informed decision making consists of gathering information, exploring possibilities, reflecting, and making decisions based on information and understanding.

The understanding gained from conducting an action research study enables the researcher to critically examine factors surrounding practice. The critical examination encourages the practitioner to seek additional information, explore choices, and make decisions based on knowledge and meaning. For example, in the medical community, patients seek second opinions to gather information that leads to informed decision making. This practice is common and is encouraged by most medical practitioners.

Practitioners in other fields engage in a similar process when faced with an important decision. In many cases, practitioners face numerous daily situations that require informed decisions. Practitioner researchers apply the skill of informed decision making to their research as well as their practice. By gathering as much relevant information as possible, practitioners are better able to explore possible solutions and choices before making a critical decision regarding practice. The degree of information gathering is based on the type of decision that must be made. Therefore, it helps to have completed the action research study prior to making decisions regarding the action plan and strategies for improving practice. Practitioner researchers face three types of decisions when designing an action plan:

- *Basic decisions*. *Basic decisions* are decisions that must be made regarding the structure of the plan, the timeline for implementation, who will be involved in the implementation, and resources needed.

- *Implementation decisions*. *Implementation decisions* include decisions regarding strategies to be included in the action plan, any necessary funding needed to implement the plan, and whether the plan will be implemented as a collaborative effort.

- *Reflective decisions*. *Reflective decisions* require a high degree of background information, time, and contemplation. They may include decisions regarding implementing the plan in multiple locations or environments, decisions based on ethical and logistical issues, or decisions involving treatments.

Informed decision making on the part of practitioners begins with the action research study. As a result of a thorough literature review, the action researcher is able to design a hypothesis or develop overarching questions. Data sets and analysis procedures are identified using the information gained from the literature review. Conclusions are drawn on the basis of information gleaned from the inquiry. Last, findings are presented that are based on experience and inquiry. Every decision made throughout the action research process is guided by educated, informed practice. The same is true when designing and implementing the action plan. The researcher uses information from the action research to identify goals and design the plan. Decisions based on information are made regarding strategies and possible solutions. Decisions made through self-evaluation are guided by experience and information gained from implementing the plan.

The process involved in informed decision making enables the practitioner researcher to become the catalyst needed to make changes in the work-based environment. Informed decision making empowers the practitioner as a professional. Throughout the design process, the practitioner makes informed decisions that are within the realm of possibility and expertise. As the action plan is implemented, the practicing professional continues to make decisions that directly affect the environment. The decisions are grounded in experience and driven by information and research, resulting in improvements and positive change in the practicing environment.

DESIGNING THE PLAN

Each action plan is unique because each is based on a specific action research study. However, the process of designing the action plan remains the same. The first step in designing the action plan is to reexamine the information presented in the action research report. A close look at the data, findings, and conclusions helps prioritize and focus the action plan. At this stage, researchers should ask the following questions:

- What initial ideas emerge as a result of a reexamination of the action research report?

- Is additional background information needed to design an effective action plan?

- What do the findings reveal regarding priorities for the action plan?

- What are the overall goals that need to be accomplished?

- Are there any individual goals? Team goals?

- How can information revealed in findings be integrated into the action plan goals?

- What general strategies emerge as a result of a reexamination of the report?

- Will the same participants be involved in implementing the action plan?

- Will the plan include colleagues, administrators, researchers, or community members?

- What roles will they play?

■ What resources and materials are needed, and how do these relate to information revealed in findings?

■ What evaluation strategies will be used?

After revisiting the action research report and reflecting on the questions, the researcher should record any initial thoughts or ideas regarding the action plan in the field journal. Continuing to record entries in the field journal helps when implementing the plan because they may provide insights and spark ideas for effecting change.

Remember that qualitative action research findings will include multiple concepts, patterns, and themes. During the initial steps in designing the action plan, the practitioner researcher selects key concepts, patterns, or themes that emerged during the action research and were included in the findings. The items are prioritized and later reexamined. The prioritized list provides many possibilities for the action plan. Next, the practitioner researcher selects one of the prioritized items gleaned from the findings. For example, findings may reveal that participants are experiencing difficulty when using lab equipment. Beginning researchers should select one or two items as the focus of the action plan. Once the plan is implemented, subsequent plans may be designed to address other items. Goals to be accomplished as a result of implementing the action plan are developed. Next, strategies are selected based on the goals to be accomplished. Last, the plan is implemented. The design process may be completed individually or collaboratively, depending on the action research inquiry.

Many researchers find it helpful to use a template during the initial stages of design. Information entered on the template is later transferred to the desired action plan format. The planning template helps organize thoughts, prioritize items, chart strategies, and identify resources needed to implement the plan. Exhibits 9.1, 9.2, and 9.3 illustrate planning templates that may be used in the early stages of action plan design.

COMPONENTS

Although every action plan is unique, several components are universal. The following information appears in all action plans:

■ Identity of the practitioner researcher, the location or site, and number of participants. The plan may include location and researcher's name. Participants are not identified, only the number of those who took part.

■ Targeted focus of the action plan based on prior inquiry

■ Overall goals of the plan

■ Specific goals

■ Team goals, if applicable

■ Strategies that will be implemented and integrated into the action plan

EXHIBIT 9.1. Sample Planning Template 1

Designing the Action Plan: Early Planning

Initial Ideas and Thoughts After Revisiting the Action Research Report:	**Prioritized Concepts, Themes, and Patterns:**
Action plan should address the recurring theme of male versus female grouping.	Student preferences regarding group members (male versus female)
This seems to be a problem in math classes at all grade levels	Student views of math instruction
Findings were shared with team members, and they are interested in a collaborative plan.	Use of graphing calculators (effectiveness)

Overall Goal of the Action Plan:

Students will work collaboratively and successfully in small groups while solving algebraic problems.

Specific Goals of the Action Plan:

Students will select group members on Mondays and Wednesdays and work collaboratively to solve problems.

Teachers will assign group members on Tuesdays and Thursdays and monitor students working in small groups, providing assistance as needed.

Students will take part in "modeled" problem solving and apply skills as they collaboratively solve problems.

Possible Strategies:	**Resources and Materials Needed:**
Teacher and student modeling	None
Student-selected groups	
Same-sex grouping	

- ■ Timeline for implementing the action plan
- ■ Evaluation techniques—formative, summative, and self-evaluation
- ■ Materials, resources, and funds needed to implement the plan

Some practitioner-based environments, such as schools and universities, have templates for action plans; however, many do not. The action plan information may be entered into a template like those shown in Exhibits 9.1, 9.2, or 9.3 organized according to the points just listed. It helps to have a rubric for evaluating the design of the action plan (see Table 9.1). Prior to implementation, the plan should be evaluated to be sure that the design is sound, clear, and concise. If the plan will be implemented

EXHIBIT 9.2. Sample Planning Template 2

Planning Template for Action Plan

Overall Goal:
Students will work collaboratively and successfully in small groups while solving algebraic problems.

Specific Goals:
Students will select group members on Mondays and Wednesdays and work collaboratively to solve problems.
Teachers will assign group members on Tuesdays and Thursdays and monitor students working in small groups, providing assistance as needed.
Students will take part in ''modeled'' problem solving and apply skills as they collaboratively solve problems.

Team Goals:
All students enrolled in team 3 math sections will self-select group members and work collaboratively to solve algebraic problems two days each week.

Targeted Concepts, Themes, or Patterns:
Student preferences regarding group members (male versus female)
Student views of math instruction

Possible Strategies:
Teacher and student modeling
Student-selected groups
Same-sex grouping

Location:
GMS/WC

Participants:
All students enrolled in team 3 math sections

Information Needed to Develop the Action Plan:
Additional information needed regarding same-sex math instruction

Resources or Funding Sources:
None

Materials and Programs:
AAUW books

Possible Evaluation Strategies and Tools:
Rubric for student problem solving (formative)
Student scores (summative)
Self-evaluation rubric

EXHIBIT 9.3. Sample Planning Template 3

ACTION PLAN TEMPLATE

NAME OF RESEARCHER/S   **DATE:** 9/24/09

SCHOOL/LOCATION:

GMS/WC

OVERALL GOAL:

Students will work collaboratively and successfully in small groups while solving algebraic problems.

SPECIFIC GOALS:

Students will select group members on Mondays and Wednesdays and work collaboratively to solve problems.

Teachers will assign group members on Tuesdays and Thursdays and monitor students working in small groups, providing assistance as needed.

Students will take part in "modeled" problem solving and apply skills as they collaboratively solve problems.

STRATEGIES:

Teacher and student modeling
Student-selected groups
Same-sex grouping

FORMATIVE ASSESSMENT STRATEGIES AND TOOLS:

Rubric for student problem solving
Survey for students (grouping and methods)

SUMMATIVE ASSESSMENT STRATEGIES AND TOOLS:

Student test and quiz scores (summative)

SELF-EVALUATION STRATEGIES AND TOOLS:

Self-evaluation rubric
Peer evaluations

RESOURCES AND MATERIALS:

AAUW books for team members

TABLE 9.1. Action Plan Rubric

Target	Acceptable	Needs Improvement
Design		
The action plan is designed in a clear, concise, and organized manner. All components are fully addressed. Overall goals are appropriate and well expressed. Specific goals are appropriate and well expressed. Strategies are well matched with the plan's focus. Timeline is detailed and organized. There are no grammatical or technical errors.	The action plan is designed in an organized manner. All components are present. Overall goals are appropriate. Specific goals are appropriate. Strategies are matched with the plan's focus. Timeline is organized. There are a few grammatical or technical errors.	The action plan is unclear and somewhat disorganized. Some components are lacking. Overall goals are somewhat appropriate. Specific are goals unclear. Strategies may or may not reflect the plan's focus. Timeline is included. There are multiple grammatical or technical errors.
Relevancy and Connectedness to the Action Research Findings		
The selected focus is relevant and connected to the action research findings. The action plan focus is identified as a recurring priority in the findings. The focus is integrated well with the strategies and the overall action plan design.	The selected focus is relevant to the action research findings. The action plan focus is identified as one of the priorities in the findings. The focus is integrated with the strategies.	The selected focus is somewhat relevant to the action research findings. The action plan focus is identified as a low priority in the findings.
Evaluation Strategies and Tools		
A variety of appropriate evaluation strategies and tools are integrated into the plan. The plan uses both formative and summative tools. A self-evaluation tool is effectively integrated.	Several appropriate evaluation strategies and tools are integrated into the plan. The plan uses summative tools. A self-evaluation tool is integrated.	Summative evaluation tools are included.

collaboratively, team members may want to evaluate it based on the evaluation rubric before implementation begins.

USING FINDINGS TO INFORM DESIGN

After the action plan has been designed, it is a good idea to revisit the findings to be sure that the focus of the plan is one of the top priorities outlined in the action research findings, strategies are aligned with the information presented in the findings, and the design reflects the information revealed through the inquiry. The findings presented in the action research report are also excellent sources that prompt ideas regarding strategies and interventions that become part of the action plan design. A careful examination of the findings may lead the action researcher in new directions, thereby discovering strategies that may be implemented and integrated into the action plan. The same is true for interventions when addressing and targeting behaviors, views, and perceptions.

When the design is complete and the researcher is satisfied with the action plan, implementation begins. One of the components of the action plan is the timeline. During implementation, the plan should be adhered to so that all goals are addressed within a reasonable amount of time. The timeline helps keep the plan on track. This is important in situations where other priority concepts, patterns, or themes identified in the action research report findings are to be targeted for subsequent action plans.

CONTINUOUS IMPROVEMENT

As the action plan is implemented, the researcher uses the timeline to record progress toward meeting the overall goals and specific targeted goals. The notes regarding progress may also be used later when evaluating the action plan. In addition to evaluating the action plan, the researcher engages in self-evaluation as part of the process. Self-evaluation should be ongoing and may be conducted throughout the action plan implementation. Through self-evaluation, the researcher is able to determine if the strategies are working. Self-evaluation also assists in determining the researcher effect on participants, implementation of the action plan, and overall evaluation of related activities.

Continuous improvement is prompted by the action research process and through the implementation of one or more action plans that address prioritized concepts, patterns, and themes. Once the action plan is implemented, the action researcher revisits the action research findings. The planning templates used in the early design phase are reviewed to target the next prioritized concept, pattern, or theme revealed in the action research findings. A new action plan is designed and implemented; this continues the inquiry and enables the entire process to begin again.

SUMMARY

The action plan is designed and implemented based on findings, generated collections of possible solutions, strategies and interventions identified to improve practice, and continuous evaluation of practice and practitioners.

The action plan follows the path of inquiry and integrates information gained from conducting the action research to design a plan of action to improve practice. The data analysis that takes place during the action research process is used to identify recurring problems and inform decisions regarding improvements in the practitioner-based setting. In addition, the action plan serves as a tool for evaluating oneself as a practicing professional. The purpose of the action plan is to target specific information gleaned from the action research study findings in order to set goals and establish a plan for meeting the goals. The action plan also serves the purpose of continuing the inquiry, which began with the action research study.

Each action plan is unique because each is based on a specific action research study. However, the process of designing the action plan remains the same. Components that are universal to all action plans are information regarding the practitioner researcher, the location or site, and the participants; the targeted focus of the action plan, based on prior inquiry; the overall goals of the plan; specific goals; team goals, if applicable; strategies that will be implemented and integrated into the action plan; a timeline for implementing the action plan; evaluation techniques, formative, summative, and self-evaluation; and materials, resources, and funds needed to implement the plan. When designing the action plan, the researcher asks questions in connection with reflection, implementation, review, and self-evaluation. In addition, the process requires the action researcher to engage in informed decision making. Informed decision making is a direct result of understanding conditions, situations, and phenomena. The process consists of gathering information, exploring possibilities, reflecting, and making decisions based on information and understanding.

KEY TERMS

Action plan
Basic decisions
Continuous improvement.

Implementation decisions
Reflective decisions

DISCUSSION QUESTIONS

1. Discuss the action plan and its relationship to the action research study.

2. Compare the factors that are the basis for designing and implementing an action plan. How do these relate to the inquiry process?

3. Compare and contract the recursive process of action research and the recursive process of designing and implementing the action plan.

4. Conduct a brief Internet search to locate information regarding professional development plans and school improvement plans. Define each. How is the action plan similar to a professional development plan or a school improvement plan? How is it different?

5. Discuss the four types of questions—reflection, implementing, reviewing, and self-evaluation—that the action researcher addresses when designing the action plan. Which two do you feel are most important and demand the most attention? Provide an explanation and give examples.

6. Discuss the rationale that supports designing and implementing an action plan as an extension of action research. Do you agree or disagree? Support your ideas with outside sources.

7. How is the action plan an outcome of inquiry? Provide an explanation and example.

8. Discuss the purpose of the action plan.

9. Discuss situations where an action plan is appropriate and where it is not. Give examples of situations where you would suggest designing and implementing an action plan. Compare the examples to situations where a plan is not appropriate. Be prepared to provide explanations to support your examples.

10. Examine the sample templates for early planning (Exhibits 9.1, 9.2, and 9.3). Which do you feel would work best in your current situation? Why?

SUGGESTED TOPICS

1. Working in pairs, discuss the action plan. Examine components. Which do you feel are most important to the design? Be prepared to offer explanations to support your thoughts.

2. How does informed decision making relate to the action plan? In small groups, generate a list of reasons that support informed decision making in action research. Be prepared to share your list with other groups.

3. In small groups, discuss the three types of informed decisions. Which do you feel is the most critical to designing and implementing a successful action plan?

4. Examine the rubric for evaluating the action plan (Table 9.1). Critique the rubric as an assessment tool. Are there any components missing? What would you add to make the rubric more effective?

ONLINE ACTIVITIES

1. Select one or two of the discussion questions provided to set up an online forum. Have students support their ideas with outside sources. Use a rubric for evaluating the postings. (*Note:* This may be completed in small groups or with the entire class.)

2. Conduct a brief Internet search to locate examples of action plans. Once you locate a plan, use the rubric for evaluation purposes (Table 9.1). Post the URL where the action plan was located and an overview of your rating based on the rubric. Then respond to at least two other posted action plans.

3. Design a simple self-evaluation rubric. Be sure to include at least three levels of assessment (such as "target," "acceptable," and "unacceptable"). The rubric should be in table format. Post your rubric as an attachment to the dedicated forum. View at least two others, and provide feedback.

4. Complete discussion question 4. Post your response; then examine and critique at least two others.

ONLINE RESOURCES FOR HUMAN SUBJECTS TRAINING AND INSTITUTIONAL REVIEW BOARD INFORMATION

Human Subjects Training

> http://cme.cancer.gov/clinicaltrials/learning/humanparticipant-protections.asp

New York University Institutional Review Board

> http://www.med.nyu.edu/irb/

Office of Human Research Ethics at the University of North Carolina, Chapel Hill

> http://research.unc.edu/ohre/

Research at the University of California–Berkeley

> http://rac.berkeley.edu/compliancebook/introduction.html

Research at the University of Virginia

> http://www.virginia.edu/vprgs/irb/sbs_help_education.html

Training Program for Researchers at Cornell University

> http://www.osp.cornell.edu/HSCompliance/index.html

United States Department of Health and Human Services

> http://www.hhs.gov/ohrp/irb/irb_guidebook.htm

University of Pennsylvania Institutional Review Board

> http://www.upenn.edu/regulatoryaffairs/human/ApplicationProcedures.html

GLOSSARY

Action plan. A framework or blueprint that is implemented to improve practice, conditions, or the environment in general. The action plan is based on the inquiry and findings. Also see *action research report*.

Action research. A common methodology employed for improving conditions and practice in classrooms as well as within other practitioner-based environments such as administrative settings, leadership settings, social settings, and community settings.

Action research report. A formal written document that allows the researcher to compile information regarding the inquiry, methods, subjects, and conclusions.

Activity codes. Illustrations of specific behaviors and interactions. Activity codes are typically interesting as they relate directly to the participants and how they interact and communicate.

Artifacts. Qualitative data in the form of informal notes, diagrams, drawings, and so on.

Assent form. Form required when a study involves minors as subjects, consisting of a set of questions with provided answers written in a format that the targeted age group would understand.

Axial coding. A process that enables the action researcher to put the data back together by making meaningful connections between categories. This is accomplished by re-examining the categories in order to identify commonalities or relationships.

Basic decisions. Any decisions that must be made regarding the structure of the plan, the timeline for implementation, who will be involved in the implementation, and resources needed.

Blog. A Web log or online journal in which a person posts public entries regarding a variety of topics.

Blogger. The person posting the entries on a blog.

Category data. See *nominal data*.

Chunks of meaning. Understanding derived from the emerging patterns and themes, which are then organized into categories with distinct attributes.

Community-based research. Research usually conducted within the practicing environment, either individually or in teams. It involves individuals who are interacting within the environment and is ordinarily intended to improve the community as a whole.

Compliance officer. A designated person who oversees and facilitates research training and approval for research conducted by individuals associated with the institution.

Concept cluster. A list of groups and categories containing related information.

Concept mapping. The process of generating ideas through brainstorming and then creating a graphic or "map" showing how the ideas, thoughts, and themes that emerge are interconnected.

Constant comparative method. A data analysis method that involves detailed coding in order to identify categories and attributes. The process, typically part of an in-depth study, is lengthy and time-consuming. The analysis results in the development of a theory that is grounded in triangulated data.

Context codes. See *setting codes*.

Continuous improvement. Improvement prompted by the action research process and through the implementation of one or more action plans that address prioritized concepts, patterns, and themes.

Cyclical method. See *recursive method*.

Data. Information collected during inquiry, either quantified statistically or in the form of interview responses, observations, or survey responses.

Data set. The complete information collected in response to research questions.

Delimiting. Describing the boundaries of the action research as it relates to the existing body of knowledge.

Descriptive entries. Detailed records of an event or activity observed by the researcher; compare *reflective entries*.

Descriptive reality approach. A systematic analysis of data sets in a manner that ensures triangulation and presents a vivid picture of what took place within a specific environment.

Descriptive storying. A re-creation of the research environment and interactions through the use of rich, descriptive language.

Discovery. Identification of recurring ideas, concepts, themes, and patterns across data sets and subsets. Discovery is ongoing and continues throughout the analysis process, from initial stages until the analysis concludes.

Electronic field journal. A private record of thoughts, similar to a print *field journal* but maintained on a computer. Compare *research blog*, which is public.

Epoche. A process that requires the action researcher to reflect and remove any biases, views, perceptions, and assumptions regarding the research environment, interactions, and related activities prior to engaging in the analysis process.

Evaluative reflection. Examine problems, issues, and concerns in order to determine their relevance; prioritize; and pursue inquiry that will lead to change and improvements.

Event codes. Codes referring to personal activities and events that take place in the daily routine and lives of the participants.

Exempt review. IRB review given to research that involves no more than minimal risk to human subjects.

Expedited review. IRB review given to a study involving minors that presents no more than minimal risk to human subjects.

Expert approach. An in-depth analysis of sources. Literature reviews written using the expert approach enable the researcher to address each source in the context of a central theme as related to the action research. This approach uses the commonalities of theme, ideas, findings, or even chronology as vehicles for organization and writing.

Field-intensive process. A research process that requires the researcher to participate actively in the environment being studied.

Field journal. A researcher's personal daily journal. Entries may consist of reflections on observations, notes regarding the research, and related information.

Full board review. A review by the institutional review board required for studies that involve greater risk to human subjects or vulnerable populations.

Generalizability. The assurance that duplicating a study with a larger number of participants would yield similar results.

Grounded theory. A research approach that requires the highest-level and most in-depth analysis. Through data collection and systematic analysis, the researcher is able to derive theory from the interactions and activities observed throughout the study.

Hypothesis statement. The researcher's prediction regarding the outcome of an inquiry. Studies that take a quantitative approach include a hypothesis statement.

Implementation decisions. Decisions regarding strategies to be included in the action plan, funding needed to implement the plan, and determining if the plan will be implemented as a collaborative effort.

Informal interviewing. A process of engaging in professional conversations with colleagues that promotes collegiality, builds collaboration, and assists the researcher in determining which questions, topics, and issues may be vital to improving practice.

Informed consent form. A document used to gain consent of any adult participating in an approved study.

Institutional review board (IRB). A team of peers at a university or school whose goal is protecting the rights and welfare of human subjects of research studies.

Interrater reliability. The assurances that multiple researchers analyzing and evaluating the same data will arrive at very similar conclusions.

Interval data. Nominal and ordinal data with equal space between all numbers.

Keyword search. An online search using a few words that are closely related to the focus of the research.

Literature review. A process that enables the researcher to identify and evaluate studies that have been conducted by scholars and practitioners. It may also serve as a fact-finding process to help the researcher narrow the research focus.

Metasearch engine (MSE). A search engine that allows the researcher to search multiple search engines simultaneously to produce a list of possible sources.

Methods codes. Codes that separate specific research processes that may emerge as the action research study progresses. Methods coding is typically used when analyzing reflective field notes.

Nominal data. Measurements that allow the assignment of persons or items into categories; also called *category data*.

Nonparametric data. Ordinal or nominal scales of measurement.

Ongoing recording. Notes entered in the field journal as needed.

Open coding. Breaking down the data and examining, comparing, and categorizing the information.

Ordinal data. Persons or objects placed into groups or categories using nominal data and ranked from lowest to highest.

Overarching questions. Open-ended questions that guide a qualitative study. The questions are revised throughout the study based on participant observer data.

Parametric data. Interval or ratio scales of measurement.

Parental consent form. Form used to gain the consent of the parent or guardian of a minor who is to participate in a study as a subject.

Participant field journal. A journal kept by a study participant or subject. A researcher may require each participant to keep a journal to record information regarding views, perceptions, and ideas surrounding the study.

Participant observer. A researcher who takes part in all activities within the environment being studied while interacting naturally with the subjects if the study.

Phrase search. A keyword search using a short phrase (enclosed in quotation marks) rather than a single word.

Primary source. A detailed firsthand description of a study.

Proactive research process. Using expertise to identify potential problems in a study and then conducting systematic inquiry to improve the conditions.

Process codes. Words, phrases, or terms that help the researcher categorize research events, sequences of activities, or any changes in the environment that take place during the research period. Process codes reveal passages and transitions as well as steps in a process, chronologies, or periods of time.

Prospect thinking. Thinking that prompts the action researcher to ask questions in advance of a research event or activity.

Purpose-of-the-study statement. See *research statement*.

Purpose statement. See *research statement*.

Qualitative data. Writing, diagrams, pictures, audio, video, and other nonquantifiable records of research outcomes.

Qualitative research. A study involving a small group of subjects interacting in a particular environment. Qualitative research studies attempt to provide insight into behaviors that occur among a specific number of subjects at one given time in a very specific setting.

Qualitative research approach. Using broad research questions matched to multiple data sets consisting of a variety of information such as recorded notes, journals, and student writing samples.

Quantitative data. Numerical information.

Quantitative research. A systematic examination of specific factors that provides numerical information as data.

Quantitative research approach. Using a hypothesis and numerical data to answer a research question.

Questioning and discussing with self. Engaging in self-reflection and exploring questions related to practice and related inquiry that may result.

Ratio data. The highest form of quantitative measurement, with equal intervals between all numbers and a true zero point.

Reactive research process. Identifying an existing problem and then conducting systematic inquiry to correct the problem and improve conditions.

Recursive method. A continuous or cyclical research process that begins with problem identification, determines findings, forms conclusions, and begins all over again.

Reflection in action. Engaging in reflection in the present by recording entries during an event, observation, interview, or research activity as it happens; compare *reflection on action*.

Reflection on action. Reflection after an event takes place.

Reflective decisions. Determinations regarding plan implementation, ethical and logistical issues, or treatments.

Reflective entries. The researcher's personal reflections, consisting of notes, thoughts, or ideas related to the action research or additional questions related to the focus of the inquiry. In action research, both descriptive and reflective field notes are unbiased and grounded in inquiry, with the purpose of gathering information in order to improve practice.

Reflective journal. A personal journal kept by a researcher.

Reflective recording. See *removed recording*.

Reflective self. The intuitive person that develops as the researcher actualizes the process of research and progresses through the inquiry to the point of implementing the action plan and sharing findings to improve practice.

Relationship codes. Codes used to note any specific relationships among participants, activities, data sets, or subsets. Personal relationship codes are typically noted when analyzing interactions between participants. Overall relationship codes are used when analyzing data sets and subsets, emerging patterns, categories, and themes.

Reliability. Consistency of measurement. In action research, the measurement instruments may include standardized tests, interview templates, questionnaires, classroom test scores, writing test results, and surveys.

Removed recording. Making reflective entries after observing or interacting.

Reporting approach. Presenting findings with little analysis other than transcribing and examining data sources.

Research. An organized and systematic means of finding answers to questions.

Researcher-as-instrument. A researcher who is able to rely on expertise, draw on experience, and employ research skills in an unbiased manner in tasks such as conducting interviews and recording notes.

Researcher's field journal. See *field journal*.

Research imagery. Reflective entries that assist the researcher in understanding the research setting, interactions, participants, and phenomena being studied.

Research objectives. Statements that outline the goals the researcher hopes to achieve as a result of an inquiry.

Research orientation. The ability to conduct action research in an unbiased manner.

Research questions. Questions that will reveal what the researchers want to find out as a result of the action research study.

Research statement. A succinct summary of the purpose, need, and design of the action research, making it clear why the research is necessary; also known as *purpose-of-the-study statements* or simply *purpose statements*.

Research umbrella. The general focus of the study aligned with any other information related to the topic uncovered while conducting the literature review; may also consist of the focus matched with other related ideas.

Retrothinking. Reviewing research events prior to making reflective entries.

Search engine (SE). Software that scans online sites to produce a list of links that contain specifically sought information.

Secondary source. Nonoriginal research, consisting of a review of other people's studies or an overview of practice.

Selective coding. Coding after identifying a core category, systematically relating the core to other categories, and validating the relationship among data sets and subsets by comparing the information for refinement and development.

Setting codes. Codes that provide information regarding the setting, location, and action research environment; also known as *context codes*.

Situation codes. Codes that provide insight regarding how the participants interact in specific situations related to the action research. Situation codes may also refer to participant perceptions, views, beliefs, and preferences.

Strategy codes. Codes that refer to specific strategies, techniques, and processes that participants use when interacting in the practitioner environment.

Structured interview. An interview conducted using a list of questions designed to gather information from the interviewee. Although the questions are typically open-ended, the list is strictly followed with each participant without any deviation.

Subsetting. Examining the data sets—organized around the overarching questions—and identifying subsets of related data in each data set.

Summative approach. A series of bulleted points or short, disconnected paragraphs. A literature review using the summative approach does not synthesize sources, nor does it identify common themes and ideas.

Tertiary source. A collection or compilation of primary and secondary sources.

Theoretical research. Research concerned with knowledge for the sake of theory and a desire to add to the existing body of knowledge; also known as *traditional research*.

Theory of symbolic interaction. A theory that implies that communication is the most natural humanizing activity, consisting of meaning, language, and thought—all leading to conclusions about oneself and the environment.

Traditional research. See *theoretical research*.

Triangulation. Analyzing multiple forms of data and finding similar results, thereby confirming the researcher's findings.

Unstructured interview. An interview that follows a blueprint of general, open-ended questions that may be added to or amended, depending on the participants' responses.

Validity. The notion that a test measures what it says it will measure. Validity also infers the soundness of the research design.

REFERENCES

Association for Institutional Research. (2001). *Code of ethics for institutional research*. Retrieved May 15, 2008, from http://airweb.org

Baskerville, R. L. (1999, October). Investigating information systems with action research. *Communications of the Association for Information Systems*, *2*. Retrieved September 2, 2007, from http://222.cis.gsu.edu/~rbaskerv/

Becker, H. S. (1998). *Tricks of the trade: How to think about your research while you're doing it*. Chicago: University of Chicago Press.

Blumer, H. (1969). *Symbolic interactionism*. Englewood Cliffs, NJ: Prentice Hall.

Bogdan, R. C., & Biklen, S. K. (1998). *Qualitative research in education: An introduction to theory and methods* (3rd ed.). Boston: Allyn & Bacon.

Burnaford, G., Fischer, J., & Hobson, D. (1996). *Teachers doing research: Practical possibilities*. Mahwah, NJ: Erlbaum.

Corbin, J. M., & Strauss, A. C. (2007). *Basics of qualitative research: Techniques and procedures for developing grounded theory*. Thousand Oaks, CA: Sage.

Craig, D. V., & Patten, K. B. (2006). Action research in the online environment: An examination of practice among graduate students. *International Journal of Learning*, *23*, 157–168.

Creswell, J. W. (2002). *Educational action research: Planning, conducting, and evaluating quantitative and qualitative research*. Upper Saddle River, NJ: Merrill Prentice Hall.

Creswell, J. W. (2005). *Educational research: Planning, conducting, and evaluating quantitative and qualitative research* (2nd ed.). Upper Saddle River, NJ: Pearson/Merrill Prentice Hall.

Dewey, J. (1929). *Sources of a science education*. New York: Liveright.

Eisner, E. W. (1998). *The enlightened eye: Qualitative inquiry and the enhancement of educational practice*. Upper Saddle River, NJ: Prentice Hall.

Emerson, R. M., Fretz, R. I., & Shaw, L. L. (1995). *Writing ethnographic field notes*. Chicago: University of Chicago Press.

Fink, A. (2005). *Conducting research literature reviews: From the Internet to paper*. Thousand Oaks, CA: Sage.

Gardner, H. (1983). *Frames of mind: The theory of multiple intelligences*. New York: Basic Books.

Gay, L. R., Mills, G. E., & Airaisian, P. (2006). *Educational research: Competencies for analysis and applications*. Upper Saddle River, NJ: Pearson/Merrill Prentice Hall.

Glaser, B. G., & Strauss, A. C. (1967). *The discovery of grounded theory*. Chicago: Aldine.

Henrichsen, L., Smith, M. T., & Baker, D. S. (1997). *Taming the research beast: Research methods in TESL and language acquisition*. Retrieved September 2, 2007, from http://linguistics.byu.edu/faculty/henrichsenl/researchmethods/RM_0_01.html

Henson, K. T. (1996). Teachers as researchers. In J. Sikula (Ed.), *Handbook of research on teacher education* (2nd ed., pp. 53–64). New York: Macmillan.

Herr, K., & Anderson, G. L. (2005). *The action research dissertation: A guide for students and faculty*. Thousand Oaks, CA: Sage.

Johnson, A. P. (2002). *A short guide to action research*. Boston: Allyn & Bacon.

Lewin, K. (1951). *Field theory in social science: Selected theoretical papers* (D. Cartwright, Ed.). New York: HarperCollins.

Lincoln, Y. S., & Guba, E. G. (1985). *Naturalistic inquiry*. Thousand Oaks, CA: Sage.

Maykut, P., & Morehouse, R. (1994). *Beginning qualitative research: A philosophical and practical guide*. Washington, DC: Falmer Press.

Meyers, E., & Rust, F. (2003). *Taking action with teacher research*. Portsmouth, NH: Heinemann.

Noffke, S. E., & Stevenson, R. B. (Eds.). (1995). *Educational action research: Becoming practically critical*. New York: Teachers College Press.

Novack, J. (1998). *Learning, creating, and using knowledge: Concept maps as facilitative tools in schools and corporations*. Mahwah, NJ: Erlbaum.

Osterman, R. K., & Kottkamp, R. B. (1993). *Reflective practice for educators: Improving schooling through professional development*. Thousand Oaks, CA: Corwin Press.

Patton, M. Q. (1990). *Qualitative evaluation and research methods* (2nd ed.). Thousand Oaks, CA: Sage.

Reason, P., & Marshall, J. (2001). On working with graduate research students. In P. Reason & H. Bradbury (Eds.), *Handbook of action research: Participatory inquiry and practice* (pp. 413–419). Thousand Oaks, CA: Sage.

Rogers, C. (1961). *On becoming a person*. Boston: Houghton-Mifflin.

Sagor, R. (2000). *Action research*. Alexandria, VA: Association for Supervision and Curriculum Development.

Schön, D. A. (1987). *Educating the reflective practitioner*. San Francisco: Jossey-Bass.

Sohng, S.S.L. (1995, November). *Participatory research and community organizing*. Paper presented at the New Social Movement and Community Organizing Conference, University of Washington, Seattle.

Taylor, S. T., & Bogdan, R. C. (1984). *Introduction to qualitative research methods: The search for meaning* (2nd ed.). New York: Wiley.

INDEX